We Will Get to the
Promised Land

We Will Get to the Promised Land

Martin Luther King, Jr.'s
Communal-Political Spirituality

H. J. LEE

**Foreword by
Peter J. Paris**

THE
PILGRIM
PRESS
Cleveland

To
my parents, Dae Kyu and Doo Nam,
my brothers, Sang Hak and the late Hak Jin,
and my sister, Hye Sook,
whose resilient, sacrificial, and caring spirits
have been and continue to be
a source of my strength and inspiration

The Pilgrim Press
700 Prospect Avenue
Cleveland, Ohio 44115-1100
thepilgrimpress.com

© 2006 by Hak Joon Lee

Printed in the United States of America on acid-free paper

10 09 08 07   5 4 3 2

Library of Congress Cataloging-in-Publication Data
Lee, Hak Joon, 1958-
    We will get to the promised land : Martin Luther King, Jr.'s
communal-political spirituality / Hak Joon Lee.
        p. cm.
    Includes bibliographical references and index.
    ISBN-13: 978-0-8298-1526-9 (alk. paper)
    1. King, Martin Luther, 1929-1968. 2. African Americans –
Religion. I. Title.
    BX4827.K53L44 2006
    286'.1092 – dc22

                                            2006012487

ISBN-13: 978-0-8298-1526-9
ISBN-10: 0-8298-1526-0

Contents

Foreword

This book represents the first study of Martin Luther King, Jr., by a Korean American scholar. I am pleased to have had the privilege of knowing and advising the author during his advanced studies here at Princeton Theological Seminary.

Hak Joon Lee deserves high praise for this comprehensive analysis of the spirituality of Martin Luther King, Jr. Since first-generation immigrants rarely attend to African American history, the importance of this study cannot be overestimated.

Lee's aim is to discuss and assess the "communal-political" nature of King's spirituality in order to show its deep roots in traditional African spirituality. Readers will soon discover that this book is no casual inquiry into King's thought and practice. Rather, it is a compelling and refreshing interpretation of African America's most esteemed religious leader.

Contrary to the views of many, however, Lee argues that King's thought and practice were *holistic* in nature. That is to say, they comprised a composite of moral, political, religious, and African elements harmoniously synthesized into an African American spirituality. Lee's approach is the book's most important contribution.

Since none of the many studies of King's thought have focused on its African roots, Lee's work persuasively addresses that neglected subject. He accomplishes his task by discussing the many similarities among South Africa's Desmond Tutu, Tibet's Dalai Lama, and America's Martin Luther King, Jr. His comparison of these three figures clearly demonstrates also how the principles that guided King's thought and practice can be relevant resources for all peoples everywhere.

Most important, this book reveals the internal coherence of King's moral, political, and theological thought, which can be a source of inspiration for building the kind of global community we need and should strive to realize.

PETER J. PARIS
Elmer G. Homrighausen Professor
Christian Social Ethics
Princeton Theological Seminary

Preface

I am not an African American. Some may wonder how an Asian American can have the audacity to write a book on the spirituality of Martin Luther King, Jr. That concern is understandable, given that spirituality refers to a lived aspect of one's life in a community, and that King was the product of the African American community. Without sharing that fundamental membership and those historical experiences in community, how could an outsider speak about King's spirituality? I humbly accept these challenging reflections. And I respond by providing some of my reasons for undertaking this project on King's spirituality.

First, as an ordained Christian minister, I am inspired by him. King is now bigger than the African American community. As Daddy King said, "He [Martin] did not belong to us, he belonged to all the world."[1] Like classical music and classic literatures, the value and legacy of his life and ministry go beyond the community of his origin. King was cosmopolitan; he worked and died for humanity as a whole, for all of God's children. He is not only an iconic symbol of African American Christianity; he is also a global moral exemplar respected by people of various religious, cultural, and national backgrounds. I can boldly claim that Martin is my brother — a model of Christian commitment and of dedication to God and humanity.

Second, Martin Luther King, Jr., is not new to me, or alien to my native culture. King inspired a democratic movement against the military dictatorship in South Korea during the 1970s and 1980s. Most Koreans of my generation remember singing together "We Shall Overcome" in Korean on our campuses, in the

---

1. Coretta Scott King, *My Life with Martin Luther King, Jr.* (New York: Henry Holt and Company, 1993), 294.

midst of dense tear gas clouds and flying rocks. King's vision and
method helped to bring about the peaceful transition of South
Korea to a democratic society.

Third, I have been involved in the Asian American and African American dialogue on practical and intellectual levels. In the
wake of the Asian American and African American conflicts in
the late 1980s through the early 1990s, including the L.A. riots,
I was involved in an intercultural ministry in the Camden, New
Jersey, area for six years out of concern for Korean and African
American racial harmony. Through that experience, I witnessed
the dehumanizing conditions of poverty, and the despair and nihilism growing out of it. I was able to confirm King's claim that
classism is a different form of segregation, depriving the poor of
their hope and dignity.

At the same time, through a series of intercultural interactions
between the two communities, sharing music, worship, and culture, I learned that African American spirituality resonated with
many aspects of my Asian spirituality. Asians, like Africans, emphasize community over individuals. The moral epistemological
starting point is not "I," but "we." Similarly, at the seminary
where I teach, I have experienced an extraordinary degree of hospitality, support, and encouragement — the spirit of *ubuntu* —
from my students. Many of my Asian American friends have affirmed my finding that Koreans and African Americans shared a
kindred spirit, grown out of their communal traditions and their
experiences of suffering.

Furthermore, the longer I live in this country, the more I find
African American concerns for racial justice are also my concerns.
Racism is not confined to African Americans. Asian Americans
are marginalized and discriminated against, dismissed as permanent strangers, no matter how long we have lived in this country.
King's and other African Americans' struggle toward the beloved
community has become my own as well.

The title of this book, *We Will Get to the Promised Land,* is a
line from the concluding part of King's very last sermon, "I See
the Promised Land," delivered on April 3, 1968, the eve of his

assassination, in Memphis. For me, this line succinctly and elo-
quently summarizes King's spirituality, which was communal and
political in nature. It poetically represents King's deepest yearning
and noble vision for the beloved community, and his unwavering
commitment to achieving it. In this phrase, with his characteristic
emphasis on the unity and interdependence of people ("We as a
people"), King stressed that the collective formation of peoplehood is the key to the construction of the beloved community,
the Promised Land, where individual creativity, dignity, and freedom are affirmed, and where mutual love and social supports
are available for their realization. It is no overstatement to say
that the idea of a community, coined in his vision of the beloved
community, was at the center of King's thought. The search for
community was the defining motif of Martin Luther King, Jr.'s,
life and thought.[2]

The symbolism of this line, such as the Promised Land and pro-
gression toward it, came from the Exodus story — a paradigmatic
narrative for African Americans in their struggles against racial
oppression. If Egypt was the symbol of slavery, Canaan signified
the land of freedom. The Exodus story adequately communicates
the complex, multilayered meanings, agonies, and history of their
existence in the United States; their collective suffering, yearning,
journey, and passage to liberation; and their self-development and
growth as a people. King, as a third-generation African American
pastor, was intimately familiar with this story. It was one of his
favorite metaphors, and it turned up frequently in his sermons.
But it was through his civil rights struggle "to redeem the soul
of America" that King elevated the Exodus story to be the paradigm of spiritual transformation for the entire nation. That is,
he sublimated the hermeneutics of the Exodus story by injecting
the element of communal spiritual formation into a traditional
African American liberationist interpretation of the story.

---

2. Walter E. Fluker, *They Looked for a City: A Comparative Analysis of the
Ideal of Community in the Thought of Howard Thurman and Martin Luther
King, Jr.* (Lanham, MD: University Press of America, 1989), 81.

King's communal spirituality and his political vision can inspire and empower all of us. In a global, pluralistic society, creating a community has become a moral requirement, not just a concern. Although we live close physically, we have not yet learned how to live together as a people. As King said, we created neighborhood, but failed to make it into brother- and sisterhood. Many people are dislocated, fragmented, and displaced from a traditional society, moving from one place to another, looking for a community where they can belong and actualize themselves.

Globalization forces us to think of humanity as one family, one community, whether we like it or not. In a global society where social Darwinism, capitalist materialism, religious fundamentalism, religious terrorism, and military unilateralism abound, and consequently where constant fear, anxiety, insecurity, alienation, and hatred are taking a psychological and economic toll in many places, King's vision of the beloved community is earnestly and desperately needed.

By upholding the concept of "we as a people," King contends that the goal of the beloved community, the well-being of humanity, cannot be achieved by one people, one race, one nation, or one religion alone. The pronoun "we" is essential; it represents kinship and solidarity. Today, the conventional boundaries of "we," "ourselves," "us," and "our" have changed with the acceleration of globalization. Even in the movement King began, the referent of "we" has constantly expanded. It moved beyond the reference to African Americans and whites to be inclusive of the poor and the oppressed of other nations. As he proclaimed, "we, as a people, will get to the promised land," it was King's firm conviction that the Promised Land cannot be reached by disparate individual persons, groups (classes, ethnicities, etc.), or nations, no matter how rich, righteous, or powerful they may be. He believed in the fundamental interdependence of all humanity, regardless of one's race, gender, religion, or nationality. The Promised Land cannot be entered unless we are all together, in solidarity with the poor and the oppressed. The Promised Land is not an otherworldly, spiritual safe haven reserved for pious individuals; it is a historical, eschatological vision of God for humanity that pulls and molds us together as God's children. The Promised Land will open its arms only when a new moral peoplehood, a new humanity, arises beyond racial, sexual, nationalistic, and religious enmities, beyond violence and conflicts, beyond egos.

King worked for the shaping of a new peoplehood in his nation and the world. As Moses did, he saw many obstacles and challenges, within and without, standing in the way of the path to the Promised Land. He sensed that he would die before reaching this goal, yet he was not discouraged. He did not give up his dream, either. He declared, "I may not get there with you. But I want you to know tonight, that we, as a people, will get to the promised land."[3] Even at the very last moment of his life, King was inviting us to this noble vision, this goal of renewing ourselves and our world together. One major challenge of the twenty-first century is figuring out how we, as a people, can work together toward this common goal of reaching the Promised Land, namely, the creation of the beloved community.

This book is proof of the interdependent nature of human existence that King so forcefully espoused. A book is a product of a community, always owing something to previous generations and scholars, and to the author's circle of supporters and friends. I owe many people for their encouragement, support, and inspiration; I could not have completed this work without them. My teacher, Dr. Peter J. Paris, was a model for me, not only in his outstanding scholarship but also in his character, which truly demonstrated the African virtue of beneficence toward me along with many others who have become acquainted with him. His kindness was exemplified by his gracious agreement to contribute the foreword for this book.

I also want to thank George Graham, who was instrumental in the publication of this book by proposing that I write a book on

3. Martin Luther King, Jr., "I See the Promised Land," in *A Testament of Hope: The Essential Writings of Martin Luther King, Jr.*, ed. James M. Washington (New York: HarperCollins Publishers, 1986), 286.

King's spirituality based on a paper on this topic that I delivered at a professional society. I extend my thanks to the King Center in Atlanta for allowing me to do research there, and to Dr. Wyatt Tee Walker, who graciously granted me a rare opportunity to interview him despite his poor health. I cannot forget my school, New Brunswick Theological Seminary, and its board of trustees, who granted me a sabbatical semester to work on this project. Also, my gratitude goes to Lynn Berg, Joanne Noel, and others who carefully read the manuscript at its various stages and provided me with useful editorial suggestions and comments. I am greatly indebted to my friend E. J. Emerson for her wholehearted support for this project and extraordinary editorial skills that considerably improved the final product. I would be remiss if I failed to thank my editor, Ulrike Guthrie, for her patience and fortitude in keeping me to the publisher's limits without compromising the content or unique voice of my work. My deepest gratitude goes to my parents, my siblings, and above all to my wife and two sons, who supported this project with remarkable patience, and who provided me with continuous spiritual and moral encouragement.

My humble prayer is that this book be used to encourage and invite people to the task of building the beloved community together, as King, with nobility and commitment, inspired us to do.

Introduction

It was a spring day in Memphis. A heavy rain beat mercilessly on the roof of Mason Temple. The cracking sound of sporadic thunder scared people off the streets. The gloomy weather of the night fit King's depressed mood.[1] Dark clouds of anxiety and fear weighed heavily on his soul. Criticism was mounting, suspicion was constantly chasing him, doubts were growing even among his faithful followers, and lethal threats were increasingly encroaching on his life. The bomb scare on the plane that morning reinforced his sense of being besieged by hostile forces.

Against this backdrop, King delivered what was to be his last sermon, "I See the Promised Land," to the mostly African American audience, gathered there despite the rain to see King in person. In many ways, this sermon, preached one day before his assassination, tells who King was, psychologically and spiritually. It discloses his deep inner struggle, as a fragile human being, between life and death, comfort and sacrifice, between the desire for longevity and the commitment to moral causes. Yet its revelatory power goes beyond the realm of his psychology. The sermon shows how King spiritually overcame the negatives impinging upon him. Sensing the increasing withdrawal of both moral and financial support from his movement for economic justice, King was more and more relying on God alone. He refused to give in to fear. The sermon discloses how King confronted harsh realities with amazing inner resources found in his personal relationship with God.

The homily began in a very introspective and even pensive mood, yet it shows how his mind was becoming free and his

---

1. Stephen Oates, *Let the Trumpet Sound: A Life of Martin Luther King, Jr.* (New York: HarperCollins, 1994), 483.

spirit unchained as he interacted with his fellow African Americans. They were with him. When King revealed the threats on his life, they moaned with him because they also were harassed and threatened by whites. When King confessed that although he did not know what would happen to him next but he wanted to do God's will, they cried with him. And when King declared, at the climax of his sermon, that he had gone up to the mountain and had seen the promised land, they roared in ecstasy because they, too, had experienced ecstatic moments of encountering God in the midst of despair and suffering. Their spirits, King's and theirs, were revived and free again through the fellowship of the saints, receiving new succor and strength from God.

King was a quintessentially African American. He shared with other African Americans a profound appreciation of their rich African spiritual heritage. They knew an enormous hidden power of spirit for healing and liberation that transcends every human-made restraint and control. With his back to the wall, King, in this sermon, demonstrated the resilience of African American spirituality. In a difficult time, King stood by the faith of his father and mother and his slave ancestors. His sermon represented the best of African American spirituality that refuses to surrender to dehumanizing forces, and keeps human dignity and integrity through unwavering trust in God. In the best tradition of African and African American spirituality, King's sermon demonstrated the victory of human spirit that proclaims God-given freedom and its blissful destiny to triumph over all the dehumanizing forces.

This book is a study of Martin Luther King, Jr.'s, spirituality. His spirituality was deeply informed by his African and African American roots, which account for its major characteristics, such as its communal-political nature. Understanding King's spirituality is the key to understanding his life, ministry, and public achievements. If the spirit is the identity and essence of a person, then an understanding of King is impossible without understanding his spirit. His public speeches, sermons, actions, decisions, and even his academic works reflect his spirituality. For example, the kind of noble and elegant passion, the forcefulness, and the creativity that King brought to the civil rights movement as a leader, preacher, and speaker were the result of his spirituality. King's moral consistency, maturity, radical vision, prophetic boldness, revolutionary spirit, and generosity were the fruits of his spirit.

Although many books have already been written on King, and the number of works on him keeps growing, the study of King's spirituality has been largely ignored by those engaged in King scholarship. Often the study of his spirituality is taken for granted or subsumed under the study of his theology, ethics, social philosophy, or biography. Yet the study of King's spirituality is different from these disciplinary approaches because it is larger than these categories. Spirituality is concerned with the total disposition and the lived quality of King's person and ministry. Therefore, the study of spirituality offers a coherent and comprehensive hermeneutical angle for understanding his identity and life — his thoughts, values, yearnings, and struggles, in their mutual connections and intersections.

The study of King through spirituality is congruent with King's own identity. King was a highly religious and spiritual person. At his core, King was not primarily a civil rights leader, a theologian, or a movement organizer; primarily he was an African American pastor who felt that he was called by God for a special task. His wife, Coretta Scott King, endorsed this perspective: "Martin was a third-generation Christian minister, and this was the moral and spiritual foundation and vital center of the faith that empowered his leadership."[2]

The study of King's spirituality is also a response to our contextual demands. King has much to offer us today, particularly after the terrorist attacks of September 11, 2001, when there is so much cultural confusion and misunderstanding on the meaning and purpose of spirituality. A popular cultural discourse of spirituality in the West is predominantly private and therapeutic in

---

2. Coretta King, "Foreword," in Richard Deats, *Martin Luther King, Jr., Spirit-Led Prophet: A Biography* (New York: New City Press, 2000), 9.

nature, with a pretense to integration often in utter indifference
to public issues and social concerns. In contrast to this surge of a
private spirituality, one also sees a diametrically opposite expression of spirituality today — the spread of religiously motivated
violence and terrorism. As the suicide bombings and massacre of
civilians in the Middle East, and the abortion clinic bombings and
other violent incidents in the United States demonstrate, violence
is committed more often than not by seemingly highly devoted —
many even characterize them as fanatical — religious persons or
groups. They use violence as a means to publicly express their
religious and political statements.

This bipolar expression of spirituality forces us to ask: How
can one overcome the polarization of spirituality — the private
spirituality that is indifferent to public affairs vs. the public spirituality that advocates violence and hatred? Is there an authentic
form of spirituality that promotes peace and justice in a global society without disregarding a personal spiritual dimension? King
offers us significant insight and inspiration in answer to these
questions.

The Origin/Sources of King's Spirituality

The study of King's spirituality logically begins with the study
of the historical and psychological factors, and the cultural and
social forces, that influenced his early spiritual formation. For
many years, King scholars have been debating about the primary
sources of King's theology and ethics. Given King's academic
achievements and intellectual potency, conventional wisdom was
that King's theology and ethics derived from his theological education at Crozer Theological Seminary and Boston School of
Theology. Over the last few decades, however, challenging this
conventional understanding, King scholars have attempted to investigate the sources of his thoughts and ideas in relationship to
the particular forms of African American Christianity, intellectual
traditions, and culture. These scholars have succeeded in identifying several distinctive African American religious and cultural

sources that contributed to the formation of his theology and ethics.

For example, James Cone argued that King's theology and ethics must be understood in relation to his upbringing in the African American church. Cone said that "the faith of the black church was the most important source of King's theology."[3] Defined by the themes of justice, love, and hope, according to Cone, King's theology was decisively influenced by the faith of the African American church.[4] William Watley took a similar approach by stressing a particular contribution of African American religious tradition to King's intellectual and religious formation. He claimed that the African American church and African American religion were "the major formative sources for King's intellectual development."[5] He showed several distinctive affinities between African American religion and the white liberal theologies that King learned at Crozer and Boston. Although Cone and Watley made significant contributions by explicating King's theology and ethics in relation to the African American church and religious tradition, it was Lewis Baldwin who provided a more comprehensive and systemic analysis of the African American sources of King's theology and ethics.

In his book *There Is a Balm in Gilead*, Lewis Baldwin offers an extensive and elaborate discussion of the roots of King's thoughts by connecting King's intellectual formation to his southern African American folk culture. Arguing that King's sense of identity and purpose was shaped primarily by southern African American religion and culture,[6] Baldwin identifies three major themes

---

3. James H. Cone, "The Theology of Martin Luther King, Jr.," *Union Seminary Quarterly Review* 40, no. 1 (1986): 21.

4. Ibid., 26. In another place, Cone states, "The Bible and the spirituality of the black slave — these were the chief sources of Martin's faith" (James H. Cone, *Martin and Malcolm and America* [Maryknoll, NY: Orbis Books, 1991], 250).

5. William D. Watley, *Roots of Resistance: The Nonviolent Ethics of Martin Luther King, Jr.* (Valley Forge, PA: Judson Press, 1985), 44–45.

6. Lewis V. Baldwin, *There Is a Balm in Gilead: The Cultural Roots of Martin Luther King, Jr.* (Minneapolis: Fortress Press, 1991), 7.

constituting the roots of King's thoughts and life: southernness, community, and Christian optimism.[7] According to him, King was quintessentially southern "not only because he was born and raised in the South, but also because his identity, commitment, sense of purpose, and quest for meaning were intimately associated with that region."[8] Likewise, Baldwin traces King's strong optimism and the idea of community to King's close-knit family and the southern African American community — their communal and religious ethos. His implicit premise is that the South, unlike the North, was less secularized and thus maintained full communal ethos and intimacy, cultural habits and religious traditions. King's vision of a community and optimism are, therefore, natural products of this region.

Yet Baldwin's approach poses several problems. If the source of King's spirituality was the southern African American culture and religion, where did the latter originate? If the southernness is such an important factor, how did King's appeal spread to African Americans in other regions? If the distinctive southern culture and ethos were the dominant sources, why have white Christians in the South failed to develop a spirit of communal orientation, inclusiveness, and nonviolence similar to that of African Americans? Although Baldwin notices a communal disposition within King, he delimits it to the individual person of King and his family and a particular regional environment, rather than identifying its influence from the broader African American spiritual tradition.

Baldwin's contention is only partially true. The concept of "southernness" itself cannot be the source of King's spirituality. The source of his spirituality goes beyond his local African American culture, back to the African communal spiritual traditions that his slave forefathers and mothers brought to this land. In fact, even the other two central themes Baldwin identifies in his book — community and optimism — originated from African spiritual heritages. These themes were prevalent among African

---

7. Ibid., 4–5.
8. Ibid., 4.

Americans in the South because of the intensive accumulation of the African spiritual traditions in the region, but they were not unique to it, for these characteristics are shared by many African peoples.

Indeed, as I discuss in chapter 1, the retained African heritages are important sources that informed African American spirituality. According to Flora Bridges, (1) the African retentions, (2) the experiences of slavery and racism, and (3) the Africanized elements of the European Christian tradition are the three major sources that together gave rise to the distinctive temperaments of African American spirituality.[9]

King's spirituality, and likewise his cultural and intellectual roots, cannot be fully understood apart from the influences of African spiritual heritages. The extraordinary degree of benevolence, forbearance, and optimism that King and other African Americans demonstrated during the civil rights movement were expressive of the communal spirituality that originated from their African spiritual traditions. Similarly, his unabated interest in religious matters and his distinctive aesthetic styles cannot be properly understood without reference to African spiritual heritages.

Given King's theological and ethical emphasis on love, integration, interdependence of humanity, the beloved community, and world-house, we can see that his spirituality was distinctively communal, implying that his proclivity for community was not accidental, but constitutive of his spirituality. So far, scholars have failed to identify the source or the origin of this communal and integrative disposition of his spirituality.[10]

---

9. Flora Wilson Bridges, *Resurrection Song: African-American Spirituality* (Maryknoll, NY: Orbis Books, 2001), 3.

10. For example, Kenneth Smith and Ira Zepp attribute the source of King's idea of the beloved community to white liberal theological concepts such as personalism and the social gospel, while Lewis Baldwin and Walter Fluker attribute it to King's early family life and experience in the southern African American churches and community. See Kenneth L. Smith and Ira G. Zepp, Jr., *Search for the Beloved Community: The Thinking of Martin Luther King, Jr.* (Valley Forge, PA: Judson Press, 1998), 129; Fluker, *They Looked for a City*, 82.

Thesis

I argue that the communal and holistic streaks of King's spirituality came from his African ancestral origin. His spirituality grew out of his family and the local African American community, both of which were communal by virtue of their roots and heritage in African communal spirituality. The son of an African American Baptist pastor, King's family genealogy goes back, via African American slaves, to African forefathers and mothers. King was raised in and worked primarily within an African American community. His spirituality was birthed in the accumulated tradition and history of African American spirituality communicated from generation to generation by their forebears. These African cosmological patterns shaped the predilections in his selection, preference, and adoption of particular schools, and in his interpretations and doctrines of white liberal theology. In turn, the communal characteristic was not unique to King's family, but shared by the African American community as a whole (though to different degrees), with its origin going back to African spiritual roots.

This discovery has profound implications for the analysis, explanation, and interpretation of King's life, theology, and ministry. His much-talked-about idea of the beloved community, which scholars have identified as "the capstone of King's thought" or "the organizing principle of all of King's thought and activity,"[11] can be properly understood only in terms of the rich and organic spiritual tradition of African peoples. The idea of the beloved community was correlated with his notions of love, integration, interdependence of humanity, world-house, and so on. The beloved community reflects his holistic African spiritual worldview: all human beings are interdependent, and therefore they should live in mutual love and care and justice. We may make a similar observation about King's extraordinary sense of hopefulness as well as his penchant for synthesis and holism, all the manifestations of his African spiritual heritages. By virtue of the

---

11. Smith and Zepp, *Search for the Beloved Community,* 129.

optimistic and communal African heritages, for example, King never gave up nonviolent resistance; *agape* was central to his deep African spiritual value of interdependence.

To trace King's roots in African spiritual tradition is fruitful to explain King's effective leadership of the civil rights movement. The massive mobilization of African American people and their resolute commitments to nonviolence during the movement were possible not only because of King's intelligent leadership but also because of their shared communal spiritual outlooks and sensibilities inherited from Africa.

Of course, it is hard to identify exactly to what extent African traditions had been amalgamated with American traditions to give rise to a contemporary form of African American spirituality, because both African and American traditions are complex phenomena. The African spirituality discussed in this book refers to the beliefs, culture, and tendencies that African slaves brought with them to America. References to African American spirituality are meant to give a picture of that community's spiritual outlook and culture during Martin Luther King, Jr.'s, lifetime. While American and African American culture has changed in the ensuing almost forty years, many of these traits remain today in the African American church.

To claim that King's spirituality was inherited from the African spiritual traditions does not mean that everything he thought, wrote, or said had come directly from these traditions. Rather, it means that distinctive sensibilities, temperaments, and modalities underlying King's thoughts and moral actions were inherited from them. Although this communal African spiritual tradition was neither formalized nor theorized, it indelibly marked the undercurrent of African American spirituality. To varying degrees, it is also spread across African American churches and communities. This spirituality, communal in nature, was altered and refined through the encounter and interaction with other forces, such as Christianity and European philosophy, in the process of historical transmission and adaptation. However, the basic dispositions are still distinctive and visible. Similar spiritual orientations are

found in the South African resistance and reconciliation movements led by Nelson Mandela, Desmond Tutu, and others, which
means that King's communal spirituality was neither accidental
nor incidental; it was clearly connected to the African peoples'
communal spiritual traditions.

The discussion of the African roots of King's spirituality adds
a more comprehensive and adequate perspective to the contemporary scholarly discourse on the cultural and social sources of
King's theology and ethics. It not only corroborates the contention of African American scholars who emphasize the southern
African American Christian roots of King's faith and public ministry, but it also advances their contentions a step further by
probing the very shape and content of African American spiritual
roots back to African spiritual origins.

The Nature of King's Spirituality

King's spirituality, which is influenced by the African American
traditions with their roots in Africa, is communal-political in
its nature and emphasis. "Communal" has multifaceted meanings and conflated usages in society, often interchanged with
terms such as "social," "societal," and "collective." The term
"community" has both empirical and normative senses. Empir-
ically, "community" refers to a human gathering with a sense
of shared identity, mutuality, intimacy, and values; it is usually
more cohesive, personal, and enduring than "society," "group,"
or "association." Normatively, it means a cosmological idealism
that upholds or idealizes a community as the goal or center of
all human strivings. Hence, "the communal" indicates a spiritual and moral thrust that seeks enduring mutuality, fellowship,
and shared understanding among persons. This term has a special meaning in African American contexts, since "racism" means
noncommunity. African Americans' struggles have been those of
searching for community.

On the other hand, "politics" is a collective human enterprise
concerned with the common affairs of a society. The term refers

to a process that coordinates various parts of society in the distribution of power, authorities, goods, and resources. To be political is an attitude or activity of people or parties to influence the regulation and government ("public affairs") of a nation or a state through various conducts and contests. For African Americans, the term "political" has a particular meaning in the context of racism. It is concerned with the struggle for recognition to be a full member of U.S. society by overcoming racism. That is, to be political is to struggle to achieve full citizenship and human rights so that one can freely and equally participate in the process of decision making and share power. Hence, "the political" is a thrust or a sensibility that is deeply engaged with or concerned about the public affairs of a nation or a state.

From the early days of King's life, the communal-political thrusts defined the trajectory of his spiritual orientation and development. His struggles against racism, poverty, and militarism were all informed and guided by his communal-political spirituality. If the communal, with its emphasis on interdependence and community, originated from African corporate religious worldviews, the political, with its emphasis on freedom and justice, emerged from the African American struggle against racial oppression. King's communal orientation was disclosed in his views of love (especially *agape*), beloved community, integration, nonviolence, and so on, whereas his political thrust was manifested in his idea of power, justice, human agency, and the prophetic ministry of the church. In short, his life was consumed by the political struggles against various obstacles to the beloved community.

The communal and the political thrusts are the quintessential characteristics of the spirituality that runs deep and wide through African Americans' history and life in the United States. The communal and political aspects are rooted in the history and traditions of the African American churches where the yearning for freedom and community were from their inception inseparable. African Americans considered the community to be the goal of every meaningful human striving under the presumption of the interdependence of humanity; they also emphasized human responsibility toward justice for the liberation of the oppressed.

Methodology

The academic study of spirituality is still a nascent field. According to Sandra Schneiders, academic study involves roughly three investigative phases in examining the spirituality of a person or a group: descriptive, analytical-critical, and synthetic-constructive.[12] Because these three phases suggest substantive domains of investigation or explanatory dimensions of the study of spirituality, this book studies King's spirituality accordingly:

1. The descriptive phase: this phase is concerned with the accumulation of the data regarding the subject under investigation. Various historical, textual, and comparative studies are employed. In studying King, chapters 1 and 2 describe various factors and forces that contributed to the formation of King's communal-political spirituality: his African heritages, his family, his church, his personal experiences, his undergraduate, graduate, and postgraduate education and experiences, and so on.

2. The analytical-critical phase: the objective of this phase is the "explanation and evaluation of the subject" using an analytical and critical thinking and method. In analyzing King's spirituality, chapters 3 to 5 explain and evaluate both meaning and implications of his communal and political spirituality for his various ideas of theology (such as God, person, love, and community, to name a few central concepts), ethics (such as justice, power, and social struggles), and ministry practices.

3. The synthetic-constructive phase: this stage pertains to the appropriation and application of the results of the investigation. In chapters 5 to 7, this objective is achieved by

12. See Sandra Schneiders, "Spirituality in the Academy," *Theological Studies* 50, no. 4 (1989).

exploring King's contributions as they are related to the contemporary social and cultural situations: religious terrorism, the war on terror, and an interreligious dialogue with Desmond Tutu and the fourteenth Dalai Lama of Tibet.

Definition of "Spirituality"

Although "spirituality" is a notoriously nebulous term to define, in a simplistic sense it has to do with the activity of a spirit — the core anima and value of a person. Manifested in the lived and experienced aspects of one's core faith or value, one's spirituality shows the particular trajectory of one's spirit. "Spirit" indicates one's capacity to be relational with others or going out beyond oneself without losing one's identity.[13] Here, I define "spirituality" as that enduring human striving, whether as a person or as a group, toward authenticity and fulfillment within a particular historical context in relation to what is believed as the loftiest, the noblest, and the highest values and ideals of human life.

As the locus of one's identity, spirituality shows how a person (or a group) is oriented in the universe. This orientation is usually informed and guided by what is believed to be *the ultimate*. Constituting the purpose and meaning of human existence, the ultimate in this case has a commanding and summoning power over a person, imparting the unity of one's life. A spiritual life calls for one undivided response to the demands of the ultimate. It encompasses the whole person — body, mind, and soul — by bringing together affectivity and knowledge, rituals and ethics, ideas and actions. In this sense, spirituality is deeper than discrete intellectual ideas and sensual stimulations.

Every form of spirituality is contextually situated, embodied in a particular person or group existing in a particular time and space. Despite doctrinal similarities, spirituality inevitably varies because of its historically contingent nature. As a lived faith and

---

13. See John Macquarrie, "Spirit and Spirituality," in *Exploring Christian Spirituality: An Ecumenical Reader,* ed. Kenneth Collins (Grand Rapids: Baker Books, 2000), 69.

experience, spirituality is always configured through a person's (or a group's) subjective appropriation of a perceived ultimate reality in a particular historical and social context. Accordingly, as the study of spirituality attends to a personal, experiential dimension of faith, it inevitably examines the historical context of the experience — how a specific faith experience, spiritual orientation, or tradition is shaped and developed in a particular historical situation.

Scope and Limit

This book does not intend to present a comprehensive historical or biographical study of King and the civil rights movement, since numerous books have already done this. Neither does the discussion of historical events in this book follow an exact chronological order, although I have tried to respect the general evolution of his thought and activity. This work analyzes several crucial sources, foundational dispositions, features, and characteristics of King's spirituality.

In discussing African American spirituality, this book does not deal with extra-Christian African American spiritual traditions such as African Islamic traditions, African Catholic traditions, African voodoo traditions, or other various sects and cults found in the African diaspora communities in the Caribbean and South America. It focuses on the African American Christian spirituality that exercised the most formative influence on King's spirituality.

Chapter 1

The African and African American Roots of King's Spirituality

The African Nature of African American Spirituality

Culture is resilient. It does not allow radical abruption. A complete discontinuity or replacement of the previous culture is inconceivable in a historical process. In the process of cultural formation and transmission, a new culture is usually additively learned, layered upon the previous traditions, which in turn clandestinely maintain and exercise their influences over the process of interpretation and incorporation of new cultural elements. Old and new elements may be seamlessly fused and reintegrated to create a plausible pattern of culture that functions effectively for the new needs of a community.

This was certainly the case for African Americans. African American spirituality did not emerge in a vacuum in the United States, despite the radical uprooting and deportation of slaves from their native lands. Rather, it originated from the African spirituality they brought with them. Their experiences have been a continuous process of cultural adjustment to and appropriation of new cultural elements to add to their foundation of African spiritual heritages. "Although the African cosmologies were eroding, they still provided the philosophical basis by which new beliefs could be assimilated."[1]

Contemporary scholars of African American studies have noted the continuity of worldviews between African peoples and

---

1. Yvonne P. Chireau, *Black Magic: Religion and the African American Conjuring Tradition* (Berkeley: University of California Press, 2003), 54.

African Americans. These scholars maintain that African American spiritual experiences cannot be properly understood without adequately probing the enduring influences of African factors on African American culture and religion.[2] Despite great geographical distances and cultural-ethnographic differences, some distinctive spiritual features, themes, and concepts remain among African Americans. Although these aspects do not retain the pure form they had had in Africa, still many distinctive features and motifs of African spirituality were preserved in recognizable form among the various African American communities.[3]

How is this possible? According to these scholars, African Americans, in the transatlantic slave trade, took their cosmologies, cultural memories, philosophical thought forms and patterns, and moral principles with them into their diaspora contexts. These elements usually refuse to disappear quickly. Despite harsh and inhumane conditions, slaves continued to think in accordance with the logic and grammar of their native culture. Gayraud Wilmore notes,

> Slavery only served to drive those [African] influences from the past beneath the surface by force and terror. But instead of decaying there, the African elements were enhanced and strengthened in the subterranean vaults of the unconscious from whence they arose — time and time again during moments of greatest adversity and repression — to subvert the attempt to make the slave an emasculated, depersonalized version of the white person.[4]

These thought forms, ideational patterns, and cultural habits were passed down through various cultural and institutional means, including folktales, dances, magic, and other alternative

---

2. Peter J. Paris, *The Spirituality of African Peoples: The Search for a Common Moral Discourse* (Minneapolis: Fortress Press, 1995), 20.

3. Ibid., 129.

4. Gayraud Wilmore, *Black Religion and Black Radicalism: An Interpretation of the Religious History of Afro-American People*, 2nd ed. (Maryknoll, NY: Orbis Books, 1983), 27.

religious beliefs, ghost stories, music, art, spiritual leaders, formal religious institutions, rituals, and practices.[5] One sees a strong continuity between African and African American spirituality, for example, in the pervasive use of artistic creations for supernatural practices. This is evidenced by the plethora of supernatural artifacts (charms, talismans, and ornaments) unearthed at plantation sites, which reveal the African origin of the spiritual practices that were popular within the subculture of the slaves.[6]

African spiritual heritages, although widely dispersed, were neither equally pervasive nor equally available among African descendants in the United States. The scope and the density of the African retention depended on various social and cultural conditions and environments, such as the locale (i.e., urban or rural) and the size of the settlement, the duration of their presence there, the degree of industrialization, the nature of a hosting religion and culture, social policies toward African Americans, and so on. Finally, not all African Americans were equally responsive to these values and sensibilities.

The survival of African elements among African American communities is usually positively correlated with the duration of stay, the size of the local slave population, and the volume of slave trades. Because the strong, organized white efforts to proselytize African Americans did not develop until the early 1700s, the argument for early African retention is more plausible. Furthermore, since African Americans lived mostly in segregated communities, African spiritual features and characteristics may have been passed on more freely from generation to generation. This was especially true in the South where slaves were able to maintain their indigenous customs and practices through the continuous arrival of new slaves and through a wider and more extensive interaction among the slaves, both newly arrived and those converted to a more Western culture. Arrivals and interactions gave

---

5. For a more detailed discussion of the contribution of these various means of retention and transmission of African spiritual values and cultural practices, see Bridges's *Resurrection Song,* chapter 2.

6. Chireau, *Black Magic,* 43.

rise to the formation of larger and more cohesive African American communities with distinctive cultural and religious features. It was highly probable that the South was a fertile (incubating and nurturing) ground for the rise of a more Africanized form of African American spirituality.

Despite harsh and inhuman conditions, the slaves retained their African spiritual perspectives. There were practical reasons for this preservation: the African spiritual and cultural heritages played a crucial role in helping them survive in alien and hostile conditions. African Americans adapted the transmitted values of their African heritages to be a source of cultural and religious resistance, to empower their communities against racism. African heritages served to create a new collective social identity over against the imposed racist view.

Oddly enough, this resistance also applied to African Americans' adoption of Christianity. They incorporated Christianity critically through their inherited African spiritual perspective and social needs. The congruence between African spiritual heritages and Anglo-American supernatural traditions, especially in the preindustrial United States, facilitated exchanges, even accommodations, between both traditions. On the basis of a perceived affinity between the African and the Anglo-American Christianity, the slaves drew upon the available Christian beliefs and symbols for new expressions of their African-derived spiritual ideas and practices.

More important, the theological and doctrinal affinities between Christianity and African religious traditions assisted the retention of African factors.[7] Certain elements of African spirituality, such as supernatural beliefs and practices, were fortified

---

7. Theophus Smith notes that "some elements of American evangelical Protestantism were sufficiently similar to the African background of early black converts to allow their indigenous beliefs and practices to continue in modified form" (Theophus Smith, "The Spirituality of Afro-American Traditions," in *Christian Spirituality: Post-reformation and Modern*, ed. Louis Dupre and Don E. Saliers [New York: Crossroad, 1989], 378).

through the adoption of the Christian spiritual values and perspectives. Christianity enabled them to articulate these elements in a philosophically and theologically more robust, sophisticated, and systematic way.

Through a creative blending of Christianity and African spiritual traditions, African Americans were able to construct a new cultural form of Christianity that was different from a white American counterpart, in terms of spiritual and moral sensibilities, temperaments, and theological emphases. Adapting various elements of African and American ritualistic practices and religious understandings according to their own particular needs and purposes, African Americans were able to empower their own communities and to critique the racist structure and culture of their new country.[8] African American spirituality, consequently, features a composite, bicultural fusion of African and Anglo-American spiritualities,[9] to the extent that it is sometimes virtually impossible to distinguish the culture of origin (Africa) from the culture of adaptation (the United States).[10]

Despite this fusion and amalgamation, however, African spiritual values predisposed African Americans to particular directions in appropriating Christianity. Slaves incorporated the Christianity into their African cosmological framework, expressing its newly appropriated meanings and values creatively through their own music, songs, prayers, sermons, and folklores.[11] These African spiritual features are still alive today in African American churches, communities, and cultural activities, and in African American–owned institutions.

Although this continuity between African American Christian spirituality and the African spiritual heritages is shown in their shared features and sensibilities, it does not indicate any established doctrine or a coherent belief system. This continuity is simply marked by persistent or recurring tendencies, sensibilities,

---

8. Bridges, *Resurrection Song*, 82.

9. Smith, "Spirituality of Afro-American Traditions," 396.

10. Ibid., 372.

11. Paris, *Spirituality of African Peoples*, 38; Chireau, *Black Magic*, 54.

and temperaments. Key features of African spirituality are the ubiquity of religion, God and the moral order of the universe, hopefulness/optimism, holism, community, family, and rituals and aesthetics. How were these retained in African American spirituality?

The Ubiquity of Religion

Peter Paris identifies the ubiquity of religious consciousness as the "single most important common characteristic" of African peoples.[12] Religion is the heartbeat of African culture; it constitutes the most comprehensive and persistent category of human understanding of reality. Any visitor to Africa immediately notices that African society is profoundly religious. John Mbiti aptly illustrates the pervasiveness of religion for African peoples, observing that "to be without religion amounts to a self-excommunication from the entire life of society, and African peoples do not know how to exist without religion."[13]

The ubiquity of religion is derived from Africans' belief in the omnipresence of spirit as the source and the preserver of life. In African cosmology, the spiritual world is believed to pervade and control the material world. African society is permeated with the symbols, vocabularies, and sentiments of the spirit. As every experience is evaluated from a religious perspective, it is attributed to a spiritual cause.

The ubiquity of religion is a distinctive characteristic of African American life as well. The omnipresence of religion is demonstrated in both cultural and institutional life. The high participation of African Americans in religious organizations shows that among the many racial and ethnic groups in the United States, they are one of the most religiously active peoples. The ubiquity of religion is theologically consonant with the Christian doctrine of the omnipresence of God: God is radically related to creation to the extent that a human existence is never separate

---

12. Paris, *Spirituality of African Peoples*, 27.
13. John Mbiti, *African Religions and Philosophy* (New York: Praeger, 1969), 3.

or hidden from God, thus engendering the possibility of a radical communion of human beings with God through rituals.

The pervasiveness of religion had a profound implication for the African American struggle against racism in the United States. Religion provided a crucial mechanism of social integration that bound individual members together into a meaningful collective body. In addition, it offered the resources for sustenance and resistance against racial oppression. The inner strength that religion offered enabled African Americans to survive despite the social conditions and cultural limitations that racism imposed.

This was equally true for King, as he was a deeply religious person. Through his faith in God, King was able to overcome the destructive powers of fear and hatred. In the last years of his life, for example, he turned unceasingly to God as he faced alienation from his supporters and experienced growing criticism and pressure from the media and the government over his stance against the Vietnam War.

God and the Moral Order of the Universe

There is a structural similarity between Christianity and African theism. A key structural similarity between Christianity and African theism is that both are monotheistic. Indeed, scholars of African religion suggest that all tribes throughout Africa share a belief in a self-existing supreme deity. This deity is the benign power who oversees every aspect of the universe — nature, history, and spirit — through its agents and delegates, both human and spiritual.[14] Such a belief in a sacred cosmos created and preserved by a supreme deity understandably resonated with the Christian idea of creation.

Although traditional African religions believed that God was both transcendent and immanent, the prominence of the concept of immanence is probably a result of African communal metaphysical thinking in which God is regarded as "the patron of the

---

14. Paris, *Spirituality of African Peoples,* 28.

family,"[15] the most senior member of a community, the top of the spiritual hierarchy, and whom one had access to through the ancestral spirits.

African religions offer a sacramental understanding of nature and humanity. The universe is not the result of chance. In the cyclical return of seasons, African people saw an orderliness of the universe that was beyond human manipulation. It is sacred, pervaded by and controlled by the divine power. The universe is not morally neutral. It is structured and ordered by a moral God. Hence, the idea of the universal moral order was not at all alien to African peoples. Africans believed that the universe is structured in such a way that good is rewarded and evil is punished; one reaps what one sows. African cosmology captures this moral conviction in the phrase, "What goes around comes around."[16] The African cosmological belief in a moral order is commensurate with the Western Christian idea of natural law. The universe is not morally neutral, but rather is structured and ordered by a moral God whose laws are ingrained in nature and to which every human being and social institution is held accountable. Because this divine law is higher and more authoritative than civil laws, violation of these universal natural laws justifies civil disobedience.

Having inherited this belief, African Americans are convinced that God rules in the universe, interacting in the process of human history. African Americans are therefore typically firm believers in God's saving action in history and the rightful vindication of the innocent. God's will and purpose will be ultimately fulfilled in history against all the forces of evil, and is therefore the source of their abiding hope, for it means their unmerited suffering under white injustice will be rewarded. African American religion had early understood God to be especially concerned with the liberation of oppressed people.

---

15. Temba J. Mafico, "The African Context for Theology," *Journal of the Interdenominational Theological Center* 16, no. 1–2 (Fall 1988/Spring 1989): 74.

16. Bridges, *Resurrection Song*, 80.

King shared this trust in God and the belief in the moral nature of the universe, which constituted the backbone of his militancy for justice. King was hopeful concerning the moral direction of history toward good and the ultimate defeat of evil. He declared, "Truth, pressed to the earth, will rise again,"[17] and "The arc of the moral universe is long but it bends toward justice."[18]

Hopefulness

Hopefulness is the third feature that characterizes African spirituality. It stems from faith in the sovereignty of God in the universe. This optimism is most eminently reflected in the African view of evil. According to John Mbiti, even though Africans are quite clear about the undeniable reality of evil, and have fought with it in various ways, they have never wavered from the belief that God did not create evil and is always on the side of good.[19] By virtue of their unwavering belief in God, African cosmology does not recognize the absolute sense of evil or original sin, instead regarding human beings as the cause of, and accountable for, misery.[20]

Because African Americans inherited this African spiritual optimism and its corollary view of evil, theodicy has a very different meaning for African Americans than it does for their white counterparts, as a practical, existential issue, not a speculative and philosophical one. Because African Americans did not frame the issue in terms of the attributes of God, the contradiction between the reality of oppression and presumed goodness and omnipotence of God did not lead most of them to deny God's existence, goodness, or omnipotence.[21] They did not step back from the conviction that God surely exists and is both good and omnipotent. God's promise of deliberation was simply being delayed; therefore, like the prophet Habakkuk, they had to wait in faith and

---

17. Martin Luther King, Jr., "Where Do We Go from Here?" in *A Testament of Hope*, 252.
18. Ibid.
19. Mbiti, *African Religions and Philosophy*, 204.
20. Paris, *Spirituality of African Peoples*, 44–46.
21. The blues, a unique musical expression created by African Americans, is the exception to this sense of hopefulness.

hope. In short, the problem of theodicy has more to do with the timing of the fulfillment of God's promise than God's attributes, not "why" but rather "when." This understanding of theodicy enabled African Americans to maintain an optimistic view of history, namely the ultimate triumph of good over evil.

For African Americans, hopefulness served as an invisible but important resource of power for their struggle, for hope can suggest a new possibility for the future; it affirms and empowers human subjectivity and agency by calling persons to change the present state according to their dream of future. The ground of their hope was religion. The substance of their hope was a firm trust in God's goodness and power to deliver them. Urged by hope beyond hope in God, they were able to bounce back; they sprang up when they were pushed or crushed down. Hope was a spiritual form of power. Hope enabled slaves not to be helpless prisoners of their present imposed condition or state.

King inherited this optimistic historical outlook. During the civil rights movement, King constantly injected his followers with a sense of hope and optimism. He encouraged them to never lose hope of victory, despite temporary disappointments, failures, or setbacks. For King and his followers, hopefulness, as a spiritual form of power, served as a great antidote to white intimidations and threats, stemming any tendency toward violent retaliation resulting from frustration, and diminishing their fear of the possible failure of the movement.

King's optimism was expressed in various philosophical and theological languages, such as "the new age," "the new era," "the spirit of time," and *"Zeitgeist."* King believed that despite various obstacles, ultimate victory for his movement was inevitable as human history was moving toward freedom and justice. He saw the evidence of this new era and age in the liberation and independence of Asian and African nations from the colonial powers. In response to this dawning of a new age, human beings were summoned to facilitate, indeed to speed up, the advent of the new order by serving as God's co-workers.

Holism

African spirituality is holistic. It refuses to divide a person into separate parts, such as mind, body, and soul. It does not compartmentalize reality by separating the sacred and the secular, the political and the economic, the religious and the social, because all are comprehensively interrelated in nature. African peoples believed that the three most important aspects of the cosmos, namely nature, history, and spirit, are "ontologically united and hence interdependent."[22] This holism prevented African peoples from seeing one reality in isolation from the rest. Instead they conceived of God, community, family, and person as interdependent, connected, and mutually sustaining.

This holistic or unified attitude toward nature, human beings, and spirits is also the reflection of communal thinking. As the ultimate goal of a universe where God, nature, history, and humanity are all united, a community represents the most inclusive and encompassing category of perceiving reality. At the height and center of a community is God. God is the source of this unity and integration: "God is radically related to everything and binds everything together."[23]

African holism is intimately related to the African virtue of practical wisdom that emphasizes problem-solving ability rather than speculative abstract analysis. Practical wisdom has to do with excellence in judgment where a person examines the problem by considering all of its possible interconnections, weighing all available options, and choosing the most plausible solution within the constraints of time, energy, and resources.[24] Holism, in its intimate connection to practical wisdom, does not indicate a closed system of thought or ideas. Rather it means an endeavoring approximation to the truth of reality, using the best available human minds.

---

22. Paris, *Spirituality of African Peoples*, 22.
23. Bridges, *Resurrection Song*, 41.
24. Paris, *Spirituality of African Peoples*, 145.

Such holism runs deep also in the African American spiritual tradition. African Americans take an integrated approach to reality; they resist the Western analytic thinking that separates myth from fact, intuition from intellect, the natural from the supernatural, and religion from science. They see as inseparably linked "the seen and the unseen, the material and the spiritual, the natural and the unnatural, the individual and the community and the community and God."[25] No incident is the consequence of pure chance or accident. Nothing and no one is isolated.

Reflecting this orientation, King's worldview and attitude toward ministry were holistic. He rejected any docetic understanding of God; religion must attend to the whole person, indeed the whole realm of human existence — the social and material as well as the personal and psychological issues of people. Likewise, King repudiated a monocausal analysis of or solution to a social problem. He refused to differentiate political problems from economic ones, or domestic from international issues; they are all intertwined. Thus the solution of one problem requires the critique and reformation of the system as a whole.

Community

The idea of community has always been at the heart of traditional African cosmology. It is sacred because it was believed to be created by the supreme deity,[26] and it is an organic spiritual entity, not a human-made institution.[27] It is understood not as an artificial collection of self-sufficient, isolated individuals, but as an organism of conspiring persons — literally breathing together, or sharing one spirit — "united among themselves even to the very centre of their being."[28]

---

25. Ibid., 67.
26. Ibid., 51.
27. Augustine Shutte, *Ubuntu: An Ethic for a New South Africa* (Pietermaritzburg, South Africa: Cluster Publications, 2001), 26.
28. Leopold Senghor, "Negritude and African Socialism," in *St. Anthony's Paper*, 15, ed. K. Kirkwood (London: Chatto and Windus, 1963), 16; cited in Shutte, *Ubuntu*, 26.

A community is first experienced in a clan, kin, village, and tribe, but is often extended to include strangers — sometimes referred to as "fictive kin." Even the whole of humanity can be understood as an extended family, with God as their parents and others as fellow siblings. Indeed, for Africans community is so central that the relationship between the living and the living dead continues after death. Ancestors are never abandoned but are believed to be reborn through its living members, through this sense of community.

The African emphasis on community is reflected in its corporate view of a person.[29] Human beings cannot live apart from a community. They become full humans through a community. Mbiti notes:

> Only in terms of other people does the individual become conscious of his own being, his own duties, his privileges and responsibilities toward himself and towards other people. When he suffers, he does not suffer alone but with the corporate group; when he rejoices, he rejoices not alone but with his kinsmen, his neighbors and his relatives whether dead or living. . . . Whatever happens to the individual happens to the whole group, and whatever happens to the whole group happens to the individual. The individual can only say: "I am, because we are; and since we are, therefore I am." This is a cardinal point in the understanding of the African view of man.[30]

The community is the goal of human existence; it is where one finds and fulfills one's humanity. The essence of being human is being communal, and vice versa. Anything that frustrates this goal is regarded as immoral. One owes one's existence, growth, and fulfillment to others, including all generations of the past, present, and future. A community serves as a natural source of growth for each person in relationships with others. A biological birth is not

---

29. See Mbiti, *African Religions and Philosophy*, 108.
30. Ibid., 108–9.

sufficient; a person must be born socially through various rites of passage and incorporation (i.e., birth, puberty, marriage, death). A person moves from one stage of a corporate life to another until death, which Africans regard as the final transition required for one's incorporation into the wider kin of both the living and the dead.

A higher degree of personhood is usually assigned to older persons who have lived long among others and to those who have contributed to the well-being of their community. Elders and persons of higher social status are to be respected, just as they are expected to be benevolent toward their juniors and followers, working for their well-being.

In the African worldview, community and individuals are continuous:

> One can only do justice to the African conception of community by visualizing it as a single person.... Each individual member of the community sees the community as themselves, as one with them in character and identity. Each individual sees every other individual member as *another self*.[31]

The relationships and transactions between the members and the community as a whole remain fully personal. "The community is the 'I' writ large and the 'I' is the community individualized."[32] To be more fully human, one must participate deeply in the life of a community. For this reason, excommunication, separation from the community, is understood as the harshest punishment possible for the commission of crimes.

The concept of *ubuntu* presents a unique African notion that crystallizes the African people's communal spirituality. The axiom *Umuntu Ngumuntu Ngabantu* (A person is a person through

---

31. Shutte, *Ubuntu*, 26; emphasis is his.
32. Lebamang J. Sebidi, "Toward a Definition of Ubuntu as African Humanism," in *Perspectives on Ubuntu*, ed. M. Gideon Khabela and Z. C. Mzonlei (Alice, South Africa: Lovedale Press, 1998), 66.

other persons) sums up the kernel of *ubuntu*.[33] In and through community, a person becomes a person in the truest sense, acquiring skills and the virtues that define a human.[34]

Ubuntu is the moral quality acquired and grown in community. *Ubuntu* is not static; rather it can be increased or decreased, enhanced or lost. Each person may display a different degree of *ubuntu,* depending on the level of growth or maturity in community he or she has achieved. A good person has a greater degree of actualized *ubuntu* in his or her life. Wickedness or evil indicates the lack or deficiency of *ubuntu* that is expressed in antisocial behavior and attitudes such as hatred, resentfulness, and bitterness toward others.

Ubuntu is evinced in such communal moral qualities as gentleness, love, modesty, respect for seniors, sharing and caring for each other, forgiveness, kindness, hospitality, and so on. In the spirituality of *ubuntu,* there is no distinction between one's own interest and the interests of others. Self-fulfillment and fulfillment of the other are inseparable. A person of *ubuntu* always treats others as if they were another self.[35]

Because of this inherent other-centered orientation, *ubuntu*ism is inclusive and humane, almost to a fault.[36] *Ubuntu*ists can easily be taken advantage of because they have a nearly unconditional, generous openness toward others. They are vulnerable to deception, manipulation, and the rapaciousness of the wicked.

An understanding of *ubuntu* is impossible without an understanding of African spiritualism. In Africa, spirit is believed to be

---

33. One finds other proverbs conveying similar communal sentiments and sensibilities. For example, here are two proverbs from the Venda Society: *Muthu u bebelwa munwe* (A person is born for others) and *Munwe muthihi a u tusi mathuthu* (One finger cannot take a sample from the pot). (J. H. Smit, "Ubuntu Africa: A Christian Interpretation," in *Ubuntu in a Christian Perspective,* ed. J. H. Smit, M. Deacon, and A. Shutte [Potchefstroom, South Africa: Potchefstroom University Press, 1999], 14).

34. *Ubuntu* is roughly translated by the English word "personhood" and "humanity," yet more accurately refers to the moral, humane quality of a person that promotes mutuality, solidarity, and community.

35. Shutte, *Ubuntu,* 31.

36. Sebidi, "Toward a Definition of Ubuntu as African Humanism," 66.

a vital force shared by humanity. All humanity participates in one spirit, and as spiritual beings, humans transcend a mere material realm, seeking relationship with others in spiritual community. Africans understand that this desire for relationship is made possible by the spiritual power that exists in humanity. To grow as a human is to both educe and inculcate to the fullest extent this spiritual quality within every person. The spiritual and the communal are almost interchangeable. The more closely we identify with a community, the more strongly we develop our own humanity, our *ubuntu,* and the more deeply we enter into the hearts and minds of others, partaking of one spirit. Because of the intrinsic spiritual and communal nature of human beings, it is the African belief that community cannot be built or maintained by legislation or institutional changes alone; there must be a spiritual transformation.

That African Americans inherited this organic communal ethos we see in their cohesive and extensive family systems, their naming rituals, their respect for elders, their relational understanding of personhood, and their emphasis on communal well-being. African American spirituality is communal in its outlook as it seeks human happiness and fulfillment in a community. Persons are virtuous to the extent they contribute toward community. If full personhood is the highest goal of a personal moral striving, it is possible only in a community in relationship to God and others. This communal understanding leads African Americans to regard the community as a corporal spiritual entity like that of an individual, and thus to seek society's transformation as well as the individual's.

In this vein, it is not surprising that African Americans share similar communal virtues with African people. Peter Paris identifies beneficence, generosity, forbearance, forgiveness, nonviolence, improvisation, practical wisdom, and justice as the major virtues shared by African peoples and African Americans. All these virtues are communal in nature and indispensable for the formation and protection of community.

The struggle against racism, joined with the African heritage of virtues they carried with them, had a profound impact on African Americans. The overcoming of social evils in the creation of a community requires the sets of virtues that support and empower these tasks. For example, the virtue of forbearance was fostered through their long-standing endurance under the adverse conditions of slavery and segregation. Forbearance was required for survival in the midst of dehumanizing situations. It is not synonymous with tolerance or acquiescence, nor is it being content with oppression or justifying injustice; forbearance is best defined as actively waiting for the time of their freedom by enduring adversities in faith, love, and hope. Their role models for endurance under suffering were biblical characters like Job and Joseph. Emulating these figures, African Americans did not allow their suffering to crush their soul and spirit. Like these figures, they believed they would emerge triumphantly from suffering when God finally vindicated their cause.

King's spirituality disclosed these communal traits of African American spirituality. His idea of community and his virtues closely resonated with the African communal spirituality of *ubuntu*. King manifested a high degree of *ubuntu* in his concern for community and his generous, benevolent treatment of others as if they were his own. His speeches and writings usually concluded with a strong communal note and vision in counterbalance to his unrelenting militancy against social evils. For example, his signature sermon "I Have a Dream" was profoundly communal in its message, tone, and ethos. In the sermon, he invited the audience to envision together that "the sons of former slaves and the sons of former slave-owners will be able to sit down together at the table of brotherhood."[37] Elsewhere in the same sermon, he urged the United States to "transform the jangling discords of our nation into a beautiful symphony of brotherhood."[38]

---

37. King, "I Have a Dream," in *A Testament of Hope*, 219.
38. Ibid.

Family

Family is the foremost unit of a community and also a micro-cosm of its wider community. The African family is communal, formed by a large, closely knit kinship of blood that is multi-generational and strongly linked in reciprocal aid and support in all areas of life — material, spiritual, and moral. Each family member is expected to contribute to the well-being of the kin group.

Peter Paris identifies the eight most distinctive values of the African family that have been preserved and transmitted by African Americans through generations:

1. the natural cohesion of blood relatives;

2. the undying presence of maternal bonding;

3. deep respect for the practical wisdom of the elderly;

4. the power of the elderly to bless or curse;

5. deference of the younger to the older siblings and the responsibility of the latter for the former;

6. unquestioned obedience to the authority of parents and the elderly;

7. a communal ethos of generosity and unselfishness, and

8. belief in life after death and the reunion of the entire family with God in the spirit world.[39]

Paris says all these values were deeply grounded in African spiritual traditions, transmitted to slaves, and passed on to later generations, down to today. For example, African Americans attach much moral value and significance to the extended family network. It is common for several generations to live together in the same house. Young married couples and their own children often live with their parents/in-laws until they become financially independent. As in African families, grandparents take a high and respected place in the African American family. Through

---

39. Paris, *Spirituality of African Peoples*, 90.

their presence and care, grandparents — and particularly grandmothers — give emotional and spiritual stability to grandchildren.
It is primarily the grandmothers who are the bearers of tradition, wisdom, and knowledge, transmitting the communal values
through their loving care and education of their grandchildren.
As a result, it is common for a very strong relational bond to exist
between grandparents and grandchildren.

In the United States, through the adoption of Christianity,
family obtained an additional meaning for African Americans.
In particular the church functioned as a kind of extended family for them. Under the influence of African communalism, the
family and the church became essentially indistinguishable. If the
church was the extension of the family, the family (as a shared
community of love) was the content of the church. The family is
now understood to extend beyond the immediate relationships
of blood, kinship, or marriage to include strangers and other
people, even all of humanity itself.[40] We still find this communal, kinship role of the church wherever African Americans form
a community.

Rituals and Aesthetics

The continuity between African and African American spirituality is also found in their practices of a ritual life, such as
ecstatic ritual performances, ritual healing, conjuration, and spirit
possession. Although time may have obscured some specific aspects of the African religious heritages, basic distinctive structures
were transmitted through oral culture.[41] Singing, religious dancing, worship styles, the ring shout, vocal delivery, ceremonial
chants, stamping, call-and-response, polyrhythms, syncopation,
ornamentation, repetition, hand clapping, foot stomping, thigh

---

40. Shutte, *Ubuntu*, 29.
41. For the African religious roots of African American preaching, see
Valentino Lassiter, *Martin Luther King in the African American Preaching
Tradition* (Cleveland: Pilgrim Press, 2001).

slapping, and heterophony are all influenced by the African ritual heritage.

With their basic communal disposition, rituals in Africa stress communion with spirits (ancestors or other spirits) through spirit possession or trance. Like African rituals, African American worship is characterized by seeking and experiencing the spirit; the difference lies in the identity of that spirit. Slaves found that the emphasis on spiritualism in African religious practices and the emphasis on the charism of the Spirit in Christian practice were compatible, both stressing the manifestation of the Spirit in prophecy, healing, and trance. Likewise, spirit possession has "a foundational status in black religion and culture,"[42] serving as a root metaphor of ecstatic performance for African peoples, overtly and covertly in various religious, cultural, and political contexts like jazz clubs, religious meetings, and political rallies. It was "the height of worship — the supreme religious act."[43]

The belief in the immediacy of the Spirit meant that improvisation was often an integral part of rituals, for the improvisation responded to the urges or prompts of the Spirit at the same time as it responded to the identified needs and demands of the participants. For example, African American preaching is grounded in and mobilizes the tones and energies of spiritual immediacy and responses.

Call-and-response is another ritual action that is both highly spiritual and communal, and it is found in almost all African American worship experiences. In particular, this rhetorical device of call-and-response — where the ritual leader enjoins or exhorts with a phrase to which the congregation or community responds, often repeatedly — emphasizes freedom, improvisation, creativity, and participation through its dynamic interaction and exchange between a speaker and the listeners. The pattern of call-and-response can continue through simple verbal variations often enjoined with changes in intonation. The phrase is improvised freely

---

42. Smith, "Spirituality of Afro-American Traditions," 377.
43. Henry H. Mitchell, *Black Belief* (New York: Harper & Row, 1975), 144.

and indefinitely, as a leader feels appropriate, as moved and led by the Spirit. It elicits the participation and engagement of the listeners with the effect of creating a bond of solidarity and unity between the chanter and the audience, and within the audience itself. Collective energies arise; collective trance and collective spirit possession are experienced, and uplifting and healing bring the group's spirit to a new level of solidarity and determination toward freedom. This participatory and improvisational dynamic of African American worship is also found in other realms of African American life, such as cultural-political practices and social activism.

The liturgical emphasis on immediacy and participation had built-in political implications for African Americans. As the indication of the mastery of music and sermon, improvisation meant for African Americans the rejection of repetition or passivity that results from dependence on received notes, stanzas, doctrines, and passages. The dynamic of improvisational exchange manifests the will to agency (subjectivity) and transformation, yearning for freedom, with the determination to refuse to be boxed into the imposed confines of social and religious structures and boundaries.

Likewise, there is an intrinsic connection between the communal experience in mass worship and social transformation in African American spiritual life. Replete with multiple political and religious symbols and metaphors, worship became a moment to express freely this desire for the community of freedom, peace, and justice. African American rituals and worship are unique in approaching ethics and therapy together, holistically addressing psychological and social needs of people at the same time. African American preachers connect the therapy and ethics in their liturgies; they perform both prophetic and priestly functions simultaneously in their rituals for the community, and as therapeutic agents they are concerned with both the psychological wholeness and the moral integrity — the sociopolitical well-being — of the community.[44]

---

44. Smith, "Spirituality of Afro-American Traditions," 384.

Worship offers a therapeutic and liberating experience for the participants coping with the stressful realities of racism in their daily lives by offering occasions for psychic release, healing, and the renewal of social cohesion.[45] It encourages the unrestrained personal expression and participation in collective worship, the affirmation of individual selfhood often denied by a society conditioned to accept racism, and the freedom to release and disclose the usually concealed or repressed self.[46]

All told, we can see that in African American churches, worship is experienced in a sustained drama with a high spiritual intensity that has profound political implication. It aims for the healing and transformation of the self and community.

The ritualistic and aesthetic aspects of African American spirituality were prominent in the styles and techniques of King's own preaching and public speech. King was adept in the skills of improvisation, parallelism, contrast, and synthesis — borrowing and appropriating cultural and religious elements from various traditions and fusing them into a new, creative, and meaningful whole. He put African American worship to use for the purpose of the civil rights struggle. King saw a deeper connection between worship and social change — a renewing and cathartic power of African American worship for social transformation. His adroit use and mastery of rich religious imagery and metaphors charmed and thrilled the audience, deeply touching and moving their souls toward committed actions for justice and reconciliation.

The Spirituals

Like rituals, music and song express a community's history, experiences, values, and religious beliefs. The African culture is defined by music as much as by stories and rituals, and so music is an integral part of African work, worship, community life, and play. Slaves brought the culture of their music and religion to the

---

45. Ibid., 377.
46. Ibid., 384.

United States, and combined the memory of the African past with the Christian gospel and stories, music and songs to create what became known as spirituals.

African American spirituals grew out of the collective experience of slavery and racism. They disclose the influences of African spiritual traditions and their amalgamation with the U.S. cultures. The very name itself and the genre of spirituals tell of the ubiquity of religion and spirit in the African American culture. A careful study of spirituals shows that even under slavery, spiritualism and communalism — the most distinctive dimensions of African spirituality — remained intact.

The spirituals conveyed a strong communal sentiment, emphasizing family and the reunion with loved ones after death, particularly with those removed from their families by slave owners. The lyrics of spirituals are full of references to father, mother, brothers, sisters, uncles, aunts, and others with whom slaves anticipated a heavenly reunion. Slavery meant a broken community; this intolerable burden of loss resulted in the metaphor of home becoming prominent in spirituals. Indeed, the metaphor of home came to be used interchangeably with that of heaven, the place where reunion with lost family members takes place, the place where family will no longer depart or be removed by others. In heaven, a perfect community is fulfilled with God, ancestors, and other missing members of one's family. Whether "home" meant the African homeland, heaven (the eternal home), Canada, or the northern United States, the metaphor symbolized a liberated beloved community. The prominence of the motifs of family and home in spirituals discloses that the slaves were expressing the basic structures of African communal life through ancestral devotion.[47]

Spirituals contained and conveyed profound political and social implications and relevance in the African American struggle against racism. As the record of the slaves' agonies, struggles,

---

47. Paris, *Spirituality of African Peoples*, 57.

and hope in the inherited African spiritual framework, spirituals show the depth and resilience of African American political struggles toward freedom and their yearning for community. They enabled African Americans to "retain a measure of African identity while living in the midst of American slavery, providing the substance and the rhythm to cope with human servitude."[48] The most prominent theme of spirituals was of African Americans as the chosen people or the children of God, a self-understanding that affirmed their human dignity and identity on a transcendent religious basis, beyond the control of any social system. The theological ideas adopted from their oppressors' religion became their moral standard and shield.

Many spirituals carried hopeful and optimistic messages. With politically and religiously laden metaphoric meanings, spirituals communicated to slaves and their descendants "incurable optimism" about the ultimate destiny of human beings in God.[49] The ground of their hope was the faith in God's sovereignty and the ultimate justice in the universe.[50] Although sorrows and melancholy are expressed, overall "spirituals are a joyful and optimistic genre, in that they continually emphasize that a better time will come through the intervention of God and that great happiness is awaiting in heaven."[51] The metaphors in spirituals (e.g., Jesus as "the bright and morning star," "water in dry places," "a doctor to the sick," "a rock in a wearied land") expressed African American people's yearning for life over death, love over hatred, hope over despair, and justice over evil, thus in the midst of suffering still proclaiming, "I ain't tired yet."

---

48. James H. Cone, *The Spirituals and the Blues: An Interpretation* (Maryknoll, NY: Orbis Books, 1991), 30.

49. Howard Thurman, *Deep River and the Negro Spiritual Speaks of Life and Death* (Richmond, IN: Friends United Press, 1975), 82.

50. W. E. B. Du Bois, *The Souls of Black Folk* (New York: Dover Publications, 1994), 162.

51. Hans A. Baer and Merrill Singer, *African American Religion: Varieties of Protest and Accommodation*, 2nd ed. (Knoxville: University of Tennessee Press, 2002), 254.

King frequently quoted spirituals in his various speeches and sermons. For example, the finale of his speech, "I Have a Dream," was from an old African American spiritual: "Free at last, free at last; thank God Almighty, we are free at last."

Racism and African American Spirituality

The African American quest for a community obtained a new impulse and urgency in the United States. Under the dehumanizing conditions of racism, African American spirituality inevitably developed a strong political character of protest and resistance. The themes of freedom and liberation were found in early forms of African American folk religion in the southern United States. The political nature of African American spirituality was a natural reaction to racism. Racism was antithetical to community. The actualization of a free, equal, and reciprocal community was the aspiration of every African American person. Yet their quest for freedom has been different from an ordinary liberal democratic quest for human rights, which usually has a strong individualistic overtone and emphasis. It has always been circumscribed and inspired by a religious dimension because of the continuous influences of the African cultural tradition of the ubiquity of religion and its holism. The combination of the slaves' penchant for justice and the African quest for community gave rise to a unique form of a politico-communal spirituality that upheld freedom, justice, and love as the core values of human beings.

The search for justice and community was also expanded and refined by African Americans' encounter with Christianity. Since the time they discovered the liberating message of the gospel, the Christian faith has been a moral and spiritual source of self-esteem and strength for the African American community. The Christian gospel was found to be truly universal and liberating despite white slave owners' hypocrisy.[52] Slaves interpreted

---

52. Peter J. Paris, *The Social Teaching of the Black Churches* (Philadelphia: Fortress Press, 1985), 111.

the Scripture with a meaning that affirmed their humanity and their African heritages. The elements of the biblical narrative were selected in light of their social and cultural experiences and values, and in accordance with the emphases of African spiritual heritages. Their appropriation of Christianity was an Africanized one, as Christianity expanded and refocused in a new social context the communal and holistic feature of the African spirituality.

The fundamental African American struggle in the United States, both materially and spiritually, can be characterized by the search for the freedom to establish a community. With the balance between individual human freedom and the quest for community, African American spirituality emphasized both the intrinsic worth and the interrelatedness of all human beings in God. The biblical basis of this principle was the *imago dei*, in which African Americans found a liberating affirmation of their dignity and worth and their search for community.[53] Created by the same God in the same image, all human beings, regardless of their skin color, are free and equal before God. Their dignity and worth are transcendent and eternal. At the same time, all human beings are interdependent as they share their common origin in God as creatures made in God's image. Therefore, a community is onto-theologically given; it is not socially constructed.

The African American Church

African American churches have an indispensable place in African American experience in the United States. They are the most enduring institution that African Americans own. African American spirituality comprises three major sources: the African religious

---

53. According to Howard Thurman, for African Americans, the understanding of the *imago dei* has developed out of their experience of racism. They intuitively caught the political implication and pastoral significance of this biblical doctrine for their future freedom and present moral-psychological well-being (Thurman, *Deep River and the Negro Spiritual Speaks of Life and Death*, 11–12).

heritages, the influences of the European American religion and culture, and the collective experiences of slavery and racism; the African American church is where all three sources are found syncretized in a creative form for their struggle for freedom and a community. Their own churches allowed African Americans to continuously affirm and celebrate their inherited African cultural, spiritual heritages. African Americans were able to establish and maintain racial solidarity through their churches by providing a common set of moral values, religious rituals, and symbols that unite African Americans. Most social activities — political, economic, social, educational, cultural, in addition to religious — took place in and around the churches. In addition to formal worship services, their churches offered various opportunities for social gatherings for African Americans, creating a safe environment in which to share their sentiments, to practice their values, and to educate their children regarding the sanctity and equality of human beings and the rightness of their quest for justice.

Spiritual Tradition

Out of this collective experience and shared spiritual heritage a distinctive form of spiritual tradition arose: "the black church tradition," which is epitomized by the principles of "the parenthood of God and the kinship of humanity."[54] A congruence exists between African cosmology and the black church tradition. The principles of the parenthood of God and the kinship of humanity are consistent with the African understanding of the Creator God and the interdependence of humanity.

The anthropology of the black church tradition represents the reconstruction of African cosmology through the incorporation of Christian theology around the idea of the *imago dei*. According to these principles, everyone is equally God's child, regardless of race and ethnicity. At the same time, having God as parent, every

---

54. See Paris, *Social Teaching of the Black Churches.*

person is also interrelated and interdependent in God. The moral content of the principles is communal.

African American people did not invent these principles. The principles of the parenthood of God and the kinship of humanity were African American people's creative appropriation and interpretation of the essence of the gospel, inspired by their African communal spirituality. In other words, one may say that the black church tradition is an expression of the African communal spirituality in a Christian framework. The African idea of the transcendent supreme deity and the notion of the communal interdependence of humanity converged and gave rise to the unique African American communal spiritual tradition.

Identified as the spiritual essence of the gospel, the principles of the parenthood of God and the kinship of humanity had a universal moral import and political implication. Eschatologically, these principles envisioned a society free from any form of racism, a society where all humanity is in a loving harmony in God. For African American people, these principles provided a theological justification for their political struggle for freedom, equality, and solidarity. As a universal moral referent, they helped to disclose the discrepancy between white people's biblical confession and their practice of racism. It is not difficult to see that King's idea of the beloved community was the outgrowth and articulation of the black church tradition, centered on these principles.

Political Aspects

The African American church was the embodiment of the communal and collective political will of its community. Essentially, in the African American church, both vital concerns of seeking freedom and creating community coincide. Through their moral authority over African American masses, African American churches served simultaneously as the base for African American community building and self-reliance, on the one hand, and the African American political struggle for self-determination, on the other. Church contributed to the well-being of African Americans through these three strategies for coping with the degrading impact of racism: (1) empowerment of individuals through the nurturing of spiritual succor and virtues in a community, (2) creating independent social spaces and institutions that could be owned and controlled by African Americans, and (3) launching into a massive movement set on tackling racist systems.

Framed by a communal spirituality, the symbiosis of the prophetic and the priestly (the political and the communal) ministries has been a distinctive characteristic of African American churches. African American Christian ministers discovered quickly in their struggle against racism that the pastoral care of individual members and the social criticism of slavery, segregation, and racism are inseparable. As W. E. B. Du Bois observes, the slave preachers carried the functions of "the healer of the sick [priestly], the interpreter of the Unknown [mystical], the comforter of the sorrowing [pastoral], the supernatural avenger of wrong [prophetic]."[55] They found that it was impossible to effectively deal with one without addressing the others. Racist social structures are culpable for personal sufferings of individual African Americans. Many of the pathological and dysfunctional symptoms found in African American families and their larger communities cannot be dealt with without addressing the problem of racism in society. King embodied the tradition of the slave preacher in one of its most productive forms.

The Exodus Story

The Exodus story offered a paradigmatic symbol of political spirituality for African American Christians. The story has a prominent place in their faith as an archetypal symbol for a religiously motivated political transformation. The symbolic imagery and metaphor are replete in spirituals, early African American gospel music, poems, and sermons. Like the Jews before them, early slaves found their most appropriate spiritual languages and symbols in the Exodus story. African American clergy, unlike

---

55. Du Bois, *Souls of Black Folk*, 119.

many other Protestant evangelicals, refused to allegorize the Exodus story as an individual spiritual pilgrimage — a personal spiritual passage to overcome the power of sin and enter heaven. Rich with such spiritual themes and motifs as evil, passage, temptations, and idolatry, and reaching the destination while overcoming stumbles and obstacles, African American Christians, and with them Martin Luther King, Jr., interpreted the Exodus story as the saga of a people in their collective spiritual journey from slavery to freedom through the rise of their new peoplehood.[56] They found in the story a direct political relevance and a theological basis for the African American struggle for liberation; it was a political paradigm of liberation.

The Exodus provided a moral framework for the spiritual interpretation of political situations affecting African Americans. It condemned a collective aspect of human sin and evil, as embodied in Pharaoh's slavery system. And it showed that slavery was not an individual problem, but a structural evil that is beyond the occasional individual goodwill of slave owners. The Exodus story conveyed God's unfailing care and intervention in human suffering.

Communal Power

Because of their roots in African communal spirituality, African Americans rejected a unilateral notion and use of power, because they were firsthand victims of just such power. Unilateral power creates isolation, separation, castes, and segregation. It goes against the solidarity of humanity. It is not based on equality, reciprocity, and cooperation, but rather on a coercive power directed toward others, or the denial of relationship.

The power exercised by the African American church has been communal in nature. Communal power is characterized not only by its rejection of injustices but also by its active openness toward the other, or keeping the conditions of communication open

---

56. See Michael Walzer, *Exodus and Revolution* (New York: HarperCollins, 1985).

to others while challenging the implications in their injustice.[57] Communal power, in its exercise, acknowledges the fundamental solidarity of humanity and the recognition of otherness, including one's enemies. Often called soul force, moral suasion, nonviolence, and so on,[58] it is based on reciprocity, collaboration, and equality. Communal power recognizes the unity between the contending parties as they strive toward a community.

Racial solidarity formed around a shared religious vision, and the communal power of the church was politically useful in effecting a change in society. It is not a coincidence that African American churches were at the center of the civil rights movement. The movement's initiating and sustaining power stemmed largely from the spiritual, moral, and cultural resources of the southern African American churches. They informed the movement's vision, character, and method. African American pastors and lay Christians were the major leaders and participants in the movement. The dissemination of information, organizational meetings, and mass rallies for the movement took place in African American churches, as training in the philosophy of nonviolence, demonstrations, and sit-ins were also organized and mobilized in the communities by the churches.[59]

The Montgomery Bus Boycott was a typical case in setting the spiritual tone and pattern for the movement, with African American clergy and lay leaders exercising leadership roles in various functions and capacities. Not only did the churches initially raise money for the boycott, but they also served as dispatch centers.[60] The most notable example of the organizational support

---

57. Paris, *Social Teaching of the Black Churches*, 115.
58. Ibid.
59. Baldwin, *There Is a Balm in Gilead*, 192. The connection between African American churches and the civil rights movement is also indicated by the fact that the SCLC (Southern Christian Leadership Conference), the movement's headquarters and leadership organization, was variously called "the social action arm of the black church," "the black church writ large," even "a church" and "a faith operation."
60. John Ansbro, *Martin Luther King, Jr.: The Making of a Mind* (Maryknoll, NY: Orbis Books, 1982), 179.

that African American churches provided for the boycott was the carpool that transported people morning and evening, day and night, for more than thirteen months of the boycott period.

Nonviolent resistance, a major method of the movement, was the expression of the communal power of African Americans.[61] The notion of nonviolence was not at all alien to African Americans because it is consistent with their African communal spiritual heritages. The inherited nonviolent communal spiritual disposition was further refined and strengthened in the United States by the slave ancestors' nonviolent, communal interpretation of the Christian gospel.

African Americans found an elective affinity between African peoples' communal spirituality and the love ethics of Jesus (see the Sermon on the Mount). Although African American churches had not developed any coherent theory of nonviolence before Gandhi, the seeds of nonviolence had indeed existed there. Historically, African American Christians have had a special penchant toward the Sermon on the Mount and Jesus' sacrificial love on the cross.[62] African Americans, by virtue of their belief in the power of spirit and the ubiquity of religion in their lives, were naturally receptive to Gandhi's idea of soul force and his method of nonviolence. Having grown up in a nonviolent, communal atmosphere, it was King who ingeniously tapped into and mobilized the deeply rooted, communal spirituality of African American people. Through his study of Gandhi, King introduced nonviolence as a coherent philosophy, method, and practice for a massive African American social movement.

During the civil rights movement, the nonviolent nature of African American spirituality was expressed in the extraordinary power of forgiveness demonstrated by the oppressed toward their oppressors. Even in the face of the most brutal white violence, African Americans generally maintained a conciliatory,

---

61. Paris, *Social Teaching of the Black Churches,* 115.
62. See Baldwin, *There Is a Balm in Gilead,* 170.

nonviolent attitude toward whites. Forgiveness is an indispensable first step toward reconciliation, and thus a community making/forming/restoring event. Forgiveness is indispensable for the restoration of a once alienated and antagonized relationship. It is integral to the building of a community; there can be no community without forgiveness. Forgiveness has a saving power for both victims and perpetrators. Without forgiveness, harbored hatred and fear bring imbalance and disintegration to them, slowly destroying the essence of their lives.[63]

Summary

African American spirituality displays distinctive characteristics and dynamics that are ritualistic, communal, political, and aesthetic.[64] Among these various dynamics, communal and political dynamics are most prominent in its social expression. In response

---

63. E. Franklin Frazier was totally mistaken in claiming that "Gandhism as a philosophy and a way of life is completely alien to the Negro and has nothing in common with the social heritage of the Negro" (E. Franklin Frazier, *Negro Church in America* [New York: Schocken Books, 1966], 75). Other scholars of African American religion have been arguing that African American adherence to a nonviolent method had to do with their Christian faith. For example, Nathan I. Huggins says that the method of nonviolence was effective in the South because of the deep tradition of "Christian stoicism" in the African American community (Nathan I. Huggins, "Martin Luther King, Jr.: Charisma and Leadership," *Journal of American History* 74, no. 2 [September 1987]: 480–81). However, his argument is only partially true to the extent that the churches were the places where the nonviolent ethos was most systemically nurtured. It is more accurate to say that Christian stoicism, which Huggins identified as the major cultural resource of nonviolent resistance, was none other than the unique African communal spiritual heritages infused into African American Christianity. For a long time, a nonviolent African American Christian tradition contributed to the moderation of African Americans in the midst of white violence in the South because the African communal heritages were most replete and abounded in the South.

64. Smith, "Spirituality of Afro-American Traditions," 372ff. Smith identifies the ritualistic, the aesthetic, and the political as the three major dynamics of African American spirituality developed through their religious and social experiences. On the basis of the aforementioned discussion of the African origin of African American spirituality, however, I add communal to the list. African American spirituality cannot be properly understood without the explication of

to hostile racism and by virtue of its inherited communal pro-clivity, African American spirituality, in its social expression, has been communal and political. If the communal takes the community as the goal of every meaningful human striving under the presumption of the interdependence of humanity, the political emphasizes human responsibility and exertion toward social transformation and justice, for the liberation of the oppressed in particular. As racism offered the external, negative stimuli for the African American search for freedom and community, African spiritual heritages have served as the positive resource for the rise of a distinctive racial identity and a political change agency to persist in this search for community. Other dynamics and sensibilities of ubiquity of religion, belief in God's natural laws and moral orders, hopefulness, and rituals and aesthetics were distilled into the communal and political spirituality. Consistent with their African spiritual origins, the ultimate goal has been to build a community where they could finally be free to actualize their lives.

The prominence of the communal and the political dynamics does not mean, however, that other dynamics and sensibilities of African American spirituality are not present or not important. As their spiritual struggles were focused on overcoming racism on personal and communal levels, other dynamics played supportive roles, rendering resilience, intellectual criticism and defense, personal succors and psychological strengths, temporary transcendence and relief. Their unwavering faith in God was the source of power and hope for African Americans in their struggle against racism. Hopefulness sustained their spirits and courage in otherwise totally disappointing conditions. Rituals and aesthetics provided them with new energies and powers to carry out the struggles. This convergence of various spiritual dynamics around the communal and the political thrusts was critical for the success of the civil rights movement under the leadership of Martin Luther King, Jr.

---

its communal dimension. Communalism is a peculiar African spiritual sensibility in which the ubiquity of religion, holism, ritual, and aesthetic experiences converge.

Chapter 2

Family, Church, and Schools in the Formation of King's Spirituality

This chapter explores the continuity between King's spirituality and African heritage, centering on such salient African spiritual features as the ubiquity of religion, communalism, holism, hopefulness, and the improvisation of rituals and aesthetics. It shows how these spiritual emphases were naturally acquired through King's family, church, and community in the South, then refined and expanded through his education at Morehouse College, Crozer Theological Seminary, and Boston University School of Theology.

Although he was not consciously aware of the influences of African spiritual factors on his life, it is highly plausible that King drank heavily from the deep well of them, particularly through community, folktales, religious institutions, music, and anecdotal family culture. Although these spiritual heritages existed not in a pure form but mixed with other cultural and religious influences, a strong sense of historical continuity between King and his slave ancestors was always present — as we see in his citation of slave spirituals. The Christianity that King learned from his parents was already Africanized, transmitted as it was through a long process of retention and adaptation from generation to generation.

Indeed, the environments where King was raised — namely, family, church, and community — were filled with the traces and marks of the rich African spiritual and cultural tradition. The African American South of King's formative years at home and at school was the place where African spiritual vestiges were most pervasively and fervently alive; indeed, Atlanta was probably more fertile with this heritage of African spiritual traditions than any other place in the United States.[1] Folktales, dance, magic, alternative religious beliefs, ghost stories, music, arts, spiritual leadership, formal religious institutions, and their rituals and practices were all readily and richly available to King.

Knowing that any person is greatly influenced by the family, religious institution, schools, and community that frame his or her formative years, we cannot lose sight of the powerful effect that the African American culture surrounding King's upbringing had on the development of his personality and the determination of his spirituality and religious attitudes.[2] King responded positively to the ideals and values of his family and the church.[3] Despite his distance from the emotionalism of African American churches, King showed no serious signs of rejection of African American religious traditions. In fact, these spiritual dispositions were expanded and articulated through his education.

African American Spiritual Features in the King Family

A look at the times and culture into which King was born provides a clearer perspective on how he was shaped by his family's spirituality.

Martin Luther King, Jr., was born on January 15, 1929. The King family retained much of the richness of the African spiritual and cultural heritage, as well as a history of protests against racism. His ancestors were the bearers and transmitters of African spiritual traditions and culture for King and his siblings. Indeed, genealogy itself was an important subject at King's home.[4]

---

1. See Baldwin, *There Is a Balm in Gilead*, 31.
2. Martin Luther King, Jr., "Autobiography of Religious Development," in *The Papers of Martin Luther King, Jr.*, vol. 1, ed. Clayborne Carson, *Called to Serve, January 1929–June 1951* (Berkeley: University of California Press, 1992), 360; hereafter, *The Papers I*.
3. Frederick Downing, *To See the Promised Land: The Faith Pilgrimage of Martin Luther King, Jr.* (Macon, GA: Mercer University Press, 1986), 42.
4. Baldwin, *There Is a Balm in Gilead*, 93.

By its close-knit yet extended nature, the King family showed a strong sense of "the natural cohesion of blood relatives" (Paris's term). King grew up with his parents, his grandparents, and other extended family members, such as cousins, uncles, aunts, and friends of the family who frequently visited his house and often boarded with them for lengthy periods of time. Love, mutual support, and cooperation were part of the normal flow of their life together. In his autobiography, King wrote affectionately about the intimate relationship that existed between his father and mother, between his parents and their children, and between his siblings and him.

The naming rituals of the King family reflect African cultural features. The African custom of naming children after other elderly family members, such as great-grandparents, grandparents, uncles, aunts, or cousins, was based on an African religious belief that the souls and spirits of ancestors and close relatives lived on through the individuals who bore the same name. Though this religious belief was adjusted by the Christian faith of African Americans, the custom remained very much a part of their culture, instilling and sustaining a sense of connectedness and solidarity in the children. King's family provides good examples. Alfred Daniel (A. D.) King, King's younger brother, born in 1930, was named after his maternal grandfather, A. D. Williams; King's older sister Christine, born in 1927, received her name from her mother's middle name. King's father, MLK, Sr., received his names, "Martin" and "Luther," from his own father's two brothers. Martin Luther King, Jr., continued the tradition by naming his daughter Bernice Albertine, after Coretta's mother Bernice and King's mother Alberta. In recognition of King's first pastorate at the Dexter Avenue Baptist Church in Montgomery, King named his youngest son Dexter.

In King's intimate relationship with his maternal grandmother, Jennie C. Parks Williams, we see the African family characteristic of the abiding presence of maternal bonding. Communal values were naturally transmitted by his grandmother, who played a pivotal role in his early emotional and spiritual formation. He practically grew up on her lap — singing, playing, and learning. She instilled in him "a strong sense of identity, self-esteem, and mission."[5] Like many other African and African American grandparents, her presence in the King family was distinctive. She was "a strong spiritual force, a bearer of culture, and a pillar of strength" in the family.[6] King referred to her as "a saintly grandmother." She was a source of extraordinary maternal care and love for King. As was rather common in his culture, King grew up calling her "Mama." The bond between them was so strong that on the two occasions when he thought she had died, King tried to commit suicide. The first time, he threw himself out of a window, falling twelve feet to the ground, because he thought that his brother A.D. had accidentally killed their grandmother while they were playing. His second suicide attempt on November 18, 1933, was in response to learning that his grandmother had died when he had left to go to a parade before finishing his homework. King believed that his grandmother's death and his personal irresponsibility were somehow connected and no accident. King was deeply unsettled by her death "because of the extreme love" he had for her; this distress led him to reflect deeply about the doctrine of immortality, eventually coming to believe that she was somehow alive and still with him. This belief in immortality, which was common in African American culture, bears a trace of the African belief in life after death and the reunion of the family in God in the spirit world.

The concepts of "love" and "forgiveness" were also prominent in King's family. King's parents told their children that Christians should not hate others. Daddy King constantly preached love and forgiveness to his congregation and to his children. He declared, "I love everybody" and "Nobody is going to make me hate." Despite his experiences of racial oppression, poverty, and hardship, it was primarily a nonviolent spirit — or the spirit of *ubuntu* —

---

5. Ibid., 110.
6. Ibid., 109.

that dominated Daddy King's life. This nonviolent spirit was passed down to King from his parents.

Through his family, King learned how to love and forgive others despite the adversities the family faced. His family's communal ethos was exhibited in their unity, loyalty, and interfamily cooperation.[7] They commonly ate together, read the Bible, offered prayers, and shared conversations around the dinner table.[8] Such experiences of love and community instilled in King a sense of self-worth, despite the dehumanizing racist environments outside their home and immediate community. Walter Fluker observes:

> The influence of his family environment gave Martin a sense of personal worth and a basis for belief in a "friendly universe." These two interrelated themes were fundamental to his emerging vision of community and in the coming years they would be given greater conceptual clarity.[9]

King's own recollection supports this observation. King said that he spent his early childhood in "a wholesome community." It was a neighborhood with a low crime rate, with people who were deeply religious, though not affluent.[10]

Through all these relationships and values, King learned early on to think of human life as more than that of an isolated individual or a nuclear family, but as an extended, beloved community.

Ubiquity of Religion

The ubiquity of religion, which is a major characteristic of African spirituality, was a distinctive feature of King's whole life, as testified to by every person who knew him. His ancestors and his immediate and extended family members were all deeply religious and dedicated to the life of the church. His father was a

---

7. Ibid., 104.
8. Ibid.
9. Fluker, *They Looked for a City*, 83.
10. King, "Autobiography of Religious Development," 360.

pastor, as were his grandfather and great-grandfather, and his father's brother. Daddy King reminisced in his autobiography that he had always been close to church.[11] He had been a licensed preacher since he was fifteen years old. Daddy King's mother, Delia Lindsay, was deeply religious as well. She took her children to country services, revivals, baptisms, and funerals. King, Sr., learned his faith from his mother, who showed him by example how to find strength in God to weather adversities.

All of King's childhood playmates attended Sunday school — because that was just what one did in his neighborhood at that time. Religion was indispensable to his life, as his autobiography sums up: "Religion has just been something that I grew up in."[12] This religious identity formed the bedrock of his life, and it remained his foundation for the rest of his life. King was not able to think of human existence without religion. In one of his seminary papers, he said that religion gives meaning and direction to life and the Universe.[13] For King, atheism was "philosophically unsound and practically disadvantageous."[14] In another paper, he noted that "by becoming properly adjusted to the divine power of religion I can become adjusted to myself and to my fellow man."[15]

Religion served as the encompassing, unifying power of every aspect of the King family's life. Religion and politics, morality and spirituality were not separate for King's parents and grandparents. As we have seen, Daddy King and Rev. Williams, as clergy, were active in social struggles for the betterment of their people in every aspect of their community life. In characteristic

---

11. Martin Luther King, Sr., *Daddy King: An Autobiography,* with Clayton Riley (New York: William Morrow, 1980), 23.

12. King, "Autobiography of Religious Development," 361.

13. Martin Luther King, Jr., "A Conception and Impression of Religion Drawn from Dr. Brightman's Book Entitled *A Philosophy of Religion,*" in *The Papers I,* 415.

14. Ibid.

15. Martin Luther King, Jr., "A Conception and Impression of Religion from Dr. W. K. Wright's Book Entitled '*A Student's Philosophy of Religion,*'" in *The Papers I,* 389.

holistic fashion, Daddy King said once, "The church is to touch every phase of the community life."[16]

Hopefulness

Despite their daily experiences of racism, a sense of hopefulness abounded in King's family. Through the loving, caring, and trustful relationship with his parents, he was able to keep an optimistic view of life in his early years. King believed that the universe is under the control of the loving purpose of God, and was, therefore, friendly.[17] In one of his seminary papers, King confessed that he had an "ever present desire to be optimistic about human nature."[18] Later, he noted in his autobiography:

> It is quite easy for me to think of a God of love mainly because I grew up in a family where love was central and where loving relationships were ever present. It is quite easy for me to think of the universe as basically friendly mainly because of my uplifting hereditary and environmental circumstances.[19]

King's optimism was derived from the unwavering faith of African Americans in God's justice and power and from a belief in the essential goodness of humanity.[20] It was consistent with the spirituality of the slaves, who did not give up hope in the midst of the most degrading conditions. Lewis Baldwin observes, "[King's] Christian optimism, rooted in a cultural heritage stemming back to his slave forebears, affirmed that in spite of human suffering and the tragic circumstances of life, God will ultimately emerge

16. Martin Luther King, Sr., "Moderator's Annual Address, Atlanta Missionary Baptist Association," October 17, 1940, CKFC; cited in "Introduction," in *The Papers of Martin Luther King, Jr.*, vol. 2, ed. Clayborne Carson, *Rediscovering Precious Values, July 1951–November 1955* (Berkeley: University of California Press, 1995), 2; hereafter, *The Papers II*.
17. Martin Luther King, Jr., "Pilgrimage to Nonviolence," in *A Testament of Hope*, 40.
18. Martin Luther King, Jr., "How Modern Christians Should Think of Man," in *The Papers I*, 274.
19. King, "Autobiography of Religious Development," 360–61.
20. Baldwin, *There Is a Balm in Gilead*, 5.

triumphant over evil and bring liberation and salvation to all people."[21]

Natural Law/Moral Order

Like many other African American Christians, King believed in the existence of God's moral order and its ultimate triumph in history — something he learned at home and in the church by hearing his grandmother and her sister tell biblical stories and African American folktales.[22] As his mother recalls:

> [Martin] remembered a lot of the Bible stories and when he was a man and he started preaching, he would remember those stories from the time he was a little boy.[23]

Martin Luther King, Jr.'s, parents taught their children the values and morality of the Bible and their own community. King learned the sanctity of human dignity from them; they repeated the lesson that "You must never feel that you are less than anyone else."[24] When King was told not to play with his white playmate by the latter's father because he was colored, Alberta told King: "You are as good as anyone."[25] King was reminded by his parents to love and respect all human beings and to treat other human beings, including the white people who mistreated them, with dignity and worth.

> It was here [home] that he got not only his first notion of the inherent worth of human personality but also the social nature of human existence — of the interrelatedness and interdependence of all life — ideas for which he later received a metaphysical grounding in Boston Personalism.[26]

---

21. Ibid. See n. 10.
22. Downing, *To See the Promised Land*, 44.
23. Mrs. Alberta King, "Martin Luther King, Jr.: Birth to Twelve Years Old"; cited in Downing, *To See the Promised Land*, 45.
24. Baldwin, *There Is a Balm in Gilead*, 117.
25. King, Sr., *Daddy King*, 130.
26. Ibid., 118.

Daddy and Alberta King taught their children high moral and spiritual values using such means as storytelling and fasting. The many biblical stories and folktales they told were infused with moral teachings and lessons about God's sovereignty, God's care for the poor and the oppressed, vindication of the righteous and the faithful, moral obligation to family and community, and hope for redemption. King must have learned naturally about God's justice, righteousness, and judgment, together with love and care. This justice and judgment were not confined to religious communities alone, but applied universally in the form of natural laws and moral order. Through stories, King was introduced to the history of African American people — their oppression, struggle, survival, and hope. King appropriated these stories as his own through his experiences in the African American community.[27]

Wisdom of Elders

Daddy King's relationship with King displayed several features of the African cultural tradition. He was a "real father" to his children, resembling the patriarchal but benevolent father of a traditional African household. He was resolute, strong, and forthright, and was a good material provider, emanating a sense of security as well as authority to his children. He provided a good role model for King in terms of manly identity and career. For example, King followed in his father's footsteps by going to Morehouse College, and acknowledged that his father's influence and example were considerable factors in his decision to enter ministry.[28]

The wisdom and advice of African American parents and elders exercise a distinctive authority in the decision-making process of a family and a community. Individuals do not make decisions alone, or by their own will. In selecting his wife, King was profoundly

---

27. Downing, *To See the Promised Land*, 88.

28. Filial or genealogical succession in terms of profession and position has not been unusual for the African or the African American family.

concerned about Daddy King's opinion. This concern demonstrates a common feature of the African family, an "unquestioned obedience to the authority of parents and the elderly."

This characteristic was revealed on another important occasion, during the Montgomery Bus Boycott (1955–56). Daddy King convened his family friends and influential social and religious leaders of the African American community (such as Dr. Benjamin Mays, the president of Atlanta University, and several other prominent businessmen and leaders) in order to discuss his son's safety and future. At the meeting, Daddy King, who feared for his son's life, demanded that King relinquish the Boycott and return to Atlanta. To put pressure on King, he summoned the elders of his community. King pleaded with his father not to hold him in Atlanta. King's future was literally in the hands of his father and the elders of the African American community. The role of Benjamin Mays at the meeting was critical to persuading Daddy King. This meeting was somewhat analogous to the African meeting of tribal elders in its deep respect for the practical wisdom of the elders in making decisions on crucial matters of a clan and a tribe.

Political Consciousness of Family

King learned his political-prophetic spirituality from his family, church, and community. Andrew Young says, "Speaking out against injustice was a way of life in Martin's family."[29] His family tradition understood the highest calling in life to be serving the community. King's selection of ministry as his future career was therefore the continuation of the long-standing family tradition of serving an African American people through ministry. King's family showed an unyielding and indefatigable spirit of resistance against racial oppression, and extraordinary care and service to the poor. King inherited a keen political awareness and a spirit of beneficence from both his paternal and maternal families.

---

29. Andrew Young, "Introduction," in King, Sr., *Daddy King*, 10.

King grew up listening to the stories about his family ancestors who dedicated their lives to the struggle of and in service to the African American community.[30] King's maternal great-grandfather, the Rev. Williams, was a slave "exhorter" on a plantation in Georgia. Later, upon emancipation, he became a Baptist preacher in Green County, Georgia. A slave himself, he not only shared the pain and suffering of fellow slaves, but as a spiritual leader, he ministered to them with spiritual encouragement and moral exhortation. Alfred D. Williams, King's maternal grandfather, grew up interacting with former slaves and hearing stories about slavery and African struggles against it. King's maternal grandmother, Jennie C. Parks, wife of A. D. Williams, was also a descendant of slaves. A. D. Williams was a religious leader, and, like his father, had been a country preacher before he settled in Atlanta where in 1894 he became the pastor of the Ebenezer Baptist Church. A. D. Williams was convinced that a minister must lead people not only in a spiritual sense but also in the social realms of a practical world.[31] Applauded as "one of Atlanta's most prominent and respected ministers," he was well known for his courageous protests against racial segregation. He served as the first president of the local NAACP. In the 1920s, he led various campaigns against racial injustice, including an economic boycott against *The Georgians,* an Atlanta newspaper that printed racist slogans and slurs.[32]

Daddy King also exercised a major influence in the formation of Martin's social spirituality.[33] According to King's sister Christine, King's "single-minded determination, faith and forthrightness" indisputably came from Daddy King.[34] Daddy King's ministry was for ordinary African Americans, reaching

---

30. Baldwin, *There Is a Balm in Gilead,* 93.
31. King, Sr., *Daddy King,* 82.
32. Ibid., 86.
33. See Andrew Young, "Introduction," 10–11.
34. Christine Farris, "The Young Martin," 57; cited in Baldwin, *There Is a Balm in Gilead,* 105.

out to the poor and serving the cause of the oppressed. It was King, Sr.'s, conviction that any social and/or economic privilege must be used to advance the cause of the poor. King, Sr., was determined not to accept the rationale of segregation. King grew up watching his father's constant fight against racism. On many occasions, young Martin was an eyewitness to his father's confrontation with it, and Daddy King made sure that his namesake understood his determination.[35]

King's father was active in the campaigns for voter registration, equal pay for African American teachers, equal funding for African American schools, and other civil and economic rights for African Americans. Daddy King led a protest to end segregated elevators at the Fulton County Courthouse. He exercised political leadership in various local and national organizations, such as the Atlanta District Baptist Young Peoples Union and Sunday School Convention, the Atlanta Baptist Ministers Union, the Atlanta Voters' League, YMCA, NAACP, the Atlanta Civic and Political League, the Atlanta Ministers Council, and the National Baptist Convention. Like his father-in-law, whenever the opportunities were given, Daddy King emphasized the significance of a socially active ministry within the National Baptist Convention.

In organizing these struggles, Daddy King was led by a Niebuhrian realist sense of social understanding. He knew that action was the only course for social change,[36] and that without collective pressure a meaningful social change was not possible. He was convinced that demonstrations, marches, and picket lines were important tools African Americans possessed in their struggle for freedom. He believed that such mass action could bring an adverse effect on the white economy, thereby putting pressure on whites for a positive change.[37] Martin recollected later, "With this

---

35. King, Sr., *Daddy King*, 109.
36. Ibid., 98.
37. See ibid., 111.

heritage, it is not surprising that I had also learned to abhor segregation, considering it both rationally inexplicable and morally
unjustifiable."[38]

The African American Church

Together with his family, the African American church was the
incubator of King's spirituality. His identity was ingrained in the
church. And through the African American church, King gained
additional African spiritual heritages.

For the Kings, the church was the extension of their family
and home. Living just a few blocks away from the church, King
went there often, not only on Sundays. In particular, King's father's church, Ebenezer Baptist Church, exercised a decisive role
in forming King's spiritual self-understanding in a communal and
political sense. In 1886, the church was built with funds given by
the descendants of slaves. King's maternal great-grandfather, the
Reverend Williams, was its minister. From the time he joined the
church at the age of five under his father's pastorate, until his
death, King maintained a membership there.

King was fascinated with African American music — gospel
songs, the spirituals, and hymns. He sang before congregations
and church conventions, frequently accompanied by his mother
at the piano; "I Want to Be More and More Like Jesus" was his
favorite song.[39] King was familiar with the various expressions
and practices of the rich African American rituals and aesthetics, having grown up listening to and watching the preaching
of his father and other speakers in the church. He "witnessed
variants of the African ring shout, such as 'shouting' and the
'holy dance' during his father's sermons."[40] He learned to mem-
orize Bible passages before he was five. King understood his faith
through the eyes of African American experiences; he confessed

---

38. Martin Luther King, Jr., *Stride toward Freedom: The Montgomery Story*
(New York: Harper & Row, 1958), 6.
39. Baldwin, *There Is a Balm in Gilead*, 163.
40. Ibid., 31.

his belief in the Almighty God and envisioned humanity as one family under God.

Throughout his life, King continued to be nourished and sustained by his deep roots in the African American church. Through its spiritual heritages, the African American church informed King's early commitment to love and justice.[41] So it was natural for King to recognize the potent collective energy of these churches and to connect it to the movement for social change. Within his lifetime, King became one of the most effective and articulate popularizers of their spiritual tradition in the United States and the world.

King's Experiences of Racism

The political thrust of King's spirituality was further intensified through his personal witness and experience of racial oppression. King recollected, "I had grown up abhorring not only segregation but also the oppressive barbarous acts that grew out of it."[42] He grew up seeing police brutality, lynchings of his people, and the intimidating and obnoxious rides of the Ku Klux Klan at night. Segregation was a social norm in the South at King's time. Like many African American children in Atlanta, he was forced to drink from a "Colored" water fountain, not allowed to sit at the lunch counters, relegated to riding a "Colored" freight elevator, sent to buy ice cream from a side window, and required to take a segregated city bus. Like most other African American children in the South, King had traumatic experiences of racism in his early years. Once, in the dining car of a train, a waiter pulled the curtain around him to segregate him from white passengers. He later expressed the feelings of humiliation and anger that the incident had evoked in him. During the Depression, King watched a multitude of poor African Americans standing in bread lines. The stories are endless.

41. James H. Cone, "Black Theology–Black Church," *Theology Today* 41, no. 1 (1984): 415.
42. King, *Stride toward Freedom*, 90.

Impelled by these experiences, King's political and social concern was later widened through his firsthand exposure to the appalling conditions of African American masses. During his Morehouse years, King took summer jobs at the Cullman Brothers' Tobacco Plantation in Simsbury, Connecticut (1944 and 1947), at Atlanta's Railway Express Company (1946), and at the Southern Spring Bed Mattress Company. Through these experiences, King was an eyewitness to the harassment and abuse African Americans received under the system of segregation and the prevailing style of capitalism. King saw how segregation was undermining African American livelihood and well-being, and how fear and anger were destroying people from within. Physical abuse, poverty, low self-esteem, family violence, and child abuse were all direct and indirect results of segregation. His personal struggle differed little from any other African American raised in the face of alienation, oppression, and subjugation. Like many, King overcame the feelings of resentment, anger, and hatred through his faith, aided by his parents' example. These early experiences of racial injustice compelled him to make a conscious note of the variety of injustices in the United States. These experiences also intensified the political tone of his spirituality and impelled him through his studies at Morehouse, Crozer, and Boston to probe this issue intellectually as well as spiritually.

The Growth of King's Spirituality

Morehouse College

King's communal and political spirituality grew and expanded through his studies at Morehouse College, which he entered in September 1944. Morehouse was an African American institution where a political awareness and a communal African American solidarity were alive and praised. It was widely recognized among African Americans for its contribution toward the betterment of their people through the education of many leaders in various professions. Morehouse helped King to deal intellectually with the unjust political, social, and economic conditions of his time and for his people.

The Kings had a special tie with Morehouse. Martin Luther King, Sr., was a trustee of the college, and its President, Benjamin Mays, was a frequent guest at King's home. Mays's influence was remarkable. King often referred to Mays as his spiritual mentor. Mentorship was exercised through frequent informal conversations on campus and in Mays's office. Mays's own observation helps us in understanding the influence he had on King: "Many times during [Martin's] four years at Morehouse, he would linger after my Tuesday morning address to discuss some point I had made — usually with approval, but sometimes questioning or disagreeing."[43] Mays remained his faithful mentor and friend throughout King's life.

King majored in sociology and minored in English at Morehouse. It was there that he also developed his oratorical skills and hermeneutical understandings as he was surrounded by eloquent and articulate professors, many of whom were also trained ministers. His study of sociology and English were useful later for his analysis of the oppressive conditions of racism and capitalism and for the articulation of the African American predicaments to the public.[44]

Morehouse helped him to remove the shackles of fundamentalism and biblical literalism from his mind. About the time he entered Morehouse, King was intellectually dissatisfied with the kind of Christianity he had experienced in the southern African American churches. He harbored some disdain toward the emotionalism expressed in their style of Christianity, which he took as reflecting a lack of intellectual rigor and seriousness. Partly in reaction to emotionalism, he was considering a career in medicine or law. It was at Morehouse College that King finally came to the decision to pursue ministry as his vocation.

---

43. Benjamin Mays, *Born to Rebel* (New York: Charles Scribner's Sons, 1971), 265.

44. Baldwin, *There Is a Balm in Gilead*, 25.

Through the influence of Benjamin Mays, George Kelsey, and other faculty members, he was able to see a different expression of Christian faith and ministry, which appreciated the intellectual vigor of theology. His teachers were outstanding scholars who studied the religious and theological changes taking place in Europe and the United States, and who became pioneers in a new kind of African American theological thinking and education.[45]

Morehouse laid a crucial intellectual and vocational foundation for King's advanced work in white educational institutions. It instilled in King a sense of spiritual identity, the intellectual focus, the openness to truth, and the self-discipline necessary for any person who wanted to succeed in higher education.

King's political concern with the plight of African Americans grew during this time. In 1947, he was elected chair of the membership committee of the Atlanta NAACP Youth Council. During his Morehouse College years, King sent a letter to the editor of the *Atlanta Constitution*, the largest-circulation newspaper in Atlanta. In the letter, King criticized white hypocrisy regarding racial purity and advocated that African Americans should have the same basic rights and opportunities, such as education, health, recreation, voting rights, and legal protection, as all American citizens.[46]

White Liberal Theology: Crozer and Boston

In 1948, King started his studies at Crozer. As Ira Zepp observed, if the African American church and community provided the *esse* of King's spirituality, then his education at Crozer Theological Seminary and Boston University School of Theology became its *bene esse*.[47] During his study at both places, the fundamentalist tendency of his early Baptist faith was further overcome through

---

45. Cf. Thomas Mikelson, "Mays, King, and the Negro's God," in *Walking Integrity: Benjamin Elijah Mays, Mentor to Martin Luther King, Jr.*, ed. Lawrence Edward Carter, Sr. (Macon, GA: Mercer University Press, 1998), 154.

46. Martin Luther King, Jr., "Kick Up Dust," Letter to the Editor, *Atlanta Constitution*, in *The Papers I*, 121.

47. Smith and Zepp, *Search for the Beloved Community*, xviii.

his exposure to modern philosophy, sociology, and the liberal theology of Paul Tillich, Walter Rauschenbusch, and Reinhold Niebuhr, among many others. King's intellectual journey underwent several stages of progress and change during this period, moving from Protestant Baptist theology, to liberal Christianity, to neo-orthodoxy, and finally to the critical appropriation and synthesis of these sources into a coherent form of Christian social philosophy.[48] Liberal education gave him a conceptual framework to deepen and expand his primary spiritual quests and commitments.

In the first years at Crozer, King was almost uncritically attracted to theological liberalism, and his early academic papers show the strong influences of liberal modernist theories and assumptions. In part, his temporary attraction to liberalism was due to his being a relative novice in theological studies, but it was also a reaction to his early experience of the fundamentalism within his Baptist tradition. Despite King's early revolt against fundamentalism and emotionalism in African American churches, it never led him to the opposite extreme of modernist humanism. It was probably the African American belief in the sovereignty and transcendence of God that prevented King from adopting wholeheartedly either radical liberal Christianity or modernism.

As his thinking grew more mature, King began to discover his own, more balanced and holistic theological perspective, which was more congruent with African American spiritual tradition. For example, in his paper "How Modern Christians Should Think

---

48. King's personal intellectual biography is well documented in his essay "Pilgrimage to Non-Violence," which appeared in several different places with slightly different contents: *Stride Toward Freedom,* chap. 4, *Strength to Love,* chap. 17, *Christian Century* (April 13, 1960). Smith and Zepp's book, *Search for the Beloved Community,* presents extensive surveys of King's intellectual biography after his study at Morehouse. Ansbro's book, *Martin Luther King, Jr.: The Making of a Mind,* is a more thorough analysis of King's intellectual development. These books have limitations, however, because they ignore the influences of African American intellectuals, churches, and family on King's life.

of Man," written in early 1950, King said that he was intellectually in "a transitional stage,"[49] implying that he was now
departing from uncritical subscription to theological liberalism,
in search of his own theological voice in the midst of a variety
of theological perspectives offered at the seminary. He identified
his position as eclecticism, which synthesizes and balances liberal
theology and neo-orthodox theology at their best.[50]

Importantly, this shift from liberalism to eclecticism was tied
to King's reflection on his own personal religious and social experiences as an African American. In "How Modern Christians
Should Think of Man," King offered a dialectic perspective on
human nature with reference to his experience in the South as an
African American. He said that he observed both the viciousness
of racism and the noble possibility of its gradual improvements in
the South.[51] One can say that, in comparison to his earlier days
at Crozer, King was now more self-conscious of his distinctive
cultural and social context.

King's final paper in George Davis's course, "Six Talks Based
on *Beliefs That Matter* by William Adams Brown," discloses this
shift in intellectual orientation more explicitly and vividly. It is
also more reflective of his African American experiences and spiritual perspectives. One sees here that his early uncritical attraction
to theological liberalism was rectified.

"Six Talks" is seminal in revealing the early contours of King's
distinctive theological and ethical perspective. King demonstrates
creative and integrative thinking rather than the simple repetition or imitation of other theologians. Many of the themes found
in this paper were later developed further in his major works,
recurring in his speeches and sermons, as we discuss in the next
chapter. One finds in this paper a rough sketch of his theology reflecting his African American spirituality: the African American
spiritual values and themes of fellowship (communality), love,

---

49. King, "How Modern Christians Should Think of Man," 274.
50. Ibid.
51. Ibid.

human dignity, the spiritual origin and purpose of human existence, the theocentric view of the church and history, hopefulness, and social responsibility are prevalent there.

Examining how some of these ideas explicate the meanings of, for example, the *imago dei* and the loving God, we see how directly King appealed to African American spiritual and social experiences. King said that a human being is more than natural instinct and necessity. Human beings have a divine origin, created not for self-sufficiency, but for fellowship; the destiny of one person is inevitably tied up with the destiny of all human beings.

King portrayed God as a personal, all-loving, and good Father, and human beings as his children.[52] King's discussion of the unity of humanity and God echoed the distinctive African American view that the whole of humanity is one family. He wrote:

Each Christian should believe that he is a member of a larger family of which God is Father. Jesus expresses the view throughout the Gospels that we are members of one family, meant to live as brothers and to express our brotherhood in helpfulness. A failure to realize this truth is a failure to realize one of the main tenets of the Christian religion. The Fatherhood of God and the Brotherhood of man is the starting point of the Christian ethic.[53]

The motifs of hopefulness and love, both preeminent ethical themes of the African American church, were also prevalent in this same paper. King said that history is in the hands of divine care and providence, and the power of love and goodness, available by God's grace, enables us to overcome evil.[54] King understood the dominion of God as a society of love,[55] arguing that this communal understanding of the dominion of God was the most consistent with the preaching and ministry of Jesus,

52. Martin Luther King, Jr., "Six Talks Based on *Beliefs That Matter* by William Adams Brown," in *The Papers I,* 281.
53. Ibid.
54. Ibid., 285.
55. Ibid., 283.

who demonstrated love as the mark of divine sovereignty. Although King did not use the term "the beloved community" in this paper, his understanding of the dominion of God is obviously identical with it.

Consistent with African American Christian spirituality, King's understanding of the church was theocentric and communal. For King, the foundation of the church is God. The church should confront human beings with the fact of the living God, and obey God rather than human beings. At the same time, he insisted that we never forget that the church is communal. He stated, "The church must stress fellowship as being more important than creed, and experience as being more important than doctrinal uniformity."[56]

King's learning of white theology did not mean abandonment of the African American spiritual heritages but a growth and strengthening of those heritages, if, as Howard Thurman notes, growth means the "re-establishment of relations in one's own terms."[57] King appropriated Western theological thoughts and philosophical theories from the vantage point of African American spiritual values. The abiding influence of the African American spiritual tradition (such as communalism, political consciousness, holism, love, and faith in the sovereign God) in King's life, thinking, and developing ministry was evident.[58] Hence it is right to contend that "the religious ideas King brought to the [Crozer] seminary were modified but not drastically altered as his intellectual sophistication grew."[59]

King himself was self-conscious about the roots of his "religious attitudes," namely, the psychological and historical factors that had affected his early spiritual formation.[60] King identified himself with the religious ideals and heritages that he had learned

56. Ibid., 286.
57. Howard Thurman, *Disciplines of the Spirit* (Richmond, IN: Friends United Press, 1977), 48.
58. See Watley, *Roots of Resistance,* 45.
59. Clayborne Carson, "Introduction," in *The Papers I,* 57.
60. King, "Autobiography of Religious Development," 361.

from his family and the church. In his autobiography, which he wrote for George Davis at Crozer, King confessed he was still feeling "the effects of the noble moral and ethical ideals" with which he grew up.[61] In the same autobiography, King traced his conceptions of God, and his optimistic view of humanity and the universe, to his heritages from African American family and church.

Throughout his studies, King remained a profoundly religious person. Despite his education at liberal theological schools, the Western judicial idea of the separation of church and state never took hold in King's mind. Rather, he believed that "religion is something broad and universal covering the whole of life."[62] King was deeply and keenly aware of the limitations of scientism and materialism fostered by capitalism. Likewise, despite his sympathy toward Marx's moral critique of capitalism, King could not buy into Marxism because it was too materialistic and too atheistic in its interpretation of human nature and history. For King, a human being was a spiritual being. To contend otherwise was to deny the very essence of humanity. Unlike many modern humanists, King believed that human beings cannot be their own saviors; they need God. Indeed, people cannot live moral life without God.

King's belief in the natural moral order of God compelled him to be interested in the teachings of George Davis at Crozer, with whom he took more than one-third of his total graduation credits. African spiritual beliefs and George Davis's evangelical liberalism shared some salient features, such as the social nature of human existence and the ethical nature of religion and the universe. As a scholar of personalism, George Davis espoused the existence of moral order in the universe and the saving activity of God in history. Davis declared, "There is a certain 'logic of events' in history, a certain definiteness of purpose and intention running through the pageant of the centuries, to which the wise

---

61. Ibid., 363.
62. King, "A Conception and Impression of Religion from Dr. W. K. Wright's Book Entitled *A Student's Philosophy of Religion*," 384.

man will not close his eyes."[63] As Watley notes, King's receptivity to evangelical liberalism was motivated by the congruence between evangelical liberalism and African American spirituality.[64] Although King was attracted to evangelical liberalism, he distanced himself from the evangelical liberal view that God's goodness and omnipotence could not be held in balance in the face of evil. King adhered to a traditional African American religious belief that always upheld God's goodness and power in an uncompromising manner, despite the existence of evil.[65] For example, in his sermon "Rediscovering Lost Values," which he preached right after completing his Ph.D. comprehensive exam, King proclaimed that all reality hinges on moral foundations, that "this is a moral universe, and that there are moral laws of the universe just as abiding as the physical laws."[66] King believed that a moral life is not possible without faith in God. His exposition on the moral order of the universe received enthusiastic responses from the congregation because it struck the core of their spiritual understanding.

King's inherited hopefulness also remained intact, and this hopefulness was further refined through his study of liberal theology and evident in the obvious absence of the idea of original sin. Despite his sympathy with Reinhold Niebuhr's Christian realism, King did not believe that sin had completely obliterated the *imago dei,* the possibility of goodness and companionship with God. Yet King's optimism was different from that of Protestant liberalism, which emphasized humanity's natural inclination and progress toward altruism.[67] His optimism was ultimately based on God's promise. For King, liberalism failed to comprehend the abysmal darkness of collective evil.

63. George W. Davis, "God and History," *Crozer Quarterly* 20, no. 1 (January 1943): 35; cited in Watley, *Roots of Resistance,* 20.
64. Watley, *Roots of Resistance,* 20.
65. Ibid., 45.
66. Martin Luther King, Jr., "Rediscovering Lost Values," in *The Papers II,* 251.
67. Smith and Zepp, *Search for the Beloved Community,* 2.

King's political consciousness also grew and was strengthened. For example, his paper on the prophet Jeremiah, "The Significant Contributions of Jeremiah to Religious Thought," written in 1948 for Professor Prichard's course on the Old Testament, shows the deepening of his concern for justice. Using Jeremiah's example, King stated that religion divorced from morality is hypocrisy, no matter what form, public or private, it may take. Religious sponsorship of the status quo is the worst disservice to Christianity.[68] King's prophetic spirit was vividly disclosed in his conclusion that "the worst disservice that we as individuals or churches can do is to become sponsors and supporters of the status quo."[69]

In this paper, King commented on Jeremiah's personal relationship with God, and his critique of "artificial worship." King also showed a great deal of interest in Jeremiah's personality and spirituality. He noted the conflict within Jeremiah between the desire for divine moral truth and an escape to a private life. King defined Jeremiah's spirituality as a form of "public pietism" that emphasizes both the prophet's unflinching social criticism and an intimate personal relationship with God.

King also noted in his paper that society tends to react negatively to people like Jeremiah, either persecuting or destroying them. To make his point, he emphatically, although mistakenly, declared, "Jeremiah died a martyr."[70] King stressed that by the ordinary standards of the world, Jeremiah's ministry — suspect, despised, and ridiculed — was a failure, but human civilization and religion itself advance and renew their power through the contribution of such persons. King's reflection on Jeremiah's life and ministry was prophetic, as his own life later evolved like that of Jeremiah, especially in his last years; like Jeremiah, King experienced extreme isolation yet was sustained by his personal

---

68. Martin Luther King, Jr., "The Significant Contributions of Jeremiah to Religious Thought," in *The Papers I*, 194.

69. Ibid.

70. Ibid., 195.

relationship with God, and as he had projected onto Jeremiah, his own life ended in a tragic, violent death.

While studying at Crozer and Boston, he remained closely connected with African American communities in the areas. For example, he preached at the circles of African American churches in the Boston metropolitan area, maintained close relationships with the students from the South, and organized a discussion group for African American students at Boston University. Indeed, it was a mutual friend from the South who introduced King to his future wife, Coretta.

That King had imbibed African American spirituality was clearly evident when he preached at African American churches. The source of his sermons was not his theological treatises but the Bible and familiar folktales and hymns, interpreted through African American religious experiences. His understanding of God, humanity, and history in his sermons tended to be explicitly African American.

King never lost sight of issues regarding race relations. At Crozer and Boston, King studied in depth the great social philosophers, such as Aristotle, Plato, Rousseau, Hegel, Locke, Ricardo, Brightman, Adam Smith, and Karl Marx. A close reading of King's intellectual life at these institutions (e.g., his term papers, and the courses and seminars he took) shows that his intellectual interest was predominantly guided by his persistent struggle with racism and search for a plausible method for overcoming it. King wrestled with such questions as: how can we eliminate the social evils of segregation and poverty in a spiritually and morally consistent way? In particular, the balance and the harmony between love (the communal) and power (the political) were at the heart of his intellectual quests: how is love, as the goal of life, related to social power relationships?[71] Is there a way to overcome an

71. For example, King endeavored to reconcile God's love and power in his theological thinking. In his essay for DeWolf's course on Christian doctrine, he criticized Calvin for the latter's emphasis on God's power and justice at the expense of God's love (Martin Luther King, Jr., "A Comparison and Evaluation of the Theology of Luther with That of Calvin," in *The Papers II*, 188).

unjust system that is consistent with the demand of love? Refusing to be satisfied with the prescribed curriculum of the schools, he set out his own intellectual inquiry to clarify these problems.[72] In his effort to achieve a plausible spiritual framework to deal with racism, King came up with an integral and refined spiritual outlook through the discovery of the affinity between African American spirituality and white liberal Christianity, to which we now turn.

King's Incorporation of White Liberal Theology, Philosophy, and Gandhism

Smith and Zepp and Ansbro say that King's theology, under the influence of George Davis and Harold DeWolf, was primarily informed by personalist philosophy, and indeed in his essay "Pilgrimage to Nonviolence," King admitted that personalism offered him a metaphysical and philosophical basis for his understanding of God.[73] However, King's attraction to personalism had an African American proclivity; the indigenous personalist motifs of African American spiritual traditions, developed while countering the always degrading white racism, naturally predisposed King toward personalist philosophy.

Personalism can be defined as the beliefs in the inherent sanctity of one's person, the social nature of human existence, and the moral nature of the universe. First, personalism is the philosophy that regards conscious personality as the highest value and reality in the universe. According to personalism, a person is at the center of value and therefore should be protected and respected by all means. Second, personalism assumed the fundamental unity and harmony of persons in the universe; the whole universe is a society of mutually interacting persons, with God at its center.

Aptly analyzed by Watley, Baldwin, and others, the African American Christian understanding of God showed a strong personalist tendency. Likewise, high personalist theological thrusts

---

72. Oates, *Let the Trumpet Sound,* 25.
73. King, "Pilgrimage to Nonviolence," in *Stride toward Freedom,* 100.

and motifs are found in African American churches. Through their heritages of African cosmology, and in their struggle against racism, African American churches have developed their own personalistic anthropology. African American churches understood God as always a personal and intimate God who listens to the cries of the oppressed and works for their liberation. African American spirituals and folktales depict God as the liberator and enabler. For example, the African American expression that "God is a mother to the motherless, and a father to the fatherless" implies a personalistic God.

African American churches affirmed and elevated the personalities of African Americans. Moral declarations, such as "You are somebody," were often heard in the church, as were many other ways of building a sense of personal worth for people, such as ritual calling and recognition of individuals in their various services and contributions to a community.[74] Along with the intrinsic value of a person, another major tenet of personalism is its belief in the social nature of human existence, which was congruent with the African American communal tradition that stressed the interdependence of humanity.

Walter Rauschenbusch

King's fascination with Walter Rauschenbusch can be explained in a similar manner. During his study at Crozer, King was attracted to Walter Rauschenbusch's social gospel. Identifying the kingdom of God as the central message of the gospel, Rauschenbusch stressed the work for social reform as the indispensable realm of Christian ministry. He believed that Christians were called to the construction of a true Christian commonwealth on earth. The object of redemption was not only individuals but also the whole society and its social institutions.

Rauschenbusch argued that a human being was fundamentally social; therefore, a human being was most moral when he or she was truly social. This meant that human goodness was in essence

---

74. Watley, *Roots of Resistance*, 35.

social goodness. He proclaimed that "Love is the society-making quality."[75] It is "the highest and the most steadfast energy of a will bent on creating fellowship."[76]

In Rauschenbusch, King found a theological framework that affirmed his ministry of social reform against racism and classism. Although the social gospel was not invented in order to address racial problems, King appropriated it for that. It may appear that the social gospel was the immediate source of inspiration of King's socially oriented Christian ministry and his conception of a community, yet King's interest in Rauschenbusch was not conceivable without the predilection of the African communal spirituality obtained through his upbringing. The communal and political spiritual orientation of African American spirituality was in natural affinity with Rauschenbusch's social reformist bent. Rauschenbusch's social ideal of the kingdom of God was not foreign to the African American search for a liberated community that was idealized in the idea of the family. Political and social concerns were not at all alien to King's faith, as they were salient features of African American spiritual tradition.

The influence of African American spirituality becomes clear when we examine King's critique of Rauschenbusch. King found his view of human nature — that a human being is essentially good like Christ, and perfectible — to be very naïve. And he felt this naïve optimism regarding human nature and social progress was problematic in dealing with the harsh reality of social evils like racism. Rauschenbusch attributed evil solely to a social system, not to human beings.

Reinhold Niebuhr

King was attracted to Reinhold Niebuhr's Christian realism because it offered an astute social analysis of the collective egoism underlying segregation and racism. The reality of sin pervades every level of human existence, as the privileged groups, to protect

---

75. Walter Rauschenbusch, *Christianity and the Social Crisis* (New York: Harper & Row, 1964), 67.

76. Ibid., 68.

their collective interests, rarely give up their privileges unless it is demanded by a countervailing power. Christian realism helped King to realize that justice is not naturally obtained; it demands a self-consciously concerted, persistent, collective human exertion.

However, King's attraction to Niebuhr's Christian realism was not unusual given King's political orientation, based on African American experiences of the recalcitrant white egoism of slavery and segregation. Niebuhr's realistic understanding of human nature was appealing to King because his experiences in the South confirmed Niebuhr's realist thesis on human collective sinfulness. African Americans saw the causal connection between white racist social systems and individual African American sufferings. They were certainly aware of the collective, intransigent nature of sin through their encounter with slave masters who were also confessed Christians. By instinct they knew slavery was not an individual problem, but a societal one; it protected white social interests.

King, despite his sympathy with Niebuhr, kept a critical distance from Niebuhr's neo-orthodox theology, particularly his pessimistic view of human nature. Niebuhr's doctrine of sin seldom acknowledges that religiously inspired social activism can change the situation. For King, such acceptance of the total depravity and corruption of humanity meant a complete surrender to cynicism and pessimism. Imbued with African American hopefulness, King had a more positive view of the possibility of societal moral transformation. King had reservations about Niebuhr's failure to see the availability of the divine grace — that is, the redemptive power of divine love — in history.[77]

Unlike Niebuhr, who sharply differentiated the operation of collective morality from that of interpersonal morality, King refused to strictly separate the two. He believed the tie between collectivity and egoism or evil is not absolute. King did not hesitate to apply the ideal of *agape* love to a collective life. Collectivity

---

77. Martin Luther King, Jr., "Reinhold Niebuhr's Ethical Dualism," in *The Papers II*, 150.

is neither intrinsically evil nor egoistic. Love and justice can be achieved through the combined efforts of spiritual renewal and proper social legislation accomplished through nonviolent resistance.

Anders Nygren

Scholars ascribe the source of King's idea of *agape* to Anders Nygren (and to George Davis). King himself primarily identified his ethics with the love ethics of Jesus, and frequently mentioned *agape* in his speeches and writings. However, the original predilection for this idea came from the penchant of African American spirituality for community, harmony, and love.

King's idea of *agape* love takes different tones and nuances from other philosophical and theological expositions of love by virtue of his African American communal underpinnings. King's idea of love is deeply associated with the African virtue of beneficence — a parallel to the Christian idea of *agape*, as both stress goodwill toward others. Beneficence is indispensable for the actualization of the community.[78]

King's emphasis of *agape* over *eros* and *philia* demonstrates the communal and corporate nature of his understanding of love. *Agape* is different from other forms of love that are dependent on the contingent human qualities of emotions and attachments. *Eros* and *philia* refer to a romantic or a friendly affection, which are motivated by the attractive qualities in each other. For King, *agape*, which is impartial love, was the first law of the universe. He declared, "The universe is so structured that things go awry if men are not diligent in their cultivation of the other-regarding dimension."[79] In comparison to *eros* and *philia*, *agape* is an other-directed love, thus the most inclusive and communal.

Love is communal in nature and itself the constitutive power of a community because it brings different parties into harmony and union. He wrote:

---

78. Paris, *Spirituality of African Peoples*, 136.
79. Martin Luther King, Jr., *Where Do We Go from Here: Chaos or Community?* (Boston: Beacon Press, 1967), 180.

Agape is love seeking to preserve and create community. It is insistence on community even when one seeks to break it. Agape is a willingness to go any length to restore community. ... It is a willingness to forgive, not seven times, but seventy times to restore community.[80]

The communal underpinning of love in King becomes evident when its close relationship with the idea of interdependence is explicated. Interdependence constituted the metaphysics of his idea of love and thus spirituality. The idea of interdependence reflects his African communal heritages and upbringing. In interdependence, neither I nor you can be an absolute; only both, and only in mutual relatedness. The present life is dependent on the past, and the future on the present. Human existence is interrelated. Anyone's life is incomplete, the same as anyone else's is incomplete; our nation is incomplete just as other nations are. King declared:

All life is interrelated. We are caught in an inescapable network of mutuality, tied into a single garment of destiny. Whatever affects one directly affects all indirectly. We are made to live together because of the interrelated structure of reality.[81]

King saw in love the power that brings forth communion among the self, others, and God. For King, love is *summum bonum*, the ultimate good toward which all human moral and spiritual exertions are exercised. In the final analysis, it is the good that belongs to and is embodied in community.

However, for King, the communal nature of love did not mean the collapsing of individuality into collectivity. Love presupposes freedom, equality, and reciprocity between the self and the other in God. If love aims at the union of a person with others, it

---

80. King, *Stride toward Freedom*, 87.

81. Martin Luther King, Jr., *The Trumpet of Conscience* (New York: Harper & Row, 1967), 68.

presupposes a healthy self-love and respect for the legitimate moral claims of each participant. In this respect, his idea of love is inseparable from the sanctity of a person.

G. W. F. Hegel

King maintained a holistic epistemological attitude during his studies. Some scholars ascribe the origin of King's holism — his synthetic and dialectic mind-set — to the influence of Hegel's philosophical method of synthesis and integration. In particular, Smith, Zepp, and Ansbro contend that King's synthetic approach to racial problems was philosophically aided by G. W. Hegel. Indeed, Peter J. Paris observed that King was a master of the Hegelian dialectical method of synthesis.[82]

However, it is probable that King's proclivity toward synthesis and dialectic was also, and primarily, influenced by this African American holistic, communal spirituality, for we see this tendency in his writings even before his serious study of Hegel. At an early stage of his theological studies, King's method of reasoning showed a holistic tendency in terms of his predilection toward dialectic and synthesis; he confessed himself to be a "victim of eclecticism," as he sought to reconcile liberal theology and neo-orthodox theology. It may therefore be more accurate to say that he was attracted to Hegel because the Hegelian idea that "the truth is whole" was congenial to African American holistic spirituality. This method of synthesis was integral to holism, for the method was useful to understand the reality as a whole in the interrelation of all relevant aspects. By extension and for example, King knew that most social problems are complex in nature, and refuse a monolithic solution.

Holism was intimately related to the African American penchant for practical wisdom. Holism rendered plausible, practical, and pragmatic values to King's decisions by enabling him to understand various aspects of a reality in their associations as

---

82. Peter J. Paris, *Black Religious Leaders: Conflict in Unity* (Louisville: Westminster/John Knox Press, 1991), 101.

well as in their most comprehensive entirety. Holism for King was manifested in his synthetic and inclusive approach to social and philosophical problems. King was satisfied by discovering a more holistic solution or method that could synthesize two opposites in fruitful harmony by affirming partial truths in each position to engender a more plausible description and understanding of an issue or a problem.

King's holism offered astute analytic power in discerning various moral challenges and opportunities. He rejected any reductionist or dualist view of a reality, as such an approach inevitably distorts one's understanding of reality. His critique of materialism and his rejection of the dichotomy of body/soul, material/spiritual, and individual/society was a reflection of his African American holism; for this same reason he refused to be a disciple of any one philosopher or theologian. While learning and appropriating diverse philosophical and theological traditions and sources, he always searched for a more holistic understanding of the reality and therefore also of the solution to the problem. For example, King appropriated the strengths of liberalism and neo-orthodoxy without falling into their respective shortcomings of naïve optimism and pessimism.

Mahatma Gandhi

One may make a similar observation regarding King's interest in Gandhi's philosophy of nonviolence. Gandhi's influence on King was distinctive in several aspects. King's six principles of nonviolence, which are examined later, were a creative adaptation and improvement of Gandhi's. Gandhi's teaching appealed to King's communal political spirituality. During his student life at Crozer, King was deeply concerned with how to reconcile the demand of Christian love with political effectiveness for social change. It was frustrating for King to accept that the ethics of Jesus, which he identified as *agape* love, could only be applied to individual relationships. He finally found the answer for his search in Gandhi's method of nonviolent resistance, which showed him a way to overcome the impasse between immoral power and powerless morality.[83]

After hearing Mordecai Johnson's lecture on Gandhi in the spring of 1950, King immediately bought half a dozen of Gandhi's books and found himself moved by Gandhi's practice of non-violence, not merely as a strategy but as a spiritual way of life. Furthermore, Gandhi's success in nonviolent struggles for the independence of India gave King empirical historical evidence as a foundation for his hope that the African American social struggle could be both moral and effective at the same time. He reached the conclusion that nonviolence was the only ethically and practically justifiable method for oppressed people.[84]

Despite the doctrinal and theological differences between Christianity and Hinduism, Gandhi's nonviolence as a transformative method was not only consistent with the love ethics of Jesus,[85] but also resonated deeply with King's African American communal-political spiritual tradition. In particular, Gandhi's nonviolent method shared significant anthropological, moral, and cosmological presuppositions with African American spirituality, in terms of interdependence of humanity, its emphasis on love and compassion, the moral nature of the universe, human potentiality for community, the redeemability of adversaries, and a unified religious worldview that refuses to separate religion from other

---

83. However, if we examine King's intellectual development leading to his wholehearted adoption of nonviolence, it was not an accident. We find that King was intellectually ready for this moral enlightenment. His school papers on human nature and the question of evil were especially revealing regarding his readiness. Written around February 1950, King's "How Modern Christians Should Think of Man" precipitated his hearing of Mordecai Johnson's lecture on Gandhi in spring 1950. King's dialectical understanding of human nature in this paper was congruent with the basic anthropological assumptions of nonviolence. Another of King's papers, "Religion's Answer to the Problem of Evil," is also revealing in the way it projects a future trajectory of King's thought on nonviolence as a method to overcome the evil of racism (Martin Luther King, Jr., "Religion's Answer to the Problem of Evil," in *The Papers I*, 428).

84. King, *Stride toward Freedom*, 97.

85. Watley, *Roots of Resistance*, 49.

domains of social life.[86] Gandhi's idea of soul force, *satyagraha,* is commensurate with the notion of the communal power that King learned from African American churches.

However, King was different from Gandhi in terms of his complex and organic understanding of power. Gandhi regarded spiritual or soul force as the only pure form of power — superior to body force or physical force. He did not ascribe any intrinsically positive meaning to any other forms of societal powers, such as political, economic, and cultural ones. The latter are inherently corruptive. On the contrary, King recognized the necessity and legitimacy of societal powers for human existence. These powers are not inherently evil, for power has been an indispensable aspect of human life as far as history continues.

Summary

King's spirituality was quintessentially African American. Built on African American spirituality, it was holistic, hopeful, communal, God-centered, ritually and aesthetically rich and articulate, and politically active. King's study of white theology added new depth and scope, conceptual clarity and critical edges to his spirituality. The synthesis was naturally facilitated by King's orientation of African holistic and practical wisdom. Liberal education provided King with appropriate intellectual and theological vocabulary, concepts, and ideas to express and communicate African American social concerns and issues. Through his study of white theology and philosophy, his African American themes and motifs obtained intellectual cogency, breadth, and social-political relevance, while white liberal ideas and concepts obtained spiritual depth and concretization through his African American spirituality. Fusing African American spirituality with liberal white theology, philosophy, and other intellectual sources, King transformed the African American spirituality into a rich and dynamic form of spirituality that was useful in overcoming systemic evils.

86. Smith and Zepp, *Search for the Beloved Community,* 51.

Through this process of incorporation, expansion, and refinement, King was ready to become one of the most articulate advocates and practitioners of African American spirituality in a modern era.

With the completion of his Ph.D. comprehensive examinations, King returned to the South seeking an opportunity to work for the improvement of his people's social conditions. It was in the South that many of these spiritual characteristics named above became more explicit throughout his ministry as he served an African American church working with African Americans. King remained a profoundly religious person throughout his life, maintaining a holistic attitude toward ministry. His optimism continued throughout his ministry, at least before his engagement with the anti–Vietnam War campaign, and his ritualistic and aesthetic styles were unmistakably and more explicitly African American. King's communal dispositions also continued through his ministry at Dexter and Ebenezer as well as during the civil rights movement, as his political commitment was further intensified through his struggle against racism, poverty, and militarism.

Chapter 3

The Communal-Political Nature of King's Spirituality

African and African American spiritual features — such as ubiquity of religion, belief in God's sovereignty, communalism, natural laws and moral orders, hopefulness, justice, and rituals and aesthetics — gave a particular form and content to King's spirituality. Among these features, the communal and the political features demand our particular attention because they constitute a foundational spiritual disposition and trajectory for King's theology and ministry. These two thrusts underlie all of King's theological ideas, philosophical understandings, ethical values, and ministry practices. Other African American sensibilities and dynamics were subsumed into these two aspects, adding nuances, vitality, and complexity to his spiritual outlooks and practices.

Communal sensibility took various shapes in King's expression, such as the interdependent nature of human existence, integration, love, the beloved community, and the world house, while the political was manifested in his ideas of justice, power, his emphasis on prophetic ministry, and his leadership in the civil rights movement. Yet in King's spirituality the communal and the political nearly always remained organically integrated, complementing each other through checks and balances. For example, the dialectical and creative tension between the political and the communal was manifested in the important concepts of King's theology, ethics, and approach to ministry, such as justice and love, resistance and reconciliation, desegregation and integration, and the priestly and prophetic ministry. By virtue of this creative tension between the communal and the political, King's spirituality was dynamic and synthetic; it was militant but not violent, confrontational but not antagonistic, transformative but not destructive.

The communal and the political did not always move or find their expression evenly, as is discussed later. In the historical development of King's public ministry, there was a shift in emphasis between the communal and the political. While King's ministry had a more communal nature in the early period of his public ministry (1955–65), it became more political in the final period (1966–68).

In this chapter, I examine how the communal and political thrusts of King's spirituality were reflected in the key concepts of his theology, ethics, and ministry.

God

King's understanding of God was both communal and political. He discussed the attributes of God primarily in terms of fellowship and goodness, both of which refer to the relational and ethical-political nature of God. These two attributes are naturally expressed in the idea of a person; that is, a person is meant to be relational and ethical.

The communal dimension is disclosed in King's understanding of God as a person. While God's personhood is qualitatively different from human personhood, both God and human beings, as persons, share the fundamental aspect of a spiritual and moral nature, which is the ability to enter fellowship.[1] For King, God was not simply a concept, impersonal object, or principle, but a person who is able to be experienced in relationship. God as a person is not only the focus of our worship and respect, but also a partner in our struggles. King noted, "So in the truest sense of

---

1. On the basis of his personalist belief, King rejected both Tillich's and Wieman's ideas of God — Tillich's definition of God as "Being Itself" and Wieman's notion of God as "supreme value" — which he considered impersonal in nature (Martin Luther King, Jr., "A Comparison of the Conceptions of God in the Thinking of Paul Tillich and Henry Nelson Wieman," in *The Papers II*, 527).

the word, God is a living God. In him there is feeling and will, responsive to the deepest yearnings of the human heart; this God both evokes and answers prayer."[2]

On the basis of this communal and personalist understanding of God, King rejected a deist view of God because it presented a remote, impersonal, monistic understanding. A deist view of God does not guarantee the true communion of human beings with God, nor does it promise the assurance of God's goodness in interaction with human beings.[3] If God remains the object beside other objects, God is not able to participate in the process of communal spiritual formation and historical transformation. To be a person means to be able to enter into companionship with others, with civil and religious responsibilities. King said that although interaction may be possible between impersonal beings, *fellowship* is not possible between them.[4] Only a person can enter fellowship and form a community. The fact that God is a person means that God is the one who empowers and encourages human agents in the struggles for justice through an intimate personal relationship.[5] Created in the image of God, human beings are endowed with some spiritual and moral capacity to communicate with one another and with God. God and human beings, as persons, work together to build the beloved community.

King understood that God is moral and political. God is working in history to bring about justice. God sides with the oppressed in their struggle for freedom and justice. The universe, created and sustained by such a moral God, bends toward justice. God is the vindicator of the oppressed, and because of this eternal companionship with God, the oppressed are not alone in their struggle for justice.

---

2. Martin Luther King, Jr., *Strength to Love* (New York: Harper & Row, 1963), 141–42.

3. King, "A Comparison of the Conceptions of God in the Thinking of Paul Tillich and Henry Nelson Wieman," 514.

4. Ibid.

5. See King's sermon, "Our God Is Able," in *Strength to Love*, 101–7.

King's synthesizing holism operated here as well. The attributes of fellowship and goodness are inseparable in a proper understanding of God's personhood. King's idea of "eternal companionship with God" emphasized the synthesis of God's personhood and goodness, the relational and moral-political aspects of the divine person working in history with humanity to build the beloved community. This idea of a personal God who cares for the oppressed was critical to King's understanding of the African American struggle for freedom and justice. God is the sustaining power against otherwise insurmountable adversities and hardship.

Anthropology

King's anthropology was also informed by his African American communal and political spiritual tradition. If his understanding of humanity as kin was the expression of communalism, his advocacy for an active and participatory human agency for social transformation was a natural expression of his political commitment. In many ways, King's anthropology was consistent with the anthropology of the black church tradition, which emphasized the interdependence and the equal sanctity of all humanity.

King's communal emphasis was evident in his corporate view of a person. He believed that the self is the self only in relation to others: without others, the self is incomplete. For King, the well-being of self and the well-being of others are inextricably connected in a community. He noted, "The universe is so structured that things do not quite work out rightly if men are not diligent in their concern for others. . . . I cannot reach fulfillment without thou. . . . All life is interrelated."[6]

King's anthropology was informed by his experience of racism. In opposition to white racist anthropology, King claimed that every human being is free and equal, and must therefore be respected. The worth of a human being is transcendental because it

---

6. Martin Luther King, Jr., "The Ethical Demands for Integration," in *A Testament of Hope*, 122.

is not determined by skin color or social status but by an intrinsic relatedness to God. For King, the sanctity and interdependence of humanity are mutually associated in God, for all human beings are interrelated as they are made in the same image of God. In God, the parent, they share a common origin and destiny. King believed that only when this sacred origin and interdependence of humanity were recognized could social division and antagonism be overcome and replaced by universal kinship.

King's belief in the intrinsic worth of every person and the solidarity of humanity compelled him to distance himself from communism and from liberal individualism. He felt that both liberalism and communism offered only half-truths about human nature. Communism treated individual human beings as a means to an end, rather than as an end in itself, suppressing the creativity and freedom of individuals,[7] while liberal individualism (and capitalism) were individualistic to the extent of denying the unity of humanity.

The political aspect of King's spirituality was disclosed in his emphasis on human agency — self-conscious human actions and decisions. A person is an agent; to be a person is to will, and to will is to act. As a moral agent, a person is open to free choice. King assumed that a human life was neither static nor predetermined. It is caught between the two possibilities of good or evil (community or segregation, love or hatred, relationship or alienation, sainthood or selfishness). An eternal civil war rages within each human.

King's dialectic understanding of human sinfulness and goodness led him to stress the necessity for continuous human efforts and endeavors for personal and social progress. There is no natural law of endless progress toward perfection in human nature, nor is a human being totally helpless under the shackles of sin and egoism. This stance implies that social progress is neither automatic nor inevitable, but requires human struggle and exertion. Every social relationship and institution, whether racial,

---

7. King, *Stride toward Freedom*, 75.

economic, or political, is something that human beings can improve and reform if they have the will to do so. King believed in the reforming possibility of humanity and society, with the future of history being very much an open frontier depending on human decisions and efforts.

King's view of agency was emboldened and empowered by the African peoples' unique spirit of hopefulness. As an optimistic, religious person, he believed that by divine grace, human beings could move toward the good. According to him, despite various limitations, human beings, created in the image of God, were the makers of their destiny and fate. King contended, "There is within human nature an amazing potential for goodness."[8] Any social progress would be inconceivable if one did not believe in the possibility of human change. A happy life is created by you, not given to you.[9] He knew that pessimism makes people the victims of fatalistic self-prophecy of human inaction, and the ensuing acquiescence to social evils.

This emphasis on agency converges with the insight of personalist philosophy. However, the emphasis on this open-ended agency was a natural consequence of African American political struggles in the United States. In their experience in the United States, African Americans learned that resignation, retreat, or pessimism did not help them at all. Ultimately, they were the captains of their own destiny in God and had to work for their own liberation. The struggle for justice requires a dedicated human moral agency.

The Beloved Community

The idea of the beloved community epitomizes King's idea of community. As some scholars have said, King's idea of the beloved community was the capstone of his social philosophy or "the

---

8. Martin Luther King, Jr., "Love, Law, and Civil Disobedience," in *A Testament of Hope*, 47.

9. King, *Where Do We Go from Here?* 28.

organizing principle of all his thought and activity."[10] Like his ancestors, King understood a community as the creative purpose of the universe. King declared, "He who works against community is working against the whole of creation."[11] King contended that the formation of a community indicated the most creative turn of human history.[12] Civilization began with a human decision to give up competition and to form a community. King believed that a true sense of human civilization arose when primitive persons put aside their stone axes and decided to cooperate with each other.

Many scholars say that theologically King's idea of the beloved community was influenced by Walter Rauschenbusch and the philosophy of personalism, as both emphasized the social nature of personality. Actually, the term "the beloved community" has its origin in Josiah Royce and R. H. Lotze, whose philosophies had had a profound influence on the development of personalism.[13] However, the primary impulse of this vision came from his African and African American communal spirituality, which understands a community as the basic unit and the ultimate goal of human existence and fulfillment.

King's idea of the beloved community was postulated on the interdependence of humanity.[14] A human life is actualized only in community through mutual dependence and cooperation; for example, the well-being of African Americans and the well-being of whites are tied together. If the suffering of African Americans diminishes the well-being of whites, the liberation of the former enlarges the well-being of the latter.

With the idea of the beloved community, King envisioned a society where each individual pursues self-excellence in a harmonious relationship with others in God. It presents a holistic vision

---

10. Smith and Zepp, *Search for the Beloved Community,* 129.
11. King, *Stride toward Freedom,* 106.
12. King, "The Ethical Demands for Integration," in *A Testament of Hope,* 122.
13. Fluker, *They Looked for a City,* 110.
14. Ibid., 128.

for all individual and collective moral and spiritual endeavors and efforts. To achieve this vision, the government should support and ensure that the talents and potentials of persons are actualized to the fullest extent; the poor and the oppressed must be given equal opportunities while their civil political rights and minimum social and economic livelihood must be guaranteed by law. It is King's conviction that the moral nature of social institutions is positively correlated with the enhancement of human dignity and harmony.

King's idea of sin is closely related to his vision of a community. In the final analysis, sin for King indicates the obstacles to the fulfillment of a community, the breakup of both personal and social harmony. On the personal level, sin disrupts inner harmony and wholeness; this disruption is manifested in various forms, including ignorance, fear, jealousy, hatred, and inferiority. On the social level, sin indicates the stumbling blocks to the creation of the beloved community, usually in the form of injustice, like segregation, exploitative capitalism, and militarism.

The vision of the beloved community has immediate political and moral implications for the movements in which King was involved. The mission statement of the SCLC reads, "The ultimate aim of SCLC is to foster and create the 'beloved community' in America where brotherhood is a reality." During the civil rights movement, the idea of the beloved community served as a spiritual moral goal and criterion against social evils. In the composition and cooperation of people participating in the civil rights movement, King saw a microcosm of the beloved community.[15] Participants at mass meetings, rallies, demonstrations, sit-ins, and freedom rides came from every segment of U.S. society — transcending differences in age, race, educational background, gender, religious affiliation, occupation; they came to work for a common cause of humanity. King attempted to broaden and expand the base of the civil rights movement to be as inclusive and diverse as possible.[16]

---

15. Smith and Zepp, *Search for the Beloved Community*, 132.
16. Ibid.

King later applied the vision of the beloved community not only to racial relationships, but also to international relationships. The idea of the "world house" arose naturally as his public ministry progressed into an international realm. King argued that the beloved community could not be realized by one race, one religion, or one nation alone; it required mutual alliances and collaboration among different races, religions, and nationalities. The foundation of his belief was the interdependence of humanity.

A Complete Life

Closely related to the idea of the beloved community was King's idea of a complete life, which was the moral content of the beloved community. Even here, his communal and holistic sensibility is prominent. The idea of a complete life was presented as the major theme of his flagship sermon, "Three Dimensions of a Complete Life." Delivered at a variety of significant occasions,[17] this sermon captures the essence of King's spirituality, which is holistic, communal, and balanced.[18]

According to King, a complete life is composed of three dimensions — length, breadth, and height — which respectively correspond to the dimensions of self, others, and God. For King, a complete life includes all three dimensions of self-actualization through the pursuit of excellence, a strong sense of social responsibility toward others, and the trust in and love for God ("an intense God-consciousness").[19]

Length: Self

The first dimension of King's idea of a complete life has to do with self-love or the authentic fulfillment of the self. On the basis of his

17. King preached this sermon on several occasions, as a candidate for the pastorate of Dexter Avenue Baptist Church in 1954, and again in Westminster Abbey, London, on his way to Sweden to receive the Nobel Peace Prize in 1964.

18. King's sermon "The Drum Major Instinct" echoes the same balance among self-love, self-recognition, and service toward others (*A Testament of Hope,* 259–67).

19. Baldwin, *There Is a Balm in Gilead,* 158.

early experiences of racism and its psychological affliction on self-esteem, King was aware of the significance of self-love for healthy, well-balanced personality and social relationships. Differentiated from either egoism or narcissism, self-love is something so basic to one's life that without it a human individual existence is distorted.[20] Assertion of selfhood, so long as it is not done at the expense of others, is a precondition for the love of others and therefore the construction of the beloved community.

In the later days of his public career, facing the challenge of Malcolm X and the black power movement, King began to more explicitly appreciate and express African American cultural heritages, history, and roots for the confirmation and validation of an African American sense of worth. King contended that a healthy self-esteem grounded in a proud historical heritage of their ancestors provided a positive and necessary psychological power for African Americans.[21]

Breadth: Others

The second dimension is concerned with others. As discussed previously, King believed that the fulfillment of the self is possible only in relation to other human beings in community.

Height: God

The third dimension of King's vision of a complete life pertains to God. King felt that faith in God stood at the center of a complete life. Standing in the traditional African and African American spiritual value of the ubiquity of religion, King was compelled to believe that without God, human existence and fulfillment are impossible. King believed that both positive self-love and love of other persons are derived from the same spiritual and moral

---

20. In his early public ministry, this dimension of self-love, personal actualization, may have seemed not to have had many chances to be properly emphasized. However, King's numerous sermons at African American churches show otherwise (See his sermons "What a Mother Should Tell Her Child" and "Training Your Child in Love").

21. King, *Where Do We Go from Here?* 42–43.

foundation, which is the dignity and sanctity of a person in God. God is the source of life. Without the relationship to God, the self cannot free itself from selfishness: even reason degenerates into immoral justification of injustice.[22]

The idea of a complete life presented a unified perspective on human existence. From early on, King realized that these three dimensions are constitutive of and indispensable for human fulfillment. He said, "Life as it should be and life at its best is the life that is complete on all sides."[23] Like an architectural structure formed and sustained by the balance of length, width, and height, the integration of life requires these three dimensions. The lack of or deficiency in any of these dimensions will cause a collapse due to distortion through imbalance and imperfection. For example, *agape,* even in its most sacrificial expression, would be incomplete without a proper regard for self-love and love of God. The love of self, love of other, and love of God are all indispensable, interrelated in mutual balance and harmony.

In short, the idea of a complete life represented a manifesto of King's spirituality.[24] The balance among the three dimensions is found in King's own life and spirituality. King wanted to fulfill

---

22. King, "Pilgrimage to Nonviolence," in *A Testament of Hope,* 36. The significance of a third dimension of spirituality is found in King's own spiritual experience, mostly notably by his "kitchen experience" during the Montgomery Bus Boycott. One midnight, after receiving an especially nasty threatening call, he was shaken to his core. In deep despair and fear coming from physical and emotional exhaustion and unceasing threats on his and his wife and children's lives, King was about to give up his struggle. He was thinking about an honorable way to step down without causing harm to the boycott. Sitting at his kitchen table, he prayed aloud to God, confessing his fear and weakness. In the middle of his prayer, King felt the divine presence; he heard God's voice speaking to him with comforting assurance: "Stand up for righteousness. Stand up for justice. Stand up for truth; and God will be at your side forever." This encounter brought to King a kind of an inner calm and courage that he had never experienced before (King, *Stride toward Freedom,* 135).

23. Martin Luther King, Jr., *The Measure of a Man* (New York: Christian Education Press, 1959), 20.

24. Robert Franklin notes, "King's image of the complete life functioned as an ethical norm which consistently informed his ministerial decisions and public action" (Robert M. Franklin, "Martin Luther King, Jr., as Pastor," *Iliff Review* 42 [1985]: 5).

himself through his ministry, which he understood as the call from God to serve humanity. That is, in the ministry of Jesus Christ, he naturally harmonized his self-fulfillment and service to others. King's spirituality was deeply rooted in his personal relationship with God and his faithfulness to the gospel: he gave his life for the betterment of his people and humanity.

King never completely departed from this early insight and vision of integral human existence. For example, during his campaign against poverty in the North, King challenged African Americans to work assiduously to improve their educational and civic standards, although he emphasized the necessity of federal governmental assistance to solve the problems of urban blights, such as poverty, illiteracy, high crime rates, and juvenile delinquency.

Desegregation and Integration

This inextricable dynamic between the communal and the political was articulated by King in terms of the relationship of integration and desegregation. If desegregation was concerned with the political side of his movement, integration dealt with its communal aspect. While integration was the goal of the struggle for the beloved community, desegregation offered its means. Desegregation and integration were therefore mutually necessary.

King was deeply aware that for the nation to be transformed into the beloved community, it needed spiritual transformation as well as judicial changes. The first step toward the goal was the removal of the injustice of segregation. Desegregation was important to the extent of restraining and binding racist actions of whites against African Americans. Changes in segregationist laws demanded massive political actions, such as nonviolent resistance.

King discerned that racism had to do not only with social institutional arrangements that subjugated African Americans for white social privileges, but also with deep spiritual states and the moral underpinnings of people and society. At the root of these institutional arrangements were the spiritual problems of fear, hatred, arrogance, greed, and anxiety. He was convinced that so long as these spiritual problems persisted, the judicial achievements of civil rights bills would be vulnerable to the racist whims and wills of whites. And these spiritual inner attitudes were "unenforceable," beyond the reach of legal enforcement.[25] To obey the unenforceable required the transformation of the heart, which is the task of morality, religion, and spirituality.

Approach to Ministry: Prophetic and Priestly

King's communal-political spirituality was disclosed in his holistic and balanced approach to Christian ministry. His ministry was both priestly and prophetic.[26] King's spirituality was prophetic in its critique of social evils and abusive powers, but priestly in its emphasis on the healing of alienated relationships through forgiveness, love, and reconciliation. The goal of ministry was the creation of the beloved community for which King recognized that both prophetic and priestly dimensions were necessary.

This balanced and holistic orientation to ministry is characteristic of traditional African American Christian clergy who perform the roles of both priest and prophet. As leaders, they are typically concerned with the psychological, spiritual, and moral well-being of their people. Knowing well their members' suffering, pain, and hurt, which are especially caused by an unjust social system, they serve as therapists and moral-political leaders of the community.

This dialectical and organic ministerial approach was evident in King. King performed the traditional roles of African American clergy as priest, therapist, and moral-political leader for the nation. As a priest-therapist, he fully sympathized with the plight of ordinary African Americans and poor whites. As a prophet, he defended the human rights of the oppressed and urged people to struggle for justice.

---

25. King, *Where Do We Go from Here?* 100.
26. See Baldwin, *There Is a Balm in Gilead,* 310.

King was a prophet with the pastor's tender heart for healing, and a pastor with the prophet's passion for justice. A prophet without the pastor's caring love could end up as a self-righteous critic, judge, and vindicator, rather than a builder of a new society. A priest without the prophet's vision and passion for justice may turn out to be a defender of the status quo, a peacekeeper rather than a peacemaker, someone who tends to the symptoms of problems rather than addressing the causes. Prophetic criticism and ministry can be a higher form of pastoral care, just as pastoral love and care should be motivations for any public criticism. Even under the duress of his prophetic ministry, King did not lose his priestly care and sensibility.

In King's public career, there was a shift in emphasis between the two dimensions during the last years of his life. If the priestly-communal side was more expressive in his early public ministry, the political-prophetic was more so in his later life, but they were never completely apart from each other. In particular, King's attitude toward the United States underwent a significant change around 1965 in response to the Watts riots, the escalation of the Vietnam War, and the rise of the black power movement.

James Cone is the scholar who perceives a radical paradigmatic shift in King's theology and ethics in this period.[27] He argues that although love was a leading concept in the early period, it was replaced by the prophetic radicalism and even separatist tendency welded into the eschatological hope in the latter period, as King's dream turned into nightmare.

Yet I do not agree with Cone's interpretation of King's radicalization in this period — his tilt toward African American separatism, in particular. Cone fails to point out King's profound differences from separatists, such as Malcolm X, despite his own political radicalization. It is true that in his later career, the political or prophetic side rather than the communal, priestly side of King's spirituality became more prominent as he grew

---

27. See Cone, *Martin and Malcolm and America.*

disenchanted by the depth of white racism. King, however, never moved outside the bounds of his communal spirituality. Although his rhetoric and politics became confrontational and revolutionary, King never completely gave up nonviolence or his vision of the beloved community. Even in his harsh critique of the Vietnam War, he never completely abandoned a priestly sensibility and love for his nation.[28] King said, "I still have a dream" in his "A Christmas Sermon on Peace." As the very title of his last major book suggests (*Where Do We Go from Here: Chaos or Community?*), he was still very much concerned about the issue of community.

The kind of political radicalism that Cone identified in the later King might come from the prevalence of his political radicalism, which overshadowed communalism in his attitude toward the United States. However, it was a shift of emphasis within his orientation, from a relative prevalence of the communal in the early period to the political in the last years. From the beginning, despite his emphasis on love, King was aware of the recalcitrant nature of collective egoism and the limitations of moral suasion and ethical appeal to eliminate social evils.

I believe that the impression of such a radical shift in King's attitude is due in part to the expansion of King's communalism beyond the boundaries of the United States; in the last few years of his life, King's communalism was expressed on a global scale for the peace and justice of humanity. King's vision of the beloved community was now expressed in his solidarity with the victims of oppression. In this context, King's undeterred criticism of the United States resulted not only from his disappointment at the depth of white racism in the nation, but also from his solidarity with the victims of poor countries. In King's view, the United States was a perpetrator of violence against the "world house."

---

28. King, untitled paper on Vietnam (The King Center Archives, April 30, 1967), 2.

Love, Power, and Justice

The triadic dialectic of power, justice, and love offers an integral perspective on King's spiritual politics and his moral quest for the beloved community. In a creative adaptation of Paul Tillich's thought, King made the triad into a kind of spiritual-moral manual for social engagement. It synthesizes the moral ideal of love with the demand for justice in the awareness of the social reality of power. This triad includes the communal (with an emphasis on love), the political (with an emphasis on justice), and the practical (with an emphasis on power), combined with the holistic (and an emphasis on their interrelatedness). The unified understanding of love, justice, and power offered him a holistic and synthesized perspective to link his empirical analysis of social relationships with the spiritual aim of the beloved community, without denying the significance of human strivings toward the achievement of justice on the onto-theological ground of human interdependence.

A political aspect of King's spirituality was first disclosed in his affirmation of the indispensable nature of power for human existence. King emphasized that power itself was not evil, but only the abuse of power. Human existence is impossible without the exercise of some form of power.

Yet the exercise of power in history is always precarious. There is no intrinsic moral guarantee that every exercise of power in history will be consistent with moral demands or requirements. Hence, clarifying the goal in the use of power is important, as power indicates the ability to achieve one's intended goal. If the use of power is disconnected from a right moral purpose, power becomes demonic. For King, the goal for power should be love. Without love, power becomes immoral, misdirected, and sentimental. Love and power are not opposites. Love is not a resignation of power, just as power is not a denial of love. Rather, love presupposes power.[29] Even *agape* love is not the denial of power. If *agape* means a voluntary self-surrender

---

29. King, "Where Do We Go from Here?" 247.

for others, the very surrender requires the exercise of power — self-determination and self-transcendence.

If love is the ultimate aim of power, it must be guided by justice. Justice, embodied in specified universal rules and principles, enlightens and guides power. It is the structure that enables power to achieve love, and love requires a just moral form or structure to regulate and coordinate various expressions and competitions of power. Hence, for King, justice was not extrinsic but intrinsic to a human spiritual quest toward love. Justice presents a minimal requirement of love. Power and justice are presupposed and preconditions for the fulfillment of love.

Because of his deep awareness of the significance of power and justice, King, even in his advocacy of nonviolence, never endorsed any absolute form of pacifism or anarchism because he felt they were anti-institutional, and therefore unrealistic in nature. He was keenly aware of the value and significance of laws and institutions for social well-being. To achieve this goal of love, the mobilization of just power to challenge the evil system is important. King continuously urged the federal government to faithfully enforce various desegregation and antidiscrimination laws.

Because King knew that love could not be achieved by employing immoral political means, such as violence, he rejected the utilitarian idea that the end justifies the means. A moral means must be consistent with the moral end it pursues; the end is pre-existent in the means. For King, positive social changes can only occur when morality and power go hand in hand.

The triadic relationship of love, power, and justice is best summed up in his declaration, "Power at its best is love implementing the demands of justice, and justice at its best is power correcting everything that stands against love."[30] Love is the legitimate goal of power to which collective moral will, resources, and the energies of a society should be directed, while justice provides the form and structure of mutuality between self-regarding loves of different persons and groups.

---

30. Ibid.

Dynamics of King's Spirituality and the Civil Rights Movement

I identify the communal, the political, the ritualistic, the aesthetic, and the intellectual as the major thrusts or dynamics of King's spirituality and the civil rights movement. Raised in African American spiritual traditions, King shared most of his spiritual dynamics with his fellow African Americans. Yet through his education at Morehouse, Crozer, and Boston, King added a new dynamic: the intellectual. These dynamics have far-reaching implications beyond King's own spirituality. They constituted the core spiritual mechanics of the civil rights movement. King welded and mobilized these dynamics of rituals (worship), aesthetics (arts and music, and oratorical skills), and intellectual astuteness for the sake of an effective social change. Embodied in King's leadership, they were instrumental in mobilizing people and sustaining the movement.

These dynamics were displayed in different combinations and emphases through various aspects of the civil rights movement. Through checks and balances, they coalesced and were refined to be a unified collective energy around the shared vision and goal. These dynamics are not mutually exclusive. Each dynamic rendered its own unique strength, energy, and creativity for the movement. For example, checked and balanced by other dynamics, the intellectual dynamic was prevented from being abstract, speculative, and purely theoretical, but empowered to be enlightening and organic.

African American spirituality provided a bond between King and his followers, for King shared the same cultural roots, experiences, and aspirations of the southern African American people. King emanated a spirituality of festive and celebrative modus vivendi, an optimistic and hopeful worldview shared by many southern African Americans. Thus King's effective leadership over African Americans was the result of his familiarity with their vocabulary, symbols, songs, gestures, and stories. They felt no alienation or distance from King. They understood the logic of

King's spirituality, and they shared his moral convictions, such as the triumph of justice over evil, God's sovereign power, and the central value of love in human existence.

King was keenly aware of the remarkable communal spiritual resources of African American people, which enabled them to survive the terror and oppression of slavery, lynching, and segregation without forfeiting their souls. He stated, "Negroes are almost instinctively cohesive. We band together readily.... In some of the simplest relationships we will protect a brother even at a cost to ourselves.... Solidarity is a reality in Negro life...."[31] King used these spiritual resources for a positive purpose. Through his leadership ability, oratorical skills, and moral integrity, King catalyzed the deep and rich spiritual energy, fervor, and communal habits of African American churches into a nonviolent, militant social movement. Gayraud Wilmore's observation of King's leadership in the civil rights movement was not only relevant, but also affirms the rough combination of these dynamics found in King's spirituality:

> King's effectiveness in those early days of the civil rights movement cannot be attributed solely to *the cogency of his ideas* [intellectual] about nonviolence as a mode of practical action. The real power of his southern campaign lay in his ability to combine dexterously a simple but profound philosophy with *the folk religion and revival techniques* [ritualistic & aesthetic] of the black Baptist preacher. He was able to elicit from the thousands who flocked to hear him throughout the South *the old-fashioned religiosity of the folk* [communal], converted into *a passion for justice* [political]. But the passion for justice was already there. Suppressed by years of subjugation and domesticated by the prudence of a mute church, it was nevertheless deeply embedded in the religion of the masses. King made the familiar religious language and the old biblical images burst into new life.[32]

---

31. King, *Where Do We Go from Here?* 159.
32. Wilmore, *Black Religion and Black Radicalism,* 177; emphasis added.

If King's quest for the beloved community was the goal of his political and spiritual engagements, the realization of this goal required not only intellectual clarity and moral coherence, but also political practicality and the motivating power to accomplish the mobilization of massive numbers of ordinary people. King critically appropriated various theological, philosophical, aesthetic, and practical elements around this consistent quest for the beloved community.

King was sufficiently intellectually articulate to be able to communicate his views to various types of audiences. He was intellectually conversant with both African Americans and whites. Using universally known hymns and symbols, he was able to effectively motivate and mobilize African Americans. Using the philosophical languages and ideas of Western liberal traditions, he was able to make the case to white America for justice and freedom.

King was a philosopher and systematic theologian by training. It was King's belief that religion should be socially active as well as intellectually respectable. To be intellectually respectable, religious ideals and principles need to be communicated through reasonable and sensible language, in terms that the public can understand. In formulating a plausible form of public theology for social change,[33] King translated his particular religious language and symbols into public terms, identifying and interpreting in spiritual terms the challenges and problems of a society. A master of intertextuality, King freely interwove various spiritual, moral, and intellectual sources for the persuasion of the public. He creatively mixed spirituals, African American proverbs, and folklore with phrases from the Bible (e.g., the Exodus, wilderness, crucifixion, redemption, and *eschaton*), Western philosophies, theologies,

---

33. Public theology is a unique genre of theology that communicates and defends the universal values of one's religion to the public. Unlike other forms of public discourse, public theology uses the relevant insights and tested wisdom of religious beliefs and doctrines to address complex collective and personal human problems, situations that are otherwise confusing and ambiguous. Properly crafted, a public theological discourse can be effective in motivating and empowering people to participate in the process of positive social change.

and political documents, such as the Declaration of Independence and the Bill of Rights, in making a public case for freedom of African Americans.

For example, *covenant* was a concept that King used in his public theology to communicate his moral values and vision to the American public. King appealed to the Declaration of Independence, the Bill of Rights, and the Constitution as the primal collective covenants of the nation as they represented the professed moral principles and standards that a nation has promised to its members and its members to each other. Relying on these covenantal creeds, King disclosed the abysmal gap between the promise and its fulfillment, between its professed creed (freedom, equality, and the pursuit of happiness) and its actual practices (discrimination and exploitation). He urged the nation to be consistent with its founding credo.

King's intellectual ability and knowledge profoundly elevated his effectiveness as a leader. This intellectual dynamic not only brought a sense of confidence to the followers of his movement, but also added a much-needed persuasive power for new audiences. King's intellectual competence counterbalanced excessive ritualistic spiritualism and emotionalism.

As the intellectual dynamic obviously provided the articulation and cogency necessary to his speeches and addresses for public persuasion, so ritualistic, aesthetic dynamics added an energizing, dramatic stimulation, and a sustaining power to the movement. During the civil rights movement, the spirituals, traditional hymns, and other freedom songs were widely sung in the mass rallies, prisons, freedom rides, and sit-ins. These songs are "group participation" songs, according to Bernice J. Reagon, which not only encouraged the participation in a common struggle, but also greatly solidified the sense of community among the participants despite their different economic, social, and educational backgrounds.[34] Similarly, dancing, clapping, foot-stomping, and the

---

34. Bernice J. Reagon, "Songs of the Civil Rights Movement, 1955–1965: A Study in Culture History," (Ph.D. dissertation, Howard University, Washington, DC, May 1975), 132–38; quoted in Baldwin, *There Is a Balm in Gilead*, 197.

raising of hands added the sense of unity as people participated in the same motions and movements.

The civil rights movement obtained sustaining power from spiritual energies generated by the mass meetings. On the grassroots level, mass meetings were a significant instrument for the political operation of the civil rights struggle. Meetings were held regularly, every Monday evening. Mass meetings offered opportunities to recruit on a regular basis. Like altar calls in many African American churches that summon worshipers to a new or renewed dedication for a high purpose of life, in the mass meeting, speakers and preachers called volunteers for marches, demonstrations, and services with new dedication and commitment to the cause of freedom.

Mass meetings were occasions for a natural expression of African American spiritual holism where the religious and political, liturgical and civic are inseparable. The connection between the political and the ritualistic was clear in the way African American Christian worship provided inspiration and energy to the movement. Religious and civic agendas were often indivisible in mass meetings. Replete with multiple political and religious symbols, mass meetings offered the occasion to freely express the African American yearning for freedom, justice, and love. Meetings proceeded in a worshipful atmosphere, typically beginning with extensive music, songs, communal reading of Scripture, sermons, prayers, and testimonies. Political speeches were mostly sermonic. Reflecting their religious nature, even the marches and demonstrations approximated African American church worship by adopting the ritualistic chant (incantation) of call-and-response as a method of inviting and empowering the marchers and demonstrators.

Through the extensive uses of ritualistic and liturgical methods and mechanisms, the mass meetings had profound therapeutic and transformative effects on the participants. Facing the brutality of lynching, mob violence, dog attacks, and harassment, the participants of the movement were sustained and encouraged by the power they obtained from worship. Spiritual songs, electrifying sermons, and testimonies at the mass meetings continuously injected a new sense of meaning, energy, and hope into people to sustain their struggles. Collective worship experiences served to solidify the unity between the leaders and the participants of the movement, renewing the sense of focus and hope for their struggles. King himself and other leaders continuously received renewing energy and sustaining support from the mass meetings.

The aesthetic and the intellectual elements were useful in persuading and mobilizing the audience. Aesthetics and politics are also intimately related. Biblical narratives performed political functions in motivating and empowering African Americans. Conversely, politics was transfigured by the inclusive and universalistic moral vision engrained in the narratives. For instance, the biblical narratives of the Exodus, the crucifixion, and the resurrection, as preached by King at mass meetings, excited the political and social imaginations of the audiences to envision a nonracist, inclusive society beyond segregation. The sermons were powerful enough to redirect their energies for the struggles.

The communal and the political were mutually balanced and checked. The political made the communal practical and feasible, whereas the communal made the political ethical and self-transcending. King said that marches and demonstrations were not the end in themselves; the goal was the creation of a community. As the political pertains to the realm of power, the power employed to achieve the goal must be a communal power to create a community. The communal without the enactments of political struggles remains a remote utopian ideal; that is, the political dynamic, with its emphasis on freedom in particular, purifies the danger of collectivism and idealism within the communal and the communal redeems the political from degeneration into utilitarian, Machiavellian expediencies.

Rooted in their communal and political spirituality, African Americans during the civil rights movement were able to maintain a creative tension between communal and revolutionary impulses, the demands of radical social transformation and reconciliation under King's leadership.

The shared dynamics of communal and political spirituality between King and his fellow African Americans explain why black power and black liberation theology failed to penetrate and mobilize African American churches into the radical direction of violent resistance: it affronted their communal sensibility.

Chapter 4

The Strength of Nonviolence in King's Struggle against Racism, Classism, and Militarism

The communal aspect of King's spirituality is reflected in his spiritual approach to collectivity. He was profoundly concerned about the well-being of a community; indeed, he treated the United States as a community or entity with a soul.[1] This approach was an expression both of his African American communalism, which takes a community as the ultimate object of one's moral endeavors, and his African American spiritual holism, which refused to separate the sacred from the profane, the religious from the political, and the part from the whole.

King considered all of society to be the object of spiritual conversion and sanctification. In Richard Lischer's phrase, King preached to and moved the nation just as a pastor preaches to and moves a congregation.[2] In King's view, collectivity, such as a nation, is a moral entity bound and guided by spiritual values and ideals, and thus is not exempt from spiritual and moral judgment. King did not hesitate to apply theological terms (e.g., soul or spirit) and spiritual outlooks (e.g., repentance or salvation) to the entire nation. He frequently talked about "social salvation."[3]

---

1. The soul of the nation, metaphorically, refers to a unique and essential spiritual-moral quality collectively shared by the nation, usually embodied in its basic values and policy directives.

2. Richard Lischer, *The Preacher King: Martin Luther King, Jr., and the Word That Moved America* (New York: Oxford University Press, 1995), 3.

3. Martin Luther King, Jr., "Suffering and Faith," in *A Testament of Hope*, 42.

Although King knew that the full actualization of this goal was impossible in history, he was convinced that all human beings are called for this task.

The spiritual approach to collective problems was evidenced primarily by the spiritual nature of the civil rights movement. As the SCLC's motto, "to redeem the soul of America," implied, the civil rights movement intended the birth of a new people and nation through a spiritual, moral, and judicial transformation. The motto was quite bold given the minority status and oppressed situation of African Americans at that time, and explicitly spiritual, visionary, and communal: King refused to confine the vision of his organization to such a narrowly defined issue as African American civil rights and freedom alone.

King expressed this spiritual approach to collective social problems concretely in his critique of racism, classism, and militarism. With a priestly concern and a prophetic vision, he wanted to deliver the nation from these demons, and create the beloved community through collective political struggles of nonviolence.

Nonviolence and Racism

From King's perspective, racism is anticommunity. It violates the transcendental worth, equality, and interdependence of humanity intended by God. Racism is based on the false belief that one race is congenitally inferior to others, and thus does not deserve equal or humane treatment. For this reason, racism inevitably engenders and condones violence, and when its logic is pursued to the extreme, it leads to genocide, for racism explicitly promulgates the view that other races do not deserve to exist.

Segregation represents a systemic institutionalization of racism supported by laws, social-cultural customs, and coercion. It is the antithesis to the beloved community because it divides people on the basis of skin color. King argued that the nation needed both spiritual transformation and judicial changes to purge it of racism and segregation.

The Montgomery Bus Boycott was the first major movement in which King engaged for the defeat of racism in the United States, and through it began to evolve his political stance. With the success of the boycott, King's struggle against segregation led to the formation of the SCLC, the Albany struggle, the Birmingham campaign, and the March on Washington on August 28, 1963, and finally climaxed in the Selma march and the subsequent passage of the Voting Rights Law in 1965.

Nonviolence: Spiritual and Political Aspects

It is ironic that King, who unswervingly adhered to nonviolent resistance, died prematurely due to someone else's violence. He used nonviolent resistance as a practical method of messianic politics against the political messianism of Jim Crow segregation and white supremacy. Nonviolence was a natural consequence of the convergence of two prominent impulses of African American spirituality: the creation of a community and the overcoming of social evils — the communal and the political. King promoted nonviolence as the collective expression of African American communal power ("soul force") in search of a free community because it offered both political viability and ethical consistency simultaneously. He believed that the creation of the beloved community required a qualitative change of citizens' hearts and structural changes in social institutions.[4]

In King's view, only three social options were available to the oppressed for dealing with their oppression: resignation, violence, or nonviolence. King noticed the first two responses were the prevailing sentiments among some African Americans due to centuries of long-suffering under white racism. He regarded the options of violence and resignation as unethical, and inconsistent with the demand of the gospel. For King, resignation was worse than violence because it indicated the absence of courage and

---

4. Martin Luther King, Jr., "Nonviolence: The Only Road to Freedom," in *A Testament of Hope*, 57–58.

passive subjection to oppression, which was in effect cooperating with evil. The oppressors used the acquiescence of the oppressed as a justification for their unjust policies. Sustained resignation inevitably hampered the development of a healthy self-esteem and self-respect in the oppressed, while at the same time it heightened and consolidated the sense of superiority in the oppressors. Eventually, it paralyzed the conscience of the oppressors.

King rejected violence because it destroys human life, dignity, and community. The parties involved in the conflicts suffer mutual harm. Violence is self-defeating because the self can neither exist nor fulfill itself without others. It aims at the survival of the self at the expense of others. History shows that violence always begets more violence, and hatred begets more hatred. Although King understood that hatred, anger, and bitterness were natural emotional responses to the centuries-long oppression of African Americans, King thought that these feelings and temperaments had to be overcome. Otherwise, such passions would harm the victims who were harboring them. These emotions and desires depersonalize the self and others, as a user of violence is usually overcome by the power of evil (see Matt. 26:52).

King believed that violence was counterproductive for the oppressed in their struggle for justice. Although violence might provide a temporary catharsis for anger and frustration, it does not bring forth any meaningful change but rather instills fear and resentment in the objects of violence. Furthermore, it tends to obscure moral issues. A clear distinction between victims and aggressors disappears as the latter begin to perceive themselves as the victims of violence as well. The emotions of anger and fear block and deprive the oppressors of the opportunity to engage in an honest self-scrutiny.

King believed that nonviolence was a more effective strategy than violence or resignation. Only nonviolence could stop the vicious cycle of violence and hatred. Such nonviolence was correlated with King's belief in the human moral capacity to do good and to fight against social evils. If the aftermath of violence is bitterness, revenge, and hatred, then the aftermath of nonviolence is friendship and reconciliation. King witnessed firsthand the positive fruits of nonviolence during his trip to India after independence, where hatred and bitterness, the typical result of violent struggles, were absent from Indians' relationships with the British, their former enemy.[5]

For King, only nonviolence offered a means of political change that was consistent with the moral goal of the beloved community. King's conviction was that if the goal is moral, the means must be moral as well. Thus, if the goal is the creation of the beloved community, the means to achieve it must be communal as well because the selection of a means inevitably affected the character of the person or the group employing the means, indicating that only communal power expressed through nonviolent resistance can serve this goal.

Spiritual-Disciplinary Aspects of Nonviolent Movement: Virtue and Control of Impulses

Controlling the emotions of fear, anxiety, and hatred has been intimately associated with spiritual disciplines. King approached nonviolence as a spiritual discipline of controlling destructive emotion and behaviors. Having learned from Gandhi the discipline and transformative power of nonviolence, King highlighted this dimension throughout the movement. By his emphasis on nonviolence, King was not only concerned with the outward behavior of nonviolent resisters — namely, restraining physical forces — but also with the transformation of their internal attitudes and spirits. King contended that those who are willing to adopt nonviolence as the technique for political change would be changed by it in the process.[6]

---

5. Martin Luther King, Jr., "My Trip to the Land of Gandhi," in *A Testament of Hope*, 25.

6. King, *Stride toward Freedom*, 89.

Recognizing the spiritual disciplinary aspect of nonviolence, King included self-purification as a necessary step of training.[7] He was clear about its social and moral educative value.[8] So in meetings before demonstrations, there was usually a training session regarding the use of the nonviolent method in which participants were repeatedly taught to love rather than hate whites, and urged to prepare to suffer violence if necessary rather than inflict it.[9] Training was usually combined with songs, prayers, and the reading of biblical passages that were nonviolent in nature.[10] King demanded that participants in the demonstrations pledge themselves to nonviolence by signing a commitment card that enumerated the ten commandments of nonviolence. These commandments show precisely that the nonviolence movement was primarily a spiritual practice rather than a political strategy:

1. MEDITATE daily on the teachings and life of Jesus.

2. REMEMBER always that the nonviolent movement ... seeks justice and reconciliation — not victory.

3. WALK and talk in the manner of love, for God is love.

4. PRAY daily to be used by God in order that all men might be free.

5. SACRIFICE personal wishes in order that all men might be free.

6. OBSERVE with both friend and foe the ordinary rules of courtesy.

7. SEEK to perform regular service for others and for the world.

8. REFRAIN from the violence of fist, tongue, or heart.

---

7. Martin Luther King, Jr., "Letter from Birmingham City Jail," in *A Testament of Hope*, 290.

8. Martin Luther King, Jr., "The Social Organization of Nonviolence," in *A Testament of Hope*, 33.

9. King, *Stride toward Freedom*, 87.

10. Ibid., 88.

9. STRIVE to be in good spiritual and bodily health.

10. FOLLOW the directions of the movement and of the captain of a demonstration.[11]

For King, nonviolence was not simply an expedient political strategy to obtain power or change the power equation, for nonviolence intends not only the transformation of an unjust system, but also the transformation of the hearts of the opponents. Indeed, King often equated white racism with moral sickness, which he believed could be cured by the disciplined love of African Americans.

Six Principles of Nonviolence

The spiritual aspects of King's idea of nonviolence are well captured in his six principles of nonviolence. With the creation of the beloved community as his goal, all six principles reflect African American communal spiritual values.

1. Nonviolence is the way of the strong

King repudiated the charge that nonviolence was the method of the weak. Nonviolence must not be confused with nonresistance or passive resistance. It may look nonaggressive physically, but it is very aggressive spiritually. King was deeply aware that the question of power was at the center of African American suffering. Instilling fatalism and nihilism, a sense of powerlessness inevitably led to condoning the oppressive system. Without the accumulation and application of power, the removal of social evil is impossible, for oppression is the result of the imbalance of power. King believed the injustices of slavery and segregation were the perpetuation of domination by the powerful over the powerless. African Americans needed to gain and use power to overturn their oppression.

---

11. Martin Luther King, Jr., "Why We Can't Wait," in *A Testament of Hope,* 537.

Power has many different manifestations in society: political, economic, military, and cultural. Because whites controlled most of these forms of institutional powers, African Americans needed a new form of power. A common perception is that the oppressed are entirely deprived of their power. King rejected this perception, believing instead that the oppressed have the most formidable form of power in their hands, a power he called "soul force" or "truth force." With this new power, King said that one could be strong without using violence.

King contended that only those who were truly strong and courageous could choose to be nonviolent because nonviolence puts a higher and more stringent moral demand on its practitioners. It requires real courage and strength of spirit to resist the evil within (such as hatred and vindictiveness) and without (mob activities and police brutalities). True strength lies in one's ability to control violent emotions and desires, and to overcome enmity with friendship.

2. The goal of nonviolence is reconciliation not retaliation

Nonviolence aims to win the friendship and understanding of the other, not to retaliate.[12]

By its very nature, retaliation destroys human relationships. Violence cannot create an environment of reconciliation. King noted, "To meet hate with retaliatory hate would do nothing but intensify the existence of evil in the universe."[13] Nonviolence intends to redeem all parties, both oppressors and oppressed, and in this way humanity works for the construction of the beloved community. King beseeched his followers to reject animosities toward whites and to actually love them. On the basis of love, nonviolence creates the conditions necessary for mutual understanding.

---

12. Martin Luther King, Jr., "An Experiment in Love," in *A Testament of Hope*, 17.

13. Ibid.

King declared the goal of nonviolence to be not defeat or humiliation, but redemption of the opponents.[14] By disarming fear and irrationality, nonviolence invites the opponents to the process of communication for the common well-being of society. Nonviolence is enacted by the community-creating power of God's Spirit. Nonviolence opens the creative and constructive energy of the human spirit for the possibility of a new mutual relationship in a community. John Raines nicely sums up the spiritual meaning of nonviolence:

> Although nonviolent resistance has a No in it, its Yes is more important. It is the Yes of honesty, of a nation restored and able to live with its own conscience. It is the Yes of that justice which is the beginning of friendship, and the end of the terrible waste of injustice and oppression.[15]

3. Nonviolence is directed against the evil, not against persons

Refusing to demonize whites, King proclaimed that whites, despite racist beliefs and practices, were human beings to be respected, not objects to be destroyed. In engaging in nonviolent resistance, King tried to depersonalize the campaign by separating evil behaviors from those who conducted them. King contended that whites were also the victims of an evil system; hence, he advocated resistance against the evil powers, not persons of the segregationist system. This ideal was deeply rooted in the notion of the fundamental interdependence of humanity, which constituted the core of the African and African American communal spirituality. Thus, even when one challenges evil behavior, the sanctity of the opponent is respected.

---

14. Martin Luther King, Jr., "The Power of Nonviolence," in *A Testament of Hope*, 12.

15. John C. Raines, "Righteous Resistance and Martin Luther King, Jr.," in *Martin Luther King, Jr.: Civil Rights Leader, Theologian, Orator*, ed. David J. Garrow, vol. 3 (New York: Carlson Publishing, 1989), 738.

4. Nonviolence relies on the redemptive power of unmerited suffering

Following African American church tradition, King believed in the redemptive possibilities of unmerited human suffering. When suffering is unearned it can be redemptive, meaning it can become a concrete expression of love toward one's enemy. King's idea of redemptive or unmerited suffering was not entirely a new construct:

> Black people have been struck not only with the similarity of what seemed to be their inexorable fate as a race and the Messianic vocation of suffering, but also with the profound, if not exact correspondence between their experience of blackness in Western civilization and the description of the Messiah.[16]

Suffering can make a person angry, cynical, or bitter toward life itself, thus poisoning his or her personality; but it can also enable and activate a previously humiliated and passive person for noble moral causes. Redemptive suffering is a transformation of the suffering for a creative purpose.[17] Unmerited suffering, suffering for the sake of justice, King suggested, has a redemptive power — a mobilizing power to stir the consciences of the oppressors and the spectators who have been silent on moral issues.

King saw in the suffering of African Americans a continuation of the suffering of Jesus Christ. The blood shed by African Americans in their struggle against injustice has a similar symbolic value for the redemption of whites and the United States as a whole. King believed that redemptive suffering and sacrifice were a necessary part of social change, and considered such suffering a virtue of his life and that of his followers.[18] He said:

---

16. Gayraud Wilmore, "The Black Messiah: Revising the Color Symbolism of Western Christology," *Journal of the Interdenominational Theological Seminary* 2 (1974): 13.

17. Martin Luther King, Jr., "Shattered Dreams," in *Strength to Love*, 79–82.

18. King, "Suffering and Faith," 41.

Now I pray that, recognizing the necessity of suffering, the Negro will make of it a virtue. To suffer in a righteous cause is to grow to our humanity's full stature. If only to save ourselves from bitterness, we need the vision to see the ordeals of this generation as an opportunity to transfigure ourselves and American society.[19]

King declared that it was the moral responsibility of African Americans to unshackle whites from bigotry, fear, and alienation, and that the objective can be achieved only through the redemptive suffering of African Americans.

5. The universe is on the side of justice

Nonviolence requires the firm belief in the final victory of good over evil, justice over injustice. As the expression of African American convictions of God's sovereignty and vindication, this belief was the source of African American optimism. King was affirmed in this truth through his experience of the triumph in the Montgomery Bus Boycott.[20] He frequently affirmed, "Truth crushed upon the earth will rise again." It was the unwavering conviction of King that those who side with truth will ultimately prevail.

6. At the center of nonviolence is agape

Nonviolence is a social expression of love. Because violence in spirit cannot create an environment of reconciliation, the spirit of anger and retaliation must be overcome first.[21] Thurman observes:

[Nonviolence] is one of the great vehicles of reconciliation because it creates and maintains a climate in which the need to be cared for and understood can be honored and effectively dealt with. The mood of nonviolence is that

---

19. Martin Luther King, Jr., "Creative Protest," an address delivered in Durham, North Carolina, during the lunch counter "sit-down" by black students (The King Center Archives, February 16, 1960).

20. King, "The Power of Nonviolence," 14.

21. Thurman, *Disciplines of the Spirit*, 117.

of reconciliation. It engenders in the individual an attitude that inspires wholeness and integration within. It presupposes that the desire to be cared for and to care for others is one with the very essence of all one's meaning and significance. It provides a working atmosphere in which this mutual desiring may be normal, reasonable, and accepted.[22]

Nonviolent resistance presupposes that humans have both the moral capacity to love and to come to recognize this love and the good it represents. Nonviolence creates the capacity to heal previously alienated relationships through love. Such love includes the possibility of suffering for the sake of the well-being of others. It means having a redeeming goodwill toward one's opponents.

In King's six principles of nonviolence, all the core values of the African American spiritual tradition — such as the sanctity of a person, interdependence, the final triumph of good, love, and reconciliation — converge. In the final analysis, it is questionable whether nonviolence is possible without acknowledging the spiritual ground of human existence. Nonviolence requires more than mere codes of nonviolent actions; it also requires a nonviolent spirit.

Political-Strategic Aspect of Nonviolence

King understood nonviolence as not only a spiritual but also a political method of social transformation. King's adoption of nonviolence was based on the deep awareness of the collective nature of social evil and the subsequent necessity of collective social action to overcome it. It was a direct outgrowth of his conviction that social evil could not be eliminated by moral persuasion alone.

Nonviolent resistance was political in that it mobilized massive numbers of people to confront social evil through the methods of marches, boycotts, protests, and noncooperation, although the goal and the motivation were spiritual. King knew that to change segregation required numerous determined people to incessantly

---

22. Ibid., 114.

challenge the system through political confrontations, describing the process as being like "a turbulent ocean beating great cliffs into fragments of rock."[23]

The success of nonviolence required careful and disciplined planning, identifying the manifestations of racism (e.g., segregation of buses, public places, schools, and lunch counters), concentrating available energy and resources, training volunteers in the philosophy and practices of nonviolence, and calling on the intense commitment of massive numbers of people for the cause.

King realized that disciplined commitment was necessary for the achievement of the intended goal. A disorganized social action inevitably lacks focus, direction, and staying power. Mob actions and riots (usually unorganized and emotional) were rarely successful; they merely served to release anger and frustration. Participants thus had to organize in units of power such as political parties, leagues, labor unions, and associations.

Strategy: Confrontation and Dramatization of Evil

By mobilizing masses for nonviolent resistance, King engaged in a massive confrontation with the system of segregation, using various tactics of radical opposition, such as mass demonstrations, marches, and civil disobedience. In many cases, King intentionally created crisis situations with the segregationist power, escalating the tension through confrontations such as sit-ins and boycotts.

As a result, some critics proclaimed King's method as being a calculating, shrewd, political strategy to earn through mass media appeal the sympathy of whites. Pointing out this confrontational aspect of nonviolent resistance, critics said that nonviolent action contains a "violent essence" in its method. For these critics, nonviolence was a disguised form of political expediency, not different from violence.[24]

---

23. King, "The Social Organization of Nonviolence," 33.
24. See Reinhold Niebuhr, *Moral Man and Immoral Society* (New York: Charles Scribner's Sons, 1932).

The critics claimed that nonviolent resistance, for its success, required the provocation of violence on the part of opponents. That is, it seems that nonviolence served to dramatize issues through the violent reactions of white racists. King's tactic appeared to support this intentional disruptive element of nonviolence. He deliberately used a tactic that heightened the tension around the living incarnation of an evil system, in people like Bull Connor of Birmingham and Jim Clark of Selma. Through his failure in Albany and in other campaigns, King recognized that focusing on a single and distinctive aspect of segregation, such as a segregated lunch counter or bus, was more strategically effective than an attack on segregation in general; it unveiled the evil face of racism, and offered a tangible symbol of victory for the participants of the struggle, thus motivating them to the next phase in the struggle.

However, from King's perspective, these strategies of creating tensions were meant to expose to the nation and the world the depth and scope of white racism's depravity and bigotry. For the creation of the beloved community, the nation needed to honestly confront its latent hostilities, prejudices, and hatred, for these were the sources of self-deception, affecting the direction of public opinions and policy formation. Without public exposure, people could not see how pervasive racism was in the very fabric of their society. Only when instances of racism were brought to the surface could they be removed.[25] King believed the tension in this case was creative because the tension offered the opportunity to squarely face and heal the problems of the nation.

Through confrontation and dramatization, nonviolence awakened in the oppressors a sense of vulnerability by unsettling their consciences. Racism was built upon the presumed moral and intellectual superiority of whites, and yet when African Americans stood up for their causes and maintained a high degree of moral fortitude and calmness in the face of vicious and brutal attacks, this had the effect of unsettling racist whites' moral psyche. It

---

25. Martin Luther King, Jr., "Meet the Press," in *A Testament of Hope,* 387.

forced them to be shameful of their moral complicity with their evil system. Thurman's comment is appropriate in this regard: "The effect of nonviolence on the offender is apt to be so threatening that the security he feels in the violent act deserts him and is thrown back upon the naked hunger for his own heart to be cared for, to be understood, to experience himself in harmony with his fellow."[26]

Dramatization was also based on savvy political calculation and was necessary to effect change in the existing power inequality between African Americans and whites. King used it to mobilize the necessary forces of goodwill for the change of the system. King knew well that whites would not voluntarily give up their privileges and powers, for, as he learned from his parents and Reinhold Niebuhr, it is the nature of collective egoism to use power to maintain the status quo. In order to bring about a change, African Americans needed a new kind and amount of accumulated power. The nonviolent method generated a moral power, offering critical leverage in addressing the power imbalance between whites and African Americans.

This strategy worked on several fronts. Dramatization galvanized the African American to correct white abuse of power. Nonviolent confrontation created an opportunity to unite all conscientious African Americans for political action. This gathered and mobilized power was used to put the pressure on whites to comply with African American demands for freedom and justice. Dramatization had the effect of sparking nonviolent resistance in local areas; it galvanized national and international opinions on the side of the movement, thus isolating the segregationists from the rest of the world with the effect of demoralizing these opponents. At the same time, it stimulated financial support for the SCLC and other civil rights organizations, together with a constant provision of volunteers. The confrontation highlighted the disparity between the professed ideals of the nation and the situation of African Americans; it invited the participation and

---

26. Thurman, *Disciplines of the Spirit,* 113.

support of conscientious whites — or at least the cessation of their opposition. The mobilization of white participation and support provided crucial power resources for the movement, on behalf of African Americans.

Nonviolence and Self-Esteem of African Americans

King was convinced of the transforming spiritual and political power of nonviolence in restoring and nurturing dignity and self-respect (i.e., a "rugged sense of somebodyness") within African American psyches, not to mention cleansing the toxic damage racism had done to their sense of selfhood and personality. Nonviolence first transformed the hearts of the practitioners of nonviolence by building up a new sense of self-esteem, honor, and respect; it called up previously unknown resources of strength and courage to face injustice and to love the opponents.[27] Nonviolence helped to restore their dignity as human beings by reclaiming their intrinsic dignity and agency endowed by God. King, through nonviolent resistance, helped African Americans to realize their potential power to transform the system.

Nonviolence had a collective therapeutic effect on the participants of the movement. King noticed the changes in moral and emotional tones and in self-awareness among the African Americans who adopted nonviolence as their approach to the issue. For example, in response to King's sermon at a mass meeting, an African American janitor in Montgomery declared, "We got our head up now." During the bus boycott, a seventy-year-old woman, Sister Pollard, walking the miles from her home, turned down an offer for a ride, saying, "My feets is tired, but my soul is rested." Paris agrees to this point by noting, "All who participated in the practices of nonviolent resistance were morally changed by them and gradually formed in accordance with the virtue of beneficence."[28]

27. King, "Pilgrimage to Nonviolence," in *A Testament of Hope*, 39.
28. Paris, *Spirituality of African Peoples*, 140.

Nonviolence challenged passivity or despair in most African Americans, and became a social outlet to express African American discontent and distress in a positive way. A long-lasting oppression instills a sense of low esteem, inferiority, and moral inertia in the oppressed. In a hopeless situation of power imbalance, the oppressed are overwhelmed with feelings of indignity, hatred, and revenge that in turn engender disunity, conflicts, and further violence among themselves as those negative emotions are vented toward their fellows.

Through nonviolent resistance, African Americans shed their psychological fatalism and defeatism, inferiority, and despair. It awoke them from the spiritual and moral slumber of resignation and cynicism. Eric Lincoln comments, "It may well be the final judgment of history that Martin Luther King's greatest contribution to Black freedom was made in Montgomery when he helped Black people free themselves from self-doubt and self-abasement."[29]

The redirection of emotions and passions toward a positive goal had a profound impact on the restoration of the moral agency of the participants. The practitioners of nonviolence exercised a spiritual and moral upper hand over the oppressors by seizing the moral initiatives. They were transformed from victims into agents.

King connected the significance of nonviolent protest to a healthy form of self-love, in that nonviolence is the only morally legitimate form of social action that respects simultaneously both the self-regarding and the other-regarding elements of love. Protest and resistance were crucial for self-love in the civil rights movement.

Nonviolent resistance has the transformative power to regenerate both individuals and a community alike, spiritually and socially. The movement represented the collective public statement by African Americans toward white society that they

---

29. Eric Lincoln, ed., *Martin Luther King, Jr.: A Profile* (New York: Hill and Wang, 1984), xiii.

would not accept ill-treatment, abuse, or contempt from anyone. Instead of acquiescence, they chose nonviolent confrontation. Consequently, the movement gave African Americans new moral dignity, racial pride, and political visibility.

> Under his leadership millions of black Americans emerged from spiritual imprisonment, from fear, from apathy, and took to the streets to proclaim their freedom....Martin Luther King, the peaceful warrior, revealed to his people their latent power; nonviolent mass protest, firmly disciplined, enabled them to move against their oppressors in effective and bloodless combat.[30]

The term "New Negro" referred at the time to a new collective consciousness of African Americans — to a new self-assertive and morally conscious personhood. King regarded the emergence of a "New Negro" as a stepping stone toward racial harmony and a new peoplehood of the nation. The genesis of a "New Negro" was beneficial for both African Americans and whites. Through the rise of African American selfhood, whites in turn could be challenged to discover their own true selfhood and identity, freed from a false sense of superiority.

Nonviolence and Black Power

King's philosophy of nonviolence was later seriously challenged by the black power movement. The proponents of black power, such as Stokely Carmichael, Malcolm X, H. Rap Brown, and leaders of the SNCC (Student Nonviolent Coordinating Committee), accused King of being an Uncle Tom — too compromising and friendly to white power. Yet King remained consistent with his method. His conflict with them vividly disclosed the distinctively communal nature of his spirituality.

---

30. Harry Belafonte and Stanley Levison, "Eulogy"; cited in Coretta King, *My Life with Martin Luther King, Jr.,* 310.

Although King refused to identify himself with the black power movement, he sympathized with black power's advocacy of self-love and power. In the cries for black power, he saw the call for the dignity, honor, and subjectivity of African Americans. Black power's call for equal selfhood and agency was compatible with King's idea of self-love as articulated in his sermon known as "A Complete Life." In particular, King found a positive contribution of black power in its calling of African Americans to a new sense of selfhood and black consciousness, to a racial pride and an appreciation of their African past and heritage. King knew that self-hatred and inferiority were the psychological legacies of slavery, and unless the mind was free from these chains, African Americans could never be genuinely free.

King and the black power movement also agreed that social change required collective power, not just persuasion. They identified the unequal distribution of power as a source of injustice in general and African American suffering in particular. King found that the call for black power was a call for the amassing of legitimate power for African American self-reliance, equality, and freedom. King was deeply aware that legitimate power was indispensable for a decent human existence and the construction of a community.

Yet King disagreed with them on how to restore self-respect and what kind of power is appropriate. It was King's firm belief that violence could never achieve permanent self-respect, nor serve as a source of power. Only nonviolent struggle could achieve the goal. King pointed out that nonviolence is not antithetical to self-love and power. On the contrary, nonviolence contributes to the enhancement of self-esteem, self-respect, and the accumulation of power.

Despite his sympathy with black power, King was critical of its separatism and its ideology of violence. It was primary for King that separatism violated the socially interdependent nature of human existence. He rejected black power proponents' idea of excluding whites from the marches because the decision would not only betray those whites who sacrificed for the civil rights movement, but also contradict the ideal of the beloved community.[31] King did not believe that the advancement of black power and the raising of consciousness necessarily should require disdain for the entire white race. King was convinced that white and African American destinies were intertwined, and therefore their fulfillment had to be addressed together.

King was not able to accept black power's rejection of America because of the optimistic nature of his spirituality. Black power meant that African Americans had given up their faith in white America's moral and spiritual ability to reform itself.[32] King noted that black power was a cry of anger, resentment, and nihilism rather than love, faith, and hope. He knew that feelings of bitterness, anger, and cynicism cannot bring about any positive social change. When bitterness is not overcome by forgiveness and love, it is often turned against the self, destroying its life essence. When despair is not cured by hope, it poisons the soul with nihilism and fatalism. King recognized that African Americans constantly needed new injections of hope through their trust in God.

King also found he could not endorse black power's advocating the use of violence. Black power based its justification for violence on self-defense. King conceded that the idea of self-defense is a widely accepted moral standard in any civilized society. When one is involuntarily placed in physical danger or the threat of danger by the assault of others, one has a moral right to protect oneself with every available means.

Yet from King's perspective, black power as a whole was a misguided response to the situation of white domination because it was based on an underestimation of the magnitude of white power. He considered that the black power appeal to violence, even a self-defensive one, would obscure the incumbent moral issues, and it would give whites a perfect excuse not only to keep

---

31. Major African American Christian denominations and their affiliated institutions unequivocally rejected the black power movement because they found that the hostile slogans and inflammatory rhetoric of black power were alien to the communal spiritual tradition of African American churches.

32. King, *Where Do We Go from Here?* 33.

African Americans in their inferior places, but also to roll back the meager achievements of the civil rights movement.

On the basis of his astute empirical analysis of power distribution in the United States, King realized that the minority status of African Americans made it impossible for them to adopt violence as a means of social change. The imbalance of power between whites and African Americans did not allow any chance of success for violent struggles. King offered spiritually based nonviolence as the feasible alternative to black power. For King, there was no other option for African Americans than to move forward with nonviolent resistance because neither separatism nor submission to white supremacy was a practical and morally viable solution. He believed that only a resolute nonviolent struggle could eventually take African Americans to the goal of true freedom, equality, and community.

Despite the differences on the issues of separatism and violence, the black power movement contributed to King's movement by adding the pressure to deal with the urban ghetto problems of the North, to which we now turn.

Nonviolence and Classism: The Northern Campaign for Economic Justice

King was realizing increasingly that the civil rights movement was incomplete without the transformation of the northern urban ghettos. Racism was not just a southern phenomenon; it had different manifestations in the North. The problem in the South was political segregation, while in the North it was an economic one, the ghetto. Like segregated public places, the ghetto was equally a spiritual, moral problem for King, and no less a violation of basic human dignity and interdependence, particularly as it was manifested through police brutality, squalid and dilapidated conditions and environments, and permanent unemployment. King knew the civil political rights of African Americans were meaningless unless they were corroborated by economic rights. Chronic unemployment was an economic form of racial exploitation and segregation. An empty stomach was as miserable as lynchings and beatings. Both types of assault corrode human dignity. Just like southern segregation, the injustice of economic exploitation had to be challenged, for both posed equally insurmountable obstacles to the creation of the beloved community.

King's campaign in the North was the expansion of the civil rights movement into a new social realm: the economy. Acknowledging that the civil rights movement thus far was concentrated in the South, King decided to expand the struggle to the North with the passage of the Voting Rights Bill. A series of urban riots, such as in the Watts ghetto of Los Angeles, brought King to a heightened awareness of the urgency of gaining economic justice through the fair distribution of power.

In his Chicago campaign, King wanted to prove the effectiveness of nonviolence for the achievement of economic justice. King tried to galvanize the political and moral powers attained through the civil rights movement to gain economic power. Since African Americans were relatively devoid of economic strength in the urban areas, one possible way to translate political and moral power to economic power was through nonviolent direct action. King noticed that since many African American neighborhoods were geographically located at the center of major cities, demonstrations could have dramatic and strategic effects, convincing conscientious whites to join the movement, thus increasing the power base and resources to deal with the established white economic structure and its unjust system.

King, however, encountered a qualitatively different social, cultural, and spiritual setting in the North. He soon realized that the achievement of economic and social rights was much more difficult than the achievement of civil political rights. Even white liberals, who had supported King's civil rights struggles, showed an entirely different attitude to the economic plight of African Americans. When King and his followers demanded equal housing, health care, and employment, they became nervous and uncomfortable because African American demands for economic justice would now cost them financially.

As King studied the causes of poverty, he came to believe that the capitalist system itself was problematic. Capitalism was based on the unashamed assertion of selfishness over the common good, and the endless pursuit of profit at the expense of human dignity. In capitalism, King discovered the driving force for the perpetuation of racism, economic exploitation, and military industry. He concluded that capitalism in its current form needed to be drastically transformed through the redistribution of power and resources.

In his critique of laissez-faire capitalism, King's economic philosophy increasingly leaned toward democratic socialism, further fueling the suspicions of FBI director J. Edgar Hoover. It should be noted, however, that King was not a democratic socialist in the sense that has been aligned with atheism. His social democratic perspective was inspired and qualified by his African and African American spirituality, specifically its emphasis on the sanctity and solidarity of human beings. From King's perspective, a truly democratic society was communal, culminating in the vision of the beloved community; human beings are accountable for the mutual well-being of others, so therefore the government should be involved in the planning and implementation of national economic policies to guarantee the basic welfare of the people. On the basis of this vision, King called for the nationalization of basic industries, massive federal assistance to urban residents, guaranteed housing, annual incomes, health care, job training programs, and so on.

The Cause for Failure

Compared to his previous achievements in the fight against segregation, King's Chicago campaign against poverty failed to bring about any meaningful changes, such as an enforceable open housing law. Several factors contributed to this failure. The North presented a complex cultural-religious context, with sets of problems that were quite different from those of the South. Unlike with segregation, it was hard to dramatize the radically evil nature of economic injustice, for it did not show blood, dead bodies, or broken bones and therefore was not dramatic enough to mobilize a large number of people. Although civil political rights were protected by the Constitution, there was no constitutional protection for the rights to adequate housing, adequate income, and adequate health care. In addition, whites in the North refused to examine the economic dimension of racism and loathed giving up their economic privileges and the status quo. Capitalism was the sacrosanct entity of the day, as it still is today.

King was not able to mobilize African Americans to mass nonviolent direct actions. Most African American churches had not developed a coherent critical theology of capitalism, not to mention its interlocking complicity with racism and militarism. At least in part, however, the failure can be attributed to the erosion of communal social capital among urban northern African Americans.[33] As secularizing forces fragmented African American life, northern African Americans did not quickly buy into King's appeal to redemptive suffering through nonviolent resistance. In addition, African American churches were less prominent and influential in the lives of urban African Americans in the North. As King's method of nonviolence required a certain form of spiritual habits and orientations, consequently his northern campaign suffered.

Nonviolence and Militarism: The Vietnam War

Through his deeper engagement with the struggle for the civil and human rights of poor people, King discovered that militarism and urban and rural poverty were all closely interconnected. King

---

33. Despite their indifference to Christianity, African American communities in the North still retained some residue of African spiritual values. For example, in their cry for separatism, self-defense, and African American supremacy, they rarely relied on violence. That is, African communal values may have had a different social expression in the North, in the form of racial separatism or Afrocentrism.

saw that like a "suction tube," the war was diverting precious resources from all domestic necessities, such as urban revitalization, education, housing, and health care. For example, in 1967 the United States was spending a half million dollars to kill one enemy Vietnamese soldier, while spending only fifty-three dollars a year for each poor person at home.[34]

King's antiwar position was the expression of his solidarity with the Vietnamese people in God. He opposed the war because it violated the dignity of the Vietnamese. He was not able to tolerate what was being done to them by the United States, with such weapons as napalm and Agent Orange, and using the tactics of indiscriminate bombings, killing civilians, and burning down entire villages. For King, the Vietnamese were not obstacles to be eliminated; they were brothers and sisters in God. Common human solidarity was deeper and more important than a national or racial or ideological unity. King saw the suffering of his own people in the suffering of the Vietnamese people — the same kind of oppression and suffering due to American white supremacy and racism. The beloved community was inclusive of *all* humanity; humanity was one and indivisible in God, as God's children. In defending his stance on the Vietnam War, King said:

> I must be true to my conviction that I share with all men the calling to be a son of the living God. Beyond the calling of race or nation or creed is this vocation of sonship and brotherhood, and because I believe that the Father is deeply concerned especially for his suffering and helpless and outcast children, I come tonight to speak for them.[35]

In U.S. foreign policies, King saw the same racial supremacy that he encountered in white segregationists in the South. The U.S. arrogance toward small nations such as Vietnam and the

---

34. King, "Speech at the Staff Retreat of SCLC," Penn Center, Frogmore, South Carolina (The King Center Archives, May 1967), 21.

35. Martin Luther King, Jr., "A Time to Break Silence," in *A Testament of Hope*, 234.

Dominican Republic was nothing but another form of the expression of its racism. King saw the same contradiction within the soul of the United States in its supremacist attitude toward the colored peoples of the world. The inconsistency between its creeds and its deeds toward African Americans was unveiled in the U.S. attitude toward people of other races in other countries. King declared:

> I don't believe that we can have world peace until America has an "integrated" foreign policy. Our disastrous experiments in Vietnam and the Dominican Republic have been...a result of racist decision making. Men of the white West...have grown up in a racist culture, and their thinking is colored by that fact.... They don't respect anyone who is not white.[36]

King believed that the war in Vietnam was destroying the soul of the nation.[37] For King, the war was immoral and criminal. The United States violated not only its own democratic values, but also the moral principles of the universe. Just as he did with segregation, King saw in the war a widening gap between promise and fulfillment, thus turning the nation even more schizophrenic. King was deeply troubled and saddened by the inconsistency of white liberals and the media in applauding the nonviolence of African Americans in their civil rights struggles while supporting military aggression against a nation that was seeking its own independence and freedom.

A Call for the Revolutionary Transformation of the United States

In the triadic interrelated evils of racism, classism, and militarism King saw profound trouble within the soul of the nation. He began to question the moral foundation of the country, finding

36. Martin Luther King, Jr., "A Testament of Hope"; cited in Cone, *Martin and Malcolm and America,* 238.
37. King, "Speech at the Staff Retreat of SCLC," 29.

racism, urban poverty, and militarism to be telling symptoms of the nation's pathology. The flaws were systemic, larger than one political party or presidency. They were deeply engrained in the soul of the nation from its very inception, as evidenced by the practice of slavery by the founding fathers.[38] King found that the problem for the United States was not the deficit of material resources, but of volition.[39] But he also noted that unless the material conditions of the nation changed, judicial changes were de facto meaningless. So, like the Hebrew prophets and like Jesus, he called for the repentance and rebirth of the United States, for a revolutionary change of society through the redistribution of the nation's power and resources. He preached God's wrath and judgment on the nation for relying on its military force instead of justice, and for serving a rich few far more than the poor majority.

In the domestic realm, King's understanding was that African American problems, the economic ones in particular, could not be solved without a white conversion to justice and kinship.

Whites treated the passage of the civil rights laws and the voting rights laws as the appropriate and complete transformation of society.[40] They invented many excuses and created mechanisms to maintain their social status quo and privileges. Despite their denials, whites harbored and expressed racist beliefs and attitudes in many subtle ways. For example, as shown in white people's hysterical opposition to open housing in Chicago, the bottom line was that whites still refused to accept African Americans as their full, equal, and mutual partners.

King maintained that a true racial integration is possible only through the equal sharing of power and resources.[41] Genuine integration should be reciprocal, and it would not be possible without white acceptance of African Americans as equal citizens. African Americans and whites each held one of two keys to the

---

38. King, *Where Do We Go from Here?* 75.
39. Ibid., 177.
40. Ibid., 5.
41. King, "Speech at the Staff Retreat of SCLC," 5.

double-locked door of the beloved community.[42] Without mutual acceptance, the creation of the beloved community would be
impossible for either of them.

King's call for a revolutionary change in value was not confined
to whites alone. King called for the full participation of African
Americans in the civil rights movement and in national political
processes. While acknowledging the unmitigated dedication and
sacrifices of many African Americans toward the achievement of
the goals, King recognized that their numbers were only modest
before the formidable task of tackling the evils of racial and economic injustice. King urged African Americans to go further than
the achievement of a middle-class dream, by challenging the nation's vulgar capitalism and militarism. King defined a new era of
struggle as the struggle for "a radical redistribution of economic
and political power."[43] He warned that African Americans should
not be optimistic by falsely believing that a racial justice could be
achieved at a small cost. Unless continuous pressure was imposed
on an enlarged scale, whites would never give up their status quo.

In calling for a revolutionary transformation of the United
States, King also called upon all conscientious citizens to be
united, organized, and mobilized for the task. This implied the
call for massive civil disobedience in place of conventional methods of nonviolence such as sit-ins, demonstrations, and marches.
Between late 1967 and early 1968, King embarked on the planning of the Poor Peoples Campaign through the coalition of
diverse racial and social groups such as labor unions, poor whites,
and academic communities.

On the international front, King was increasingly aware of the
danger that the United States posed to international peace and
justice as the greatest purveyor of violence. He challenged the
hypocrisy of the U.S. government, which promoted nonviolence
for African American struggles for freedom while engaging in
highly violent warfare in Vietnam. The United States was "on

---

42. King, *Where Do We God from Here?* 22.
43. King, "Speech at the Staff Retreat of SCLC," 7.

the wrong side of a world revolution" by siding with the small minority of the rich, powerful, and reactionary leaders of the undeveloped countries in the name of anticommunism. King called for an international coalition among those countries to resist the militarism of the United States on the basis of his recognition that the freedom and well-being of African Americans were dependent on the freedom and well-being of other oppressed peoples in the world.

Summary

King's critiques of racism, classism, and militarism were launched from his holistic, communal spiritual vision of the beloved community. King's holism enabled him to see the social problems in their mutual linkages. However, despite his deep awareness of the entrenched nature of white racism, and the economic dimension of oppression, King did not substantially alter his fundamental communal, nonviolent spirituality, though this awareness may have eventually radicalized his perspective, tone, and rhetoric. In his call for revolutionary transformation of values, King still adhered to the fundamental communal values of his spirituality, and insisted on nonviolent resistance as the only morally legitimate method.

Despite his distress and disillusionment over the Vietnam War and white resistance to economic justice, King nevertheless did not lose hope; however, the meaning and the object of his hope changed from the historical reforming possibility of the United States to an eschatological vindication in God. As a descendant of African Americans, it was impossible for King to completely surrender to despair and nihilism. Instead, as was typical in the tradition of African American spirituality, King received a renewed sense of hope from his unfailing trust in God.

Chapter 5

The Shared Communal Spirituality of King and Desmond Tutu

The African roots of the communal aspect of King's spirituality are particularly evident in light of Archbishop Desmond Tutu's spirituality. Despite their differences in style and denominational affiliation, the two share similar spiritual and moral perspectives on racial oppression and the use of nonviolent resistance for liberation and reconciliation. There is great similarity in their theological and philosophical understandings of love, community, forgiveness, human dignity, the moral order of the universe, and so on. Almost all of the African spiritual features that we have noticed in King are also present in Tutu's personal and public spirituality. These parallels further serve to demonstrate that King's communal spirituality was no accident, but rather a shared spiritual heritage among African peoples.

One may claim that the source of this similarity between both civil rights leaders was King's intellectual and moral influence on Tutu. For example, in studying the source of Tutu's spirituality and ethics, Lewis Baldwin claims that King's theology and ethics profoundly influenced Tutu in terms of the idea of the *imago dei*, the social nature of human existence, and the interdependent structure of reality.[1] Indeed, Tutu was one of the most persistent followers and creative adapters of King's ideals in the South African context. One cannot deny King's contribution to the development of Tutu's theology and ethics into its current form. King's idea of the beloved community informed Tutu's

---

1. Lewis V. Baldwin, *Toward the Beloved Community: Martin Luther King, Jr., and South Africa* (Cleveland: Pilgrim Press, 1995), 108.

South African vision of a multiracial, democratic, and egalitarian nation.

A deeper look, however, reveals that their similarities are more substantial than a mere personal intellectual and moral influence of one on the other. The similarities are rooted in their shared communal and holistic African spiritual heritage. Although King may have served as a source of inspiration and a role model for Tutu, the archbishop's communal spirituality is not something he learned from King; it grew out of his own African roots. It is actually because of this shared spiritual orientation that Tutu was amenable to King's theology and ethics. In King, he saw his own African spiritual kindred. Let us look at their similarities in detail.

The Ubiquity of Religion

Tutu was born in 1931, two years later than King. Tutu is a profoundly religious person; like King and many other Africans, religion is at the center of his life. Tutu felt that God had called him to speak and work for justice. Just as the SCLC served as the base of King's movement, the South African Council of Churches (SACC), of which Tutu was general secretary, was the base of Tutu's social ministry. Tutu confessed that the foundation and ground of his struggle against apartheid was not political but spiritual, and that in his life, spiritual concern overrode political considerations. His works of justice are an extension of his pastoral identity as a parish priest in the Anglican Church.

Like King, Tutu distanced himself from political radicals who espoused a materialistic interpretation of history and who were advocates of violence. He acknowledged the presence of God wherever he went and in whatever he did. God's sovereignty has always been the source of his power and hope. Tutu declared, "Ultimately we owe loyalty not to any human authority, however prestigious or powerful, but to God and to His Son, our Lord Jesus Christ alone, from whom we obtain our mandate. We must obey the divine imperative and word whatever the cost."[2] He has never been apologetic about his faith, although he has been careful to avoid imposing his religious views upon others.

Holism

Influenced by a unified worldview of Africa, Tutu takes a holistic approach to reality. Refusing to accept a strict dichotomy of the sacred and the secular in his life, the basis of his holism is religious. God is the Lord of the universe and all life, encompassing secular and spiritual, sacred and profane, material and spiritual. For him, God is the God of all the spheres of human life, including politics and economics. The incarnation of God in Jesus means that God takes the whole of history and the whole of human life seriously.[3] In God, there is no dichotomy, no compartmentalization of reality. The world as God's creation cannot be divided, because it is the world of one God.

> Our God cares that children starve in resettlement camps. . . . The God we worship does care that people die mysteriously in detention. He is concerned that people are condemned to a twilight existence as non-persons by an arbitrary bureaucratic act of banning, without giving them the opportunity to reply to charges brought against them.[4]

For Tutu, religion is not concerned merely with personal matters but inevitably has public implications and consequences, for Christians are demanded to make public choices in light of the gospel. Although there are things about which Christians and the church should be neutral, Christians cannot be neutral to any situation of injustice and oppression, such as apartheid. A morally neutral religion is moribund; in the situations of oppression, the

---

2. Ibid., 153.
3. Ibid., 154.
4. Ibid., 155.

question is not about whether to be involved or not, but rather which side religion takes, that of the powerful or that of the oppressed.

As Tutu's holism is essentially theologically grounded, it is inseparable from the struggles of justice. God is the judge of the world. God sides with the poor and the oppressed. The world is not religiously and ethically neutral, because God is a moral God. What happens in the marketplace, courtroom, and Parliament has equal religious significance to God.[5] This understanding had an immediate theological implication for Tutu's understanding of the church and its mission. Because it represents God, the church cannot be neutral to politics but has a social responsibility to work for justice.

Tutu did not separate the works of the Truth and Reconciliation Commission (TRC) from his own spiritual values and convictions, but appropriately brought to bear spiritual resources on the task of the commission. Tutu brought with him the Christian theological principles and African spiritual resources to enhance the work of the commission — to sharpen moral and pastoral sensitivities. Tutu publicly declared that theology undergirded his work in the TRC.[6] All these aspects reflected his African spirituality, which views human existence as spiritually governed and controlled, and maintains that the universe is a unified whole, without divisions or compartmentalization.

Moral Order

Tutu insists that resistance to immoral, unjust laws, such as various kinds of apartheid laws, is morally imperative for Christians. Tutu said without hesitation that if apartheid were biblical and Christian, he would cease to be Christian. The basis of Tutu's rejection of apartheid was the moral nature of the universe created

5. Ibid., 39.
6. Desmond Tutu, *No Future without Forgiveness* (New York; London: Doubleday, 1999), 87.

by God. Like King, Tutu has a firm moral conviction that God is moral, and that the universe is governed by moral order and rules. Right and wrong do matter. God is not only concerned with individual salvation but also with the redemption of socio-political systems and economic conditions.[7] God is not a neutral God who abstains from the mundane realities of human conflict, but rather is just, compassionate, involved, and active. God is the liberator God of the Exodus, and continues to set people free from all kinds of bondage so that nothing can thwart God's goal.[8]

God, revealed in Jesus Christ, profoundly cares about the plight of the poor, the dispossessed, and the powerless. The resurrection of Jesus Christ proclaims that right will prevail. Goodness and love, justice and peace are not illusory, or mirages that forever elude our grasp.[9] They are moral realities in God, revealed in Jesus Christ. The church cannot be politically and socially neutral. Tutu has proclaimed the Christian gospel as "subversive of all injustice and evil."[10] He writes,

> Christ has assured us that His Church is founded on rock and not even the gates of Hell can prevail against it. The Resurrection of Our Lord and Savior declares for all to know that life will triumph over darkness, that goodness will triumph over evil, that justice will triumph over injustice, and that freedom will triumph over tyranny.[11]

Tutu feels assured of the ultimate defeat of evil and the final victory of justice. For Tutu, resurrection is the proof of this historical truth. Because God is just, no power that stands up against justice can prevail because doing so is against God, and hence any attacks on justice are self-defeating.

---

7. Desmond Tutu, *Hope and Suffering*, ed. John Webster (Grand Rapids: Eerdmans, 1983), 38.

8. Ibid., 155–56.

9. Desmond Tutu, *Crying in the Wilderness: The Struggle for Justice in South Africa*, ed. John Webster (Grand Rapids: Eerdmans, 1982), 36.

10. Tutu, *Hope and Suffering*, 125.

11. Ibid., 158.

Hopefulness

Tutu's belief in the moral nature of the universe was intimately correlated with hopefulness and optimism. As with King, faith in God is the bedrock of Tutu's faith and hope. Out of this spiritual conviction, he injected the sense of hope and worth into the hearts of black people under apartheid. He preached that they should not fear the white rulers. He repeatedly encouraged them to never doubt the victory of freedom and justice in God. With both a sense of humor and oratorical power, Tutu dissipated fear in his black audiences.

Like King, Tutu believes in the reforming possibility of human beings and society. In his antiapartheid struggles and his leadership in the TRC, Tutu was working on the premise that human beings could change, that they are endowed with the potential to be good. He noted, "Although there is undoubtedly much evil about, we human beings have a wonderful capacity for good. We can be very good. That is what fills me with hope even at the most intractable situations."[12]

Tutu refused to reduce the perpetrators of apartheid to demons. Like King, he differentiated deeds from persons, sin from sinner. Tutu made an interesting point that when we turn perpetrators into demons by depriving them of moral agency, we in effect dispense them of any moral accountability for the heinous deeds that they have committed. In addition, this declaration meant abandonment of all hope for their moral rehabilitation. For Tutu, this goes against the grain of the communal spirituality of *ubuntu*.

Community

Tutu's spirituality is deeply communal. For Tutu, as for King, the organizing principle of his vision, ideas, and practices was the community. All his important theological concepts and ideas turned around the vision of a fully liberated, reconciled community — "a new South Africa that is just, nonracial, and

---

12. Tutu, *No Future without Forgiveness,* 253.

democratic, where black and white can exist amicably side by side in their home country as members of one family."[13]

Tutu's communal spirituality is best described by the idea of *ubuntu*. As mentioned in chapter 1, *ubuntu* understands interdependence as the fundamental principle of human existence. In our interdependence with others, we experience the fullness of God's creation and the fulfillment of ourselves. For Tutu, a "self-sufficient human being is subhuman."[14] No one can be human alone. He continues:

> We need other human beings in order to be human. We are made for togetherness; we are made for family, for fellowship, to exist in a tender network of interdependence.... This is how you have ubuntu — you care, you are hospitable, you're gentle, you're compassionate and concerned.[15]

Almost as one voice with King, he says that "a human being can be a human being only because he belongs to a community."[16] Our humanity is so intertwined that the suffering and dehumanization of a person cannot exist without the suffering and dehumanization of others.[17] By dehumanizing others, one inevitably dehumanizes oneself. An ethical implication of this communalistic cosmology is obvious. Apartheid was sin because it separated people into artificial racial castes — creating disunity, alienation, and distrust. The abolition of apartheid was not the final goal; it was only the instrument to the ultimate goal of unity and love in God. The struggle against apartheid was the struggle

---

13. Desmond Tutu, *The Words of Desmond Tutu*, ed. Naomi Tutu (New York: Newmarket Press, 1989), 29, 32, 41.

14. Desmond Tutu, "God's Dream," in *Waging Peace II: Vision and Hope for the 21st Century*, ed. David Krieger and Frank Kelly (Chicago: Noble Press, 1992), 37.

15. Desmond Tutu, handwritten speech, Morehouse Medical School Commencement, May 15, 1993; cited in Michael Battle, *Reconciliation: The Ubuntu Theology of Desmond Tutu* (Cleveland: Pilgrim Press, 1997), 65.

16. Tutu, *Crying in the Wilderness*, 99.

17. Tutu, *No Future without Forgiveness*, 103.

for reconciliation and friendship. And, in that quest, forgiveness is an indispensable process.

Tutu sees the congruence between the Bible and the traditional African worldview of *ubuntu* in terms of their emphasis on the interdependent nature of human reality and solidarity in God the Creator. He contends that the African communal worldview is more congenial to the biblical outlook than the Western individualist view.[18]

Tutu sees *ubuntu* in God's creation and redemption story. Tutu identifies unity, love, and reconciliation as the goals of the universe: "The unity of the entire creation was God's intention from the very beginning of creation."[19] The primal state of the universe was harmony, unity, and fellowship. God declared that it was not good for a man to live alone. When sin destroyed this unity, all relationships — God and humanity, man and woman, humanity and other creatures — were alienated. Under the power of sin and brokenness, creation now cries out for reconciliation and restoration of its unity. From the beginning of history, there has been a cosmic movement toward unity and reconciliation. All God's activities in history point toward this goal of restoring the primal unity. God sent the Son to achieve the unity, harmony, and reconciliation. Atonement, at-one-ment, means the overcoming of alienation, hostility, and division. Tutu claims that Jesus Christ "came to restore human community and brotherhood which sin destroyed."[20]

Unity is not uniformity, however, which abolishes our distinctiveness, our cultural otherness. God created human beings as male and female, in their sexual diversity. For Tutu, differences are necessary and to be celebrated for the richness and fullness of life that they represent; the differences complement each other, supplying strength to weakness and necessity to want. Differences mean that no one is self-sufficient; we need each other for fulfillment.

---

18. Battle, *Reconciliation*, xiii.
19. Tutu, *Hope and Suffering*, 159.
20. Ibid., 166.

The influence of *ubuntu* was found in the conciliatory tone of Tutu's voice even as he attacked the injustice of apartheid.[21] Like King, Tutu displayed communal virtues such as patience, love, generosity, and forgiveness. Despite the constant threats of physical violence, harassment, and blackmail, Tutu extended the hand of fellowship to whites, not retaliatory violence or civil war. Tutu reminded blacks that despite their racist activities and attitudes, "[Whites] belong together with us in the family of God, and their humanity is caught up in our humanity, as ours is caught up in theirs."[22]

Despite his wholehearted appreciation of *ubuntu,* Tutu saw the potential collectivist danger of *ubuntu,* especially when individual freedom and creativity are not properly emphasized:

> Of course this strong group feeling [*ubuntu*] has the weaknesses of all communalism; it encourages conservation and conformity. It needs to be corrected by the teaching about [each individual's] inalienable uniqueness.... We need both aspects to balance each other.[23]

For Tutu, the collectivist danger of *ubuntu* was corrected by his Anglican Christian spirituality. Throughout his struggle, Tutu

---

21. Battle, *Reconciliation,* xiii. In the 1970s and 1980s, Tutu struggled with the question of self-defensive use of violence. Tutu challenged nonviolence as the absolute and only means to achieve justice. One may infer that Tutu did not share the depth of King's commitment to nonviolence. However, Tutu's reference to the possible use of violent means was more rhetorical than literal. It intended to challenge white Afrikaners for their moral complacency, their complicity with apartheid, by warning them of the impending catastrophe when justice was constantly delayed and denied. His strategy was effective, because blacks constituted the numerical majority in South Africa. Tutu never got involved in armed struggles or violent resistance. Rather, he distanced himself from exponents of radical South African black theology — their advocacy of retaliatory violence and their Marxist orientation — because he believed the latter threatened the integrity of the gospel by allowing the sociological variables to control the theological content.

22. Desmond Tutu, "Where Is Now Thy God?" cited in Battle, *Reconciliation,* 47.

23. Desmond Tutu, "Some African Insights and the Old Testament," in *Relevant Theology for Africa: Report on a Consultation of the Missiological Institute Lutheran Theological College,* 44; cited in Battle, *Reconciliation,* xiii.

maintained a balanced tension between the promotion of communal well-being and respect for individual freedom.

Tutu's vision of a new society for South Africa grew out of the synthesis of Christianity and *ubuntu*ism. It was an expression of a Christian ideal of the dominion of God interpreted through the African spirituality of *ubuntu*. A new society is a shared society. Tutu called for a redistribution of wealth and equitable sharing of resources. Contributing to each other creates a society that is more compassionate and caring, where everyone is welcome. His vision is congruent with King's idea of the beloved community. According to Tutu, in a new society the emphasis is placed on sharing and giving rather than competition and pursuit of self-interest and self-aggrandizement. Tutu rejected any kind of narrow racial ethnic caste system, tribalism (whether Zulu or Afrikaner), or black nationalism.

Someone may raise a question regarding the apparent tension between the communal value of *ubuntu* and the frequent intertribal wars waged in Africa. How, one might ask, can one explain the existence of intertribal wars if *ubuntu* is such a pervasive value in Africa? In a traditional Africa, especially in the situation of intertribal power struggles and wars, *ubuntu* was usually confined to the members of one's tribe and harmless strangers or visitors. It was expressed in an ethnocentric, tribalistic form to promote intragroup cohesion and commitment.

The interaction of African spirituality with Christianity, Islam, and Western philosophies gradually added a more universal scope and depth to *ubuntu*. As mentioned before, the principles of the black church tradition, the parenthood of God, and the kinship of humanity were a universal expression of the African communalism appropriated through Christianity. In South Africa, the scope and content of *ubuntu* were substantively broadened and universalized by the incorporation of Christianity and Islam.

In King, Tutu, and Nelson Mandela, we witness a very noble, inclusive, and universalistic expression of communalism that overcame tribalism and ethnocentrism. This communalism finds expression in King's vision of the beloved community; for Tutu and Mandela, it was expressed in the TRC and a new, inclusive vision of South Africa. The creative synthesis of African communal spirituality with a universalistic interpretation of Christianity enabled all three leaders to stem any tendency toward excessive individualism, collectivism, or violence in the course of political struggles.

The Imago Dei

Tutu constructed an alternative liberating anthropology by synthesizing the Christian idea of the *imago dei* with *ubuntu*. He simultaneously emphasized the intrinsic worth of a person and the interrelated nature of human existence with a just and reconciled community as the ultimate goal of his movement.

Tutu's understanding of the *imago dei* is quite similar to King's. Tutu said, "Each person is not just to be respected but to be revered as one created in God's image."[24] For both King and Tutu, the *imago dei* denotes the onto-relational theological reality with universal moral binding power. For both of them, the *imago dei* means the infinite quality of a person as God's child. The *imago dei* means a fundamental solidarity among human beings as children of the same God. Representing the same image of God, all human beings are interrelated. Hence, the *imago dei* constitutes the universal human identity, deeper than any racial, ethnic, and/or cultural self.

God is understood as the source of both the individuality and the communality of humanity. In God, everyone is unique, yet at the same time interrelated. One is qualified and complemented by the other. In light of *ubuntu*, the *imago dei* is not an individualistic notion. In light of the *imago dei*, *ubuntu* is not a collectivist concept. *Ubuntu* is interpreted in terms of the *imago dei*. That is, all human beings are one in their shared metaphysical quality in the *imago dei*. The purpose of each person is to contribute to and receive life from each other. As the values of individuals derive

---

24. Tutu, *No Future without Forgiveness*, 197.

from the community, the goal of the community is to promote and enhance the well-being of individuals. Therefore, whereas the idea of the *imago dei,* in its Western context, highlights the individual moral faculty or rationality, in an African and African American Christian context it emphasizes both the individual and communal dimensions of human existence.

In fighting against the discriminatory anthropology of white Americans and Afrikaners, the communal spirituality of King and Tutu, respectively, has served as the resource of both their critique of racism (resistance) and the vision of a new community (reconciliation). Tutu's *ubuntu* theology offers a third alternative to the Afrikaner theology of racial election and retaliatory African liberation theology, while King's anthropology did the same for the white segregationist Christianity and the Nation of Islam's separatism. They understand segregation and apartheid as direct contradictions to the *imago dei* and community. In the situation of oppression, King's and Tutu's understandings of the *imago dei* and community take on a strong political meaning and relevance. If the *imago dei* means the human rights of blacks, community means a racism-free society.

Critique of Racism

For King and Tutu, racism constituted a primary context of their political and social activities. Tutu's, like King's, primary opponents were not non-Christians persecuting the Christian faith, but self-proclaimed pious Christians who were distorting the truth of the gospel. As King struggled against segregation, Tutu struggled against the apartheid system. For Tutu, apartheid was not merely a political issue but more profoundly a spiritual issue, for it frustrated human fulfillment and community. Apartheid exalted a biological element over a biblical and theological value. The apartheid system claimed that a biological attribute, such as skin color, determines human worth. Apartheid was a completely arbitrary ideology to protect the privileges of whites at the expense of blacks. It was supported by various legal, ideological, cultural, military, and religious apparatuses.

From Tutu's perspective, apartheid is wrong because it not only denies the fundamental sanctity of blacks, but in the final analysis, it claims that humanity is created for division, fear, and hostility. Artificial separation of human beings on the basis of skin color is blasphemous. It is against God's intention for humanity: freedom in community. As such, it denies God, who created all humans in the divine image. Apartheid contradicts the gospel, which claims that God created humanity for community and love. Apartheid deprives both whites and blacks of any possibility of mutual understanding or community; it impedes the development and realization of their potentials.

The impact of apartheid on the psychological and physical well-being of blacks in South Africa was enormous. All the laws of apartheid, such as the Pass Laws and the forced removals of people, dehumanized blacks. (To curtail freedom of movement, a black person over age sixteen was required to carry a pass.) These laws undermined the blacks' sense of dignity. Moreover, by suppressing their freedom, apartheid removed the condition and context of blacks' moral responsibility and fulfillment because, according to Tutu, responsibility and moral actions presume the existence of human freedom. In place of the apartheid system, Tutu called for the establishment of a nonracial, genuinely democratic society.[25]

Like King, Tutu shows a dialectic understanding of the relationship of love and justice. He rejects the attenuated doctrine of reconciliation, which avoids confrontation with the system of social evils.[26] No forgiveness, no love is possible without addressing the problems of injustice. Peace cannot be equated with acquiescence to unjust relationships and conditions, and reconciliation is not situated somewhere between justice and injustice, avoiding

---

25. Tutu was equally critical of capitalism, for its unashamed appeal to self-interest and individualism and its emphasis on competition, both of which conflict with the African communal spirituality of *ubuntu*.

26. Tutu, *Hope and Suffering*, 38.

conflict and confrontation.[27] As we see in God's reconciliation with the world through the crucifixion of God's Son, reconciliation is costly; it requires sacrifice, repentance, and works of justice.

In dismantling apartheid, Tutu used international pressure, just as King used mass media and the support of conscientious northern liberals and other citizens. Tutu urged the world to exert economic sanctions against South Africa. He called on the church to participate in works of justice in solidarity with suffering blacks.

The Truth and Reconciliation Commission

In postapartheid South Africa, Archbishop Tutu served as the head of the Truth and Reconciliation Commission (TRC). The TRC shows that his spiritual approach to a collective problem was parallel to King's attempt to redeem his nation. Tutu applied *ubuntu* to the task of reconciliation and nation building in South Africa. If the antiapartheid movement was directed toward liberation and overcoming injustice, the work of the TRC was pointed toward reconciliation and the creation of a new nation as a community. The TRC was inspired by African *ubuntu* Christian spirituality embodied in the life of Tutu, Mandela, and other movement leaders. Its primary aim was the restoration of community by healing a traumatized people and rehabilitating the perpetrators into a new order. The TRC symbolized South Africa's collective determination to choose harmony over vengeance, reparation over retaliation, *ubuntu* over victimization.[28] The TRC was a creative and audacious project, designed to bring healing to the nation, avoiding further bloodshed without compromising the demands of truth. The TRC's task was to investigate human rights abuses and political crimes committed both by supporters and opponents of apartheid between 1960

27. Ibid.
28. Tutu, *No Future without Forgiveness*, 45.

and May 10, 1994. To carry out the task, the commission was empowered to grant amnesty for those who truthfully confessed their complicity in human rights violations. The amnesty granted by the TRC was an exceptional, unrepeatable, one-time event.

As the TRC motto ("Truth hurts but silence kills") indicates, the TRC was premised on the power of public confession to heal alienated relationships and to prevent the recurrence of similar atrocities. Rather than retribution, the ultimate goal was healing and reconciliation.[29] Tutu noted that it was different from Chile's secretive blanket amnesty.[30] Compared to the clandestine amnesty hearing, the TRC imparted more accountability upon the perpetrators. The TRC did not grant a blanket amnesty but rather a conditional one — and only to those who truthfully confessed everything that they had done. It did not dispense responsibility because it required truth telling. It was a bold new experiment — the truth in exchange for granting impunity to the offenders. By emphasizing public confession, the TRC aimed to nurture a culture of accountability, respect for basic human rights, and forgiveness through honesty and repentance.[31]

The TRC was the social and political expression of *ubuntu*. It was profoundly spiritual. Although its task, purpose, and function were conceived to be quasi-judicial, its underpinning was spiritual. Among the members of the commission, three were active, ordained ministers, and its chairperson was an archbishop. This decision reflected Nelson Mandela's spiritual conviction that the restoration of a community requires spiritual healing beyond mere judicial action. By appointing clergypersons, he intended to bring a vibrant, new spiritual currency of forgiveness, healing, and restoration into the commission's operation — elements that are often missing in politics.

As desired, the African ubiquity of religion was evident in the commission. There was no separation of spirituality and politics. "The President [Mandela] must have believed that our work

29. Ibid., 26.
30. Ibid., 27.
31. Ibid., 79.

would be profoundly spiritual," said Tutu. "After all, forgiveness, reconciliation, reparation were not the normal currency in political discourse."[32] Prayers were spoken at the beginning and at the end of their meetings. The testimonies at the hearings of the Human Rights Violations Committee were accented with frequent prayers, hymns, and ritual candle lighting to commemorate the deceased victims.[33] Upon Tutu's proposal at the first meeting (and later at the end of the term), the commission held a retreat in order to enhance their spiritual and moral sensitivities.[34] Tutu confessed that he had requested the worldwide Anglican Communion to regularly intercede for the success of the TRC. It was the shared understanding of most of the commission members that the task they were undertaking was religious and spiritual, so it was natural that spiritual resources be appropriately drawn upon.[35]

According to Tutu, the TRC depended on the relational truth of sharing pain and suffering rather than the "forensic factual truth" supported by scientific evidence. Similarly, the TRC put the emphasis on restorative rather than retributive justice. When retributive justice is served in society, little consideration is given to the victims, not to mention the possibility of reconciliation between the victims and the perpetrators. The restorative justice sought by the TRC was grounded in the traditional African communal jurisprudence of *ubuntu*. Tutu said that the goal of African jurisprudence is not punishment, but the restoration of breached relationships by redressing the imbalances and seeking to rehabilitate both the victims and the perpetrators. In the spirit of *ubuntu,* the TRC gave victims an opportunity to be healed, and perpetrators a chance to be rehabilitated and reintegrated into the community. The TRC was not preoccupied with past evils

---

32. Ibid., 80.
33. Ibid., 81.
34. Ibid.
35. Ibid., 82. For a more detailed understanding of the significance of spirituality and theology for the formation and operation of the TRC, see ibid., 80–87.

and wrongdoings; rather it was future-oriented for a reconciled community. Tutu contends,

> Thus to forgive is indeed the best form of self-interest since anger, resentment, and revenge are corrosive of that *summum bonum*, that greatest good, communal harmony that enhances the humanity and personhood of all in the community.[36]

Critics said that the TRC was unfair to the victims, for once amnesty was granted, the victims lost their rights to litigate the perpetrators in civil courts to seek compensation for their damages.[37] However, the generosity of South Africans was the key to the function of the commission. The TRC was not the instant invention of political expedience. It made use of the richly available spiritual and moral resources of African cultures and traditions. The TRC was based upon the African *ubuntu* anthropology that human beings are bound up in a delicate network of interdependence.[38] According to Tutu, the interim Constitution of South Africa provided a judicial foundation for the TRC in the spirit of *ubuntu*. Its postscript declared, "There is a need for understanding but not for vengeance, a need for reparation, but not for retaliation, a need for *ubuntu* but not for victimization."[39]

The TRC was the historical-political experimentation of reconciliation, theologically inspired by Jesus Christ, but rendered possible and practical by virtue of African peoples' spirituality. That is, it was a reflection of a longstanding spiritual outlook and moral commitment of South African black people, under the leadership of Tutu and Mandela. It was neither hastily nor expediently conceived. It manifested a deliberate consideration of both the reality of the current historical conditions and the future well-being of the new South Africa. More specifically, the

36. Ibid., 35.
37. Insufficient reparation for victims was another point of critique.
38. Tutu, *No Future without Forgiveness*, 35.
39. Ibid., 45.

design of the TRC was the expression of practical African wisdom, which enabled the TRC to take into account the reality of power politics to use its limited resources most effectively for the greatest good of the country, and to harmonize the requirements of justice with the reality of history (e.g., disparity of power). Instead of wasting limited resources on endless contentions, litigations, investigations, and conflicts, the TRC applied them to the rebuilding of the nation.

Not only would such litigations be prolonged, exhausting, and expensive, there would also be no guarantee that they would lead to the discovery of the truth. Since the system of apartheid destroyed most criminal evidence, or conspired to cover up the crimes, thus making it difficult to prove the cases beyond reasonable doubt, there could be no real closure to the suffering. The Nuremberg Trial model was not feasible; there was no guarantee for retributive justice as the judicial system of the nation was still controlled by white interests. Tutu acknowledged that the TRC was not perfect, but he believed it was the best that could be achieved.

Instead of dwelling on past wrongs, Tutu used the commission as an opportunity to cultivate "the culture of accountability and respect for human rights" which was, in his opinion, indispensable for a new postapartheid South Africa.[40] He recognized that the construction of a new community requires a supportive, spiritual-moral ecology of self-discipline, a healthy self-love, and commitment to justice. Like King, he knew that changing the political system alone could not bring about the desired transformation of society. A culture of peace and justice was required for a new South Africa.

Summary

King and Tutu shared the same moral vision that human beings cannot be human apart from a community; all human beings

---

40. Ibid., 79.

belong to one family of God. They both believed that human solidarity was built into our very essence. If for Tutu this idea was summed up in *ubuntu,* for King it was coined in the concept of the interdependence of humanity, epitomized by his vision of the beloved community.

A striking similarity in the contour and nature of communal spirituality in both King and Tutu shows, despite enormous geographical distance and despite King's generational distance from Africa, how much King and Tutu share in spiritual orientation and perspective. The communal ethos and practices of African American Christianity, whose roots go back to Africa, substantively informed King's idea of the beloved community, which constituted the core of his communal spirituality.

African spiritual traditions were more explicit and immediate for Tutu than King. Tutu was aware of the significance and meaning of the African spiritual heritage for theological reconstruction and political struggles. He engaged in intellectual and moral conversation with these resources and expanded the scope of a communal vision of *ubuntu,*[41] while King was less self-consciously aware of the influence of the African spiritual heritage upon his own spirituality, and his vision of the beloved community in particular.

The struggles of resistance and reconciliation led by both King and Tutu drew upon the rich spiritual and moral resources of African and African American cultures and traditions available to them. *Ubuntu* was the source of African peoples' patience, benevolence, and forgiveness. The communal spirituality of *ubuntu* especially served as a crucial resource for the task of reconciliation. Tutu's appeals and preaching would not have been effective if they were not resonant with the audiences' communal spirituality. J. H. Smit is correct in saying, "It was *ubuntu* that gave blacks the moral courage to persevere in spite of all the injustice

---

41. Influenced by the advance of feminist theology, women's rights, and other human rights movements, Tutu applied the vision of *ubuntu* to new ethical realms, including women's and children's rights (Tutu, *Crying in the Wilderness,* 120).

[under apartheid]."[42] The nonviolent revolution of South Africa would not have been possible without the historical tradition of *ubuntu,* just as the civil rights movement was made possible through the communal spiritual tradition of African Americans. King noticed that, even in the worst situations of riots and arson, there was a remarkable absence of African American violence against persons. Similarly, Tutu noticed the remarkable capacity of South African blacks to forgive, which was an indication of the magnanimity and nobility of their spirit flowing from *ubuntu.*[43] By virtue of *ubuntu,* many South African blacks, despite the abuses of the apartheid system, still maintained their humanity and compassion, unscathed by bitterness. This shows that communal spirituality does not belong to one extraordinary moral individual alone, such as King or Tutu, but to African peoples as a whole.

We see that the African spirituality of *ubuntu* survived among the African descendants in the United States and in South Africa. Despite hundreds of years of racial oppression, the communal spirituality of *ubuntu* is still abundantly available among the African descendants in the United States and in South Africa and has been powerfully manifested through social movements seeking justice and reconciliation.

---

42. J. H. Smit, "Ubuntu Africa: A Christian Interpretation," in *Ubuntu in a Christian Perspective,* ed. J. H. Smit, M. Deacon, and A. Shutte (Potchefstroom, South Africa: Potchefstroom University Press, 1999), 12.

43. Tutu, *No Future without Forgiveness,* 103.

Chapter 6

The Contemporary Relevance of King's Spirituality for Religious Terrorism and the U.S. War on Terror

In this chapter I reflect upon the lessons and insights of King's communal-political spirituality as they are applied to our contemporary sociopolitical context. Global society is increasingly pluralistic; it is more interdependent than in King's time. Globalization has brought different peoples, cultures, and religions together into a single arena, making conflict not only likely but inevitable. While in King's era nationalism, the cold war, and political ideology were the major sources of contention and conflict, many of today's social conflicts revolve around religion. Religious terrorism and U.S. supremacy, exemplified by the war in Iraq, pose major threats to global peace and justice.

Although the U.S. war on terror and religious terrorism seem to be totally different, upon close scrutiny they reveal a similar logic and the same dynamics of supremacy. In this chapter, we see how King's communal-political spirituality offers resources of critique and an alternative to the theocratic spirituality of religious terrorism and U.S. supremacy.

Religious Terrorism

Western society faces increasing challenges of religious terrorism. Many religious conflicts are instigated and perpetuated by radicals driven by zealous and destructive spirituality. The toxic ramifications of absolutist and fundamentalist spirituality on our

158

society are enormous, as shown in the September 11, 2001, tragedy, the war in Iraq, and other incidents of religious conflict.

If terrorism is a public act of violence to make or promote a group's political cause, then religious terrorism shows the most unrelenting, unflinching, and extreme form of terrorism of the early twenty-first century. What distinguishes religious terrorism from other varieties is that religion provides its motivation, justification, and organizational resources. Religious terrorists, more than other terrorists, do not hesitate to risk their own lives to achieve their intended goals through violence. They believe they are soldiers at war summoned by God to redeem civilization and humanity. In pursuing their goals with fanatic zeal and commitment, they are more resilient and uncompromising than secular nationalists or revolutionaries. The shocking aspect of religious terrorism is that vicious actions are not done by obviously bad people but rather by those who are well educated and seemingly pious. For example, Mohamed Atta, the mastermind of the September 11, 2001, attacks, was the son of a renowned Egyptian lawyer. Baruch Goldstein, a Jewish terrorist who killed over thirty Palestinian people in Hebron, was a trained professional M.D., educated at Albert Einstein College of Medicine in the Bronx, New York. Why is terrorism committed by religious groups or individuals? And why is it occurring at this juncture of history?

In its origin, cause, and assumptions religious terrorism is closely tied to religious fundamentalism or theocracy.[1] This does not mean that all religious fundamentalists or theocrats are terrorists, but rather that religious terrorists share a similar ethos and faith identity with fundamentalists or theocrats. Understanding religious fundamentalism requires the study of its historical ideology and the social contexts of its rise. Although I do not discuss this complex issue here in its entirety, I maintain that the rise of religious fundamentalism, in its contemporary socio-cultural form,

---

1. Theocracy is a religious polity and belief system that aims to establish a particular religion as the sole foundation for the political and cultural life of a nation.

has to do with the experience of fragmentation or dislocation caused by the advance of industrialization and globalization.

Jeffrey Hadden and Anson Shupe define fundamentalism as "a proclamation of reclaimed authority over a sacred tradition which is to be reinstated as an antidote for a society that has strayed from its cultural moorings."[2] Fundamentalism is characterized by its antimodern religious ideology.[3] A study of the variety of fundamentalisms shows that fundamentalism has emerged as a reaction to the loss of influence of traditional religious values and moralities. Fundamentalists disapprove of the separation of sacred from secular, which they believe has caused the secularization of their societies. They see themselves as the sole interpretive authority over the canons and assume the self-designated role of guardians of their sacred revelation and truth. Fundamentalists perceive that their world is under assault by outside cultures or alien forces, so they feel it is their religious duty to take action to defend it or, more radically, to try to bring their version of religion back to the center of a cultural and public life.

Fundamentalism can be politicized into religious terrorism when fundamentalists believe their political goals cannot be achieved by ordinary political or judicial processes. Religious terrorists approach the struggle with a sense of cosmic significance, employing millenarian or apocalyptic language and symbols to defend the unusual nature of their time and movements. They spiritualize violence as *jihad,* a holy war, to achieve their perceived noble goal, and permit social laws and moral limitations to be overridden in the process. They believe their violent actions are authorized and sanctioned by God in the conflict between God and Satan, good and evil.

This apocalyptic understanding of time and struggle inevitably leads to the satanization of the opponent. Satanization has the

---

2. Anson Shupe and Jeffrey K. Hadden, "Is There Such a Thing as Global Fundamentalism?" in *Secularization and Fundamentalism Reconsidered,* ed. Jeffrey K. Hadden and Anson Shupe (New York: Paragon House, 1989.)

3. See Bruce Lawrence, *Defenders of God: The Fundamentalist Revolt against the Modern Age* (San Francisco: Harper & Row, 1989).

effect of treating the opponents as subhumans; with such an attitude in place, the opponent cannot be salvaged, but only destroyed. As a consequence of this attitude, the possibility of dialogue or bargaining between conflicting parties is removed because such measures are considered betrayals of one's own religious ideals and purity.

Fundamentalism as a new social phenomenon is found in every major religious tradition. There are Jewish, Christian, Buddhist, and Islamic fundamentalists and religious terrorists, as we have seen in recent historical examples, such as Goldstein, Aum Chinrikyo, abortion clinic bombings, the Christian Identity group, the World Church of the Creator, and Timothy McVeigh. The global presence of fundamentalism means that the rise of fundamentalism today is related to globalization — its expansion and intensification — as globalization is mostly experienced as a secularizing, commodifying, and alienating force to indigenous cultures. The pervasive expansion of Western culture and materialism, through MTV, video, and movies, interferes with the process of socialization in various societies, and the traditional moral fabric of the community is being undermined by the increasing commodification of social values.

In particular, in many poor, non-Western societies, globalization is perceived as the continuation of Western colonialism in the name of modernization. In those societies, the age-long trauma of colonialism and oppression, along with the hatred and suspicion it entails, often plays a conspicuous role in the formation of this negative perception. A sense of violation results from the perceived intrusion of Western secular values and mores, evoking ostensibly extreme religious responses to protect the identity and dignity of a sacred tradition and the society they represent.

To further complicate the problem, the benefits of modernization are not fairly shared among the members of many underdeveloped countries. Endemic inequality and the injustice of undemocratic authoritarian regimes are often sponsored by a foreign government, such as the United States. Lacking the checks and balances of democratic systems, and blocked from the adequate venues or institutional cultures of reasonable public discourse, people find their religious passions inflamed into fanaticism. When society experiences exploitation, disempowerment, fragmentation, and alienation, religious fundamentalism appeals to many people as the only apparent alternative avenue to maintain their honor, authenticity, and dignity.

Many religious fundamentalist groups are at the forefront of political movements. They assume the leadership role for the downtrodden and the oppressed in their fight against injustice under the banner of traditional identity and cause. They offer the basic social safety nets for dispossessed, displaced people, as they become involved in social service programs and institutions, particularly in local and regional areas that the governments of their countries often disregard or neglect.

Critique of Religious Terrorism

What would be King's spiritual response to religious terrorism? King himself was deeply aware of the challenges of the massive structural changes taking place in the world (such as globalization, though the term was not yet popular during his time). King lamented the lag of the spiritual and moral realm behind the breathless pace of scientific and technological advances. He noted, "The richer we have become materially, the poorer we have become morally and spiritually."[4] In particular, he recognized the danger of the increasingly materialistic orientation of Western civilization in a shrinking world. The shallow spiritual ground of Western civilization posed the danger of self-destruction for humanity because without spiritual grounding, human beings are easily swayed by selfish goals and egoistic interests pursued at the expense of others. King believed the technological-material and the spiritual-moral advances should go hand in hand. He noticed

---

4. King, *Where Do We Go from Here?* 171.

that without learning how to live together morally and spiritually, humanity would perish together.[5]

There are parallels between King and religious fundamentalists. As for fundamentalists, religion was at the center of King's life; King was involved in and led a religiously based movement. King and fundamentalists alike acknowledge the power of religion to inject hope and power into people under oppression and alienation. As a leader of a religiously inspired social movement, King had firsthand experience of religion's power for social change and transformation.

King and many fundamentalists equally emphasized public participation in society and the responsibility of religion, refusing to accept a split between the sacred and the secular. King's life continually intersected with the social politics, laws, and foreign policies of the United States. King contended that social policy could not be isolated from a spiritual and moral dimension, and any viable social transformation could not take place without spiritual renewal.

King did not hesitate to use millennial language and symbols to empower and mobilize people and to criticize social evils. He identified himself as an extremist — indeed, dedication, zeal, and commitment characterized his life. King was one of the most poignant and formidable critics of U.S. foreign policy and its militarism, as evidenced by his anti–Vietnam War campaign.

Despite these similarities, King's spirituality does show a sharp contrast with that of fundamentalists. Although King understood himself to be an extremist or a nonconformist, he was a different kind of an extremist; an extremist for love, peace, and justice. He never swayed from his conviction that violence cannot be overcome by violence. Although King, like fundamentalists, believed that civilization needs a spiritual ground, King's conception of spiritual renewal was very different from that of fundamentalists. King functioned in the legal frame of religious freedom, under the

---

5. Martin Luther King, Jr., "Gay Lecture," Baptist Theological Seminary (The King Center Archives, April 19, 1961), 4.

separation of the church and state, but culturally or ethologically he appealed to the shared moral sentiments and consciences of people using public theology.

The Ecumenical Nature of King's Spirituality

King challenges us to rethink the meaning of religious commitment, zeal, and spirituality. He offers a valuable criterion to distinguish a genuine and productive form of religious and political zeal from a false and misguiding one. In contrast to fundamentalism, which excludes others, King's spirituality was ecumenical. He avoided the dangers and mistakes so often committed by many religious zealots — that is, to promote the interests of one's own group at the expense of others. From his perspective, any form of supremacy and unilateralism (nationalistic, racial, religious, and military) is anticommunity, thus antihumanity; the goal of a spiritual life was *agape,* serving others with genuine goodwill. He felt assured upon observing that many spiritual traditions similarly upheld love or compassion as the essence of their religions. Although King acknowledged the possibility of many different expressions of spirituality, he believed that an authentic spiritual person was not self-centered, but God- and other-centered. In light of his idea of "a complete life," for King, a mature spirituality liberates a person from self-centeredness to a responsibility to and care for humanity in a universal sense.

King's ecumenical spirituality was a natural and logical outgrowth and extension of his communal spirituality. At the center of this ecumenical spirituality was his belief in the sanctity and interdependence of humanity. In dealing with the various challenges of the civil rights movement and his antiwar actions, King always put the idea of human dignity and solidarity above any narrow allegiance and loyalty. As an eloquent expression of his communal spirituality, King conceived of humanity as one family in God. For example, he did not distinguish the value and dignity of Vietnamese from those of U.S. citizens. King critiqued the U.S. economic and military policies from this perspective of universal humanity rooted in his communal spirituality. Despite his dedication to the causes of African Americans, in the final analysis, King placed the well-being and the common good of humanity above his race, his conscience above parochial allegiance.

King saw and connected the struggle of African Americans in the worldwide context of liberation and independence of the oppressed from racism, colonialism, and economic exploitation. He believed that the civil rights movement of African Americans was inevitably tied with various liberation movements of the oppressed in the rest of the world. King did not see the issues of racism, poverty, and militarism as issues confined to African Americans alone. Rather, he understood these as problems facing humanity as a whole. He wanted to empower African Americans to be the catalyst for the spiritual and moral revolution of the nation and all humanity. It was King's conviction that a person of conscience must live by "a world perspective" rather than by a parochial vision or loyalty alone.

Out of his communal spirituality expressed in ecumenism, King rejected all forms of bigotry, bias, and prejudice within his own community and beyond it. For instance, when he heard anti-Semitic epithets in Harlem, King solemnly declared that "bigotry in any form is an affront to us all."

King practiced this ecumenical vision and value in his own ministry. He worked closely with a wide range of other activist groups, such as union leaders, socialists, and pacifists. King believed that the church must urge and assist its members to develop a world perspective.[6] Having a world perspective means conceiving of humanity as one family and exercising love and care for the broader concerns of all. Otherwise, in King's view, human beings could not rise above the shackles of prejudices and biases. King applauded the efforts of the Roman Catholic Church, the WCC (particularly its resolution condemning the war as immoral and its encouragement to seek an alternative), and other religious bodies in taking stances on global peace and justice.

---

6. Ibid., 3.

King's communal ecumenicity was also found in his affirming attitude toward other religions. He did not antagonize or reject other religions. King believed that other religions also possess the truth and wisdom of God in their shared insistence on love and peace. He declared, "Religion at its best has always sought to promote peace and good will among men. This is true of all of the great religions of the world. In their ethical systems, we find the love ethic standing at the center."[7] According to King, love is the force that all the great world religions have seen as "the supreme unifying principle of life."[8] He also declared that love is the key that unlocks the door which leads to ultimate reality.[9]

King was eager to work with people of other religions and philosophies to promote peace and justice in the nation and the world. King's relationships with South African religious leaders, Jewish and civil rights organizations, Catholics, poor whites, and labor unions attest to this point. The civil rights movement reflected and actualized this ecumenical spirituality. From the early days of his movement, he invited the participation of other religious groups and civic organizations. King believed religious communities, such as Jews, Muslims, Buddhists, and Hindus, among others, had a duty to engage in the social struggles against racism, poverty, and militarism. He was certain that if religious communities worked together and took a courageous stance against war and for peace, their cooperation would make a great impact on the world.[10]

King's ecumenicity, however, did not mean a shallow religious universalism. King's ecumenicity was deeply rooted in his African American spiritual tradition. As Harding says, although King's spirituality was grounded in one place, one base, and among one people, namely, African Americans, at the same time he reached

---

7. Martin Luther King, Jr., "Interview on World Peace," *Redbook* (The King Center Archives, November 5, 1964).

8. King, *Where Do We Go from Here?* 190.

9. Ibid.

10. King, "Interview on World Peace," 2.

far beyond that ground and that base.[11] He saw no contradictions in being grounded and reaching out as part of "one motion of spirit and life."[12] King's African American spirituality served as his foundation to stand on, while also sustaining him and bringing him growth. Like the roots of a tree, it provided him with the strength not only to weather the harsh winds, cold rains, and heavy snows, but also to reach out and to explore new possibilities for the life of his people, his nation, and all humanity.

King did not have serious difficulties in harmonizing global ethical demands with his own particular spiritual tradition. His spirituality did justice to both particular and universalistic dimensions of Christianity by avoiding a shallow universalism or a narrow parochialism. This harmony was the sign of his spiritual maturity, which allowed him to retrieve the best universal values of his spiritual traditions and to connect them to the relevant concerns of his contemporary society.

At the foundation of King's spirituality was his commitment to the ministry of Jesus Christ, interpreted through his communal-political lens. For King, Jesus represents a new humanity, the second Adam. In Jesus, every Christian is virtually a universal citizen, a citizen of the dominion of God. Christians are called to serve God and humanity, not just their own religious institutions, ethnic groups, and/or nations.

King's ecumenicity shows the true depth and scope of his communal spirituality. He was compelled by his faith to look at all human beings as his brothers and sisters, beyond the enclaves of race, nationality, class, and tribes. In contrast to the zealous, violent, and exclusive spirituality of religious fundamentalists and terrorists, King's spirituality is instructive and worth emulating for all of us who are living in an increasingly interdependent world.

---

11. Vincent Harding, "Dangerous Spirituality," *Sojourners* 28, no. 1 (January–February 1999): 29.

12. Ibid.

The U.S. War on Terror and U.S. Supremacy

Because King's spirituality is such a contrast and alternative to that of religious fundamentalists, what would he say about the war on terror? King's critique of the Vietnam War has striking prophetic value and relevance for us in understanding the immoral nature of the U.S. war in Iraq. Although the George W. Bush administration claims that the U.S. war on terror is a response to religious terrorism, there are dangerous similarities of underlying logic and dynamics between the two. King's critique of the Vietnam War provides clues and insights to substantiate this claim. A connection can be made between King's argument against the Vietnam War and the argument he might have made against the current war in Iraq based on the idea of U.S. supremacy.

U.S. supremacy pursues economic, military, and cultural hegemony over the world. Supremacy is based on the belief that one or one's group has superiority rather than equality in human relationships. It is the claim that "my race or my nation is better than yours." Supremacy always attempts to impose its views, visions, and values upon others. In times of peace, U.S. supremacy is expressed in a benefactor-to-beneficiary relationship. In times of war or crisis, however, it is expressed in the subjugation and domination of others (e.g., the Japanese internment in the United States during World War II, and the current racial profiling of Arab Americans).

One characteristic of supremacy is the rejection of human sanctity and interdependence. By striving toward domination, supremacy inculcates segregation and division among people. Supremacists refuse to treat other human beings as equal to themselves. U.S. supremacy subtly values the lives of U.S. citizens, whites in particular, more than those of others. It does not respect the universality of basic human rights and often treats other human beings as necessary collateral damage in the process of achieving its goal.

King, in his critique of the Vietnam War, saw the connection between white supremacy in the South and U.S. military supremacy in Vietnam: both treated people of color as subhuman. The U.S. supremacy in Vietnam was in continuity with the same white supremacist attitudes and ethos that King had experienced in the South in its blatant form, and the white backlash in the North in its subtler form. He realized that this supremacist value pervaded the entire fabric of U.S. institutions. It was out of this radical awareness that he repeatedly called for a transformation of the entire society. The U.S. war on terror, in its current form, is a result of the supremacist policy of the Bush government. From the beginning, the policies of the Bush administration have been unilateral and anticommunity in many aspects. It withdrew U.S. support for the Anti-Ballistic Missile Treaty, the Nuclear Test Ban Treaty, and the International Court on War Crimes, among other international agreements and laws. International laws, treaties, and agreements are considered to be useful to the extent that they support U.S. interests and domination.

U.S. supremacy is expressed in foreign policy by the assertion of military power and the unilateralism epitomized in the Bush doctrine of preemptive strike, a policy that permits the use of violence when there is merely some suspicion of another nation's intentions. For supremacists, the United States represents the best values of humanity, equating universal morality with the American way of life. Supremacists claim that those who are against them are wrong because they alone are right. George Bush declared, "Either you are with us, or you are with the terrorists."[13]

The events of September 11, 2001, were a watershed, as supremacist elements were consequently unleashed in foreign policies in the name of security and patriotism. Those ominous supremacist elements hidden within the U.S. soul, which King pointed out during his criticism of the Vietnam War, have now been unleashed in the aftermath of the World Trade Center attacks. The war in Iraq is the public expression of U.S. supremacy.

---

13. George W. Bush, Address to a Joint Session of Congress and the American People, September 20, 2001, *www.whitehouse.gov/news/releases/2001/09/20010920-8.html.*

The 9/11 attacks gave a pretext to invade Iraq by provoking the supremacist ethos within the U.S. collective psyche. The supremacy ethos of the United States, which sanctifies violence, stifled the debate on Iraq. Fostering fear by linking terrorism with weapons of mass destruction, the Bush government exploited 9/11 to pursue U.S. supremacy by military means.

This supremacist element cannot be more clearly evidenced than by our treatment of the detainees and prisoners from this war on terror, especially in Guantánamo Bay, Afghanistan, and Iraq. Since the invasion of Afghanistan, thousands of people have been detained by the United States. Prisoners under U.S. control, including those who may be innocent, are imprisoned and held without due process. Evidence proves that they are routinely humiliated sexually and tortured; some are even killed. Released government documents show that the U.S. government has sanctioned interrogation techniques and methods that violate the UN Convention against Torture. Many detainees and prisoners are routinely denied access to their lawyers and families. Some detainees are secretly transferred to other countries for torture and ill-treatment. Hundreds of detainees continue to be held without charge or trial, and many have already died in U.S. custody.

Such criminal behavior demeans not only those victims but also our nation and our common humanity. Although these abuses, tortures, and killings are squarely against the core constitutional values of our nation and humanity, there has been a persistent lack of accountability among high governmental officials and politicians who are responsible for these policies. Such apathy and callousness reflect the state of our spirituality, the soul of our nation, as we elect and empower the leaders who formulate and enact these policies. There is clearly a supremacist streak in those political extremists who took over the political center, planting a flag camouflaged in the name of traditional moral values, security, and patriotism after September 11, 2001. Our arrogance continuously misreads moral situations, and misleads our policies.

Evaluation

The reaction of our society to the 9/11 tragedy shows the spiritual poverty and immaturity of our nation. According to King, as with an individual, the character of a nation is tested in times of crisis. Rather than reflect, our nation reacted in arrogance, seeking revenge. In anger, fear, and hurtful pride, we have become a victim-turned-perpetrator.

Although tragedies, such as the 9/11 events, may offer us a rare opportunity to see our basic weaknesses and moral fallacies, U.S. citizens allowed themselves to be misled by the Bush government. There was no serious analysis of a larger cause and effect of 9/11, such as a review of our foreign policy in the Middle East, the history of colonialism, the economic exploitation of other countries, ecological destruction, and the impact of our cultural products (e.g., Hollywood movies, videos, and the mass media) on the lives of others.

King's example is instructive in this regard. During his campaign against the Vietnam War, King even demanded that the nation examine historical and social realities from the "enemy's point of view." King's comments on North Vietnam apply to our situation with regard to the war on terrorism:

> Surely we must understand their feelings even if we do not condone their actions.... Here is the true meaning and value of compassion and nonviolence, when it helps us to see the enemy's point of view, to hear his questions, to know his assessment of ourselves, for from his view, we may indeed see the basic weakness of our own condition. And if we are mature we may learn and grow and profit from the wisdom of the brothers who are called the Opposition.[14]

In light of King's wisdom, we have to ask, why do many average Muslims hate the United States? Why did the Middle East cheer terrorists? Rather than dismiss them simply as "evil" or claim they hate Americans because of our freedom and democracy, we

---

14. King, untitled paper on Vietnam, 1.

have to examine our culpability in contributing to the injustice in the Middle East. Many Muslims point to U.S. control and domination in the Middle East, a narrow pursuit of U.S. national interest at the expense of theirs, as the main cause for their hatred and militancy against the United States. The history of Western colonialism in the Middle East, the U.S. support of authoritarian regimes in the Middle East, such as Egypt and Saudi Arabia, the disdain for their ways of life and culture, the U.S. support for the Israeli occupation of Palestine, all add fuel to such toxic attitudes. As a nation we need to confront the undeniable fact that our almost unconditional support of Israel is another source of the Muslim and other Middle Eastern discontent, thus providing the infesting ground for the rise of religious terrorism. The Israeli and Palestinian conflict is more than a local conflict. Our attitude toward Israel greatly influences the Middle Eastern, and in particular the Muslim, understanding of the fairness of U.S. policy.

Collective paranoia following September 11, 2001, suspended all critical, reflective thinking and criticism. The Bush government has exploited this fear to silence its critics. As critics of the war in Vietnam were vilified by the Johnson government as traitors, enemies of our soldiers, and/or communists, so critics of the war in Iraq are regarded as unpatriotic or anti–United States. As the National Security Agency's secret eavesdropping program spies on American telephone calls and emails without warrants or oversight, citizens' constitutionally guaranteed civil liberties are also substantially compromised. It is obvious that democratic values and ideals are undermined when dissension is suppressed, secrecy prevails over openness, and the fallibility of governmental policies is simply not open for discussion.

The fallout from the 9/11 event made it difficult to think, talk, and live in terms of a common humanity. Civil liberties of citizens, especially Arab Americans, are severely violated through racial profiling and detention without trial for unlimited periods of time. Patriotism and nationalism discourage and undermine both ecumenical spirit and human solidarity as a whole. Tied with implicit Christian theocracy, a jingoistic form of civil religious spirituality is pervasive in this cultural milieu of patriotism and nationalism.

The war on terror is damaging the long-term national interests of the United States and any possibility for global peace. U.S. unilateralism and the war in Iraq, which neglected and violated international laws and agreements, seriously weakened the United Nations and undermined global peace. It is self-contradictory to believe that one can implant freedom and democracy by military invasion. If the goal is democracy and global peace, the means to pursue such noble goals should be commensurate with it, such as international cooperation and dialogue.

Bush's war on terror has generated *more* terrorists. It has promulgated *more* violence and distrust. The war in Iraq has claimed many innocent lives, including women and children, more already than the tragedy of 9/11. Our inhumane treatment of prisoners and detainees has become a new source of the rising tide of anger and anti-U.S. sentiments. The Guantánamo military camp and Abu Ghraib prison have become symbols of U.S. imperial supremacy. They are inflaming world opinions against us, and providing recruitment energy for terrorists. The United States, usurping all moral support in the aftermath of the 9/11 incident, is now one of the most disliked nations. We are regarded, even by our own allies, as a rogue superpower. We cannot win the war on terror by terrorizing others, and further terrorizing ourselves with fear.

In the economic realm, the war in Iraq is taking away valuable resources from the poor and social programs. By the end of 2005, the United States has spent more than $200 billion on Iraq when our entire foreign aid budget for 2002 was $10 billion. It is painful to witness how precious resources, which are already limited, are being wasted on unnecessary and unjustifiable warfare. The cost of the Iraqi war is high; it has robbed the poor of essential social services — and some of those poor are the dying or injured soldiers currently overseas.

The war in Iraq has fattened the military-industrial complex. King, citing President Eisenhower, frequently warned about the rise of the military-industrial complex in the United States; unfortunately, the alliance between the state, military, and big business is now a reality. The neo-conservatives, who advocated greater military spending and U.S. global supremacy, were closely associated with the defense and oil industries.[15] Dick Cheney is a former CEO of Halliburton, an oil company that received lucrative contracts in Iraq without even making bids.

The war on terror in general, and the war in Iraq in particular, poses several questions for the soul of the nation. What happened to our sense of honor, human decency, and idealism as a nation and a people? The Guantánamo and Abu Ghraib prison abuse, tortures, and murders are symptoms of the malaise within the soul of the nation. As King did at the time of the Vietnam War, many Americans feel an unspeakable, deep sorrow for and disappointment in our nation because it has given up decency, human rights, and justice in exchange for arrogance, fear, and brutality.

It is questionable whether a military supremacist policy can be effective in a highly interdependent society. In an increasingly interdependent society, various forms of international pressures can be more effective than military interventions in promoting justice. The cases of South Africa, Libya, and Iraq show that international sanctions under U.N. supervision can work effectively to bring forth the intended changes in international relationships without resorting to military invasions. In the case of Iraq, as a postwar discovery disclosed, the U.N. arms inspections and international economic sanctions were found to be working far more effectively than once imagined.

It was King's conviction that world peace was possible only when the fundamental interdependence, reciprocity, and equality

---

15. George Soros, *The Bubble of American Supremacy: Correcting the Misuse of American Power* (New York: Public Affairs, 2004), 180.

of humanity are radically affirmed.[16] We are so interdependent that even the success of our struggle against terrorism depends on the support of the peoples of other nations where terrorists operate. Alienating them makes the task of overcoming terrorism not just difficult but practically impossible. The solution to the problem is not in violence and revenge, but in dialogue and the removal of injustice. King's critique of U.S. supremacy at the time of the Vietnam War is telling and relevant for us today to examine the war in Iraq:

> God did not appoint America to be the policemen of the whole world. And America must recognize that she has not the capacity nor the power nor has she earned the moral right to be an American power, an Asian power, an Atlantic power and a South American power. And who is America to tell people what government they must choose? America is still following this terrible posture of trying to force her will down the throats of other people. We have got to tell America this in no uncertain terms. If we don't tell her and if America doesn't do something about it, she is going to destroy herself by the misuse of her own power.[17]

In order to check the rise and spread of religious terrorism, the removal of injustice is crucial for the defanaticization of religion. The removal of these barriers to justice requires the unyielding political engagement of religious communities. Supremacist interest and value cannot be transformed without a radical redistribution of economic and political power, because supremacy was based on and maintained by the monopoly or hegemonic control of power and privileges. Just peace is more important than just war. Justice requires just peace. King paid necessary attention to the root causes of conflicts, especially in developing countries:

---

16. King noticed, "I also think peace is jeopardized by extreme nationalists who fail to see that in the world today we cannot live alone, that all the nations of the world are interdependent" (King, "Interview on World Peace," 2).

17. King, "Speech at the Staff Retreat of SCLC," 25–26.

The maintenance of peace requires the promotion of justice and for almost seventy-five percent of the world's population, justice requires development. When progress and development are neglected, conflict is inevitable. We of the West must come to see that the so-called wars of liberation which loom on the world horizon are attempts of the people of under-developed nations to find freedom from hunger, disease and exploitation.[18]

King's ecumenical spirituality challenges us in times of violence and terror. Religious communities should promote nonviolence. Official religious and institutional advocacy of violence is too dangerous and stands against a general human spiritual quest, besides contradicting the teaching and wisdom of major religions. It is a challenge for each religious community to condemn and isolate this theocratic element within its own community. Conscientious individuals and religious communities need to stand up for prophetic ministries by refusing to be bound by parochial allegiances.[19]

The promotion of nonviolent spirituality is important because it not only cuts the vicious cycle of violence, but also prevents victims from turning into perpetrators. As violence comes out of a violent spirit, the former cannot be uprooted without the removal of the latter. As King so persuasively advocated, there can be no genuine global peace and justice without the affirmation of the sanctity and solidarity of all human beings. From his perspective, when we give up any redeeming possibility of others, we are giving up a part of our own humanity.

We cannot rely on our military might alone to overcome the violence of terrorism. A reckless war, no matter how shocking and awesome its military power may be, cannot remove the roots of hatred; rather, it intensifies enmity, resentment, and bitterness.

---

18. Martin Luther King, Jr., "Statement at *Pacem in Terris II* Convocation," Geneva (The King Center Archives, May 28–31, 1967), 2.

19. Baldwin, *Toward the Beloved Community*, 177.

While acknowledging the fact that, historically, war has sometimes served as a negative good by preventing the spread of an evil force, King proposed nonviolent conflict resolution as an alternative to war. Conflicts must be resolved through dialogue, fair negotiation, and other nonviolent means. The imposition or insistence of one voice cannot be fruitful. There is a threat to international peace when nations believe that they can survive alone, without others, and therefore pursue the way of monologue rather than dialogue.[20] In the last years of his life, King attempted to develop an all-encompassing philosophy of peace from his theory of nonviolent resistance. In pursuing his vision of the beloved community on a global level, he sought the application of nonviolence to international problems through a massive international coalition against injustice.[21]

---

20. King, "Interview on World Peace," 4.
21. King, *Trumpet of Conscience,* 63.

Chapter 7

The Ecumenical Spirituality of King and the Dalai Lama

As the world has become more dangerous, divided, and violent, the echo of King's call for the collaboration of different religious groups and nations underscores the sense of urgency that exists today. We cannot remain neutral or indifferent to the spiritualities of other people. The events of September 11, 2001, were an example of how the practice of another religion — militant Islam in this case — really does significantly matter to us. To a large extent, the achievement of global peace today is dependent on how religious communities can reshape their spiritualities in ways that are commensurate with common values, such as peace, justice, and the dignity and solidarity of humanity. In the final analysis, the ideas of a global ethic, human rights, and religious dialogue are all grounded in and dependent on the type of spirituality the participants, consciously or unconsciously, embody and practice, for spirituality gives motivation and energy to all ideals.

In this chapter, I explore the possibility of ecumenical spirituality through a conversation between Martin Luther King, Jr., and the fourteenth Dalai Lama of Tibet. The *Boston Globe* called the Dalai Lama "the Tibetan Buddhist leader who has succeeded Mahatma Gandhi and Martin Luther King, Jr., as the world's most eminent apostle of nonviolence."[1] Through a comparison of the two leaders, I identify several distinctive parameters of an ecumenical form of spirituality that would offer hope for the achievement of global peace and justice. I show that despite doctrinal and metaphysical differences, King and the Dalai

1. *Boston Globe,* Editorial, Monday, August 7, 2000.

Lama share many common characteristics of ecumenical spirituality rooted in their particular religious traditions, and that such commonality strengthens the possibility of collaboration among different religions for global peace and justice.

Interdependence

Interestingly, like King, the Dalai Lama takes the idea of interdependence as the foundation of his spirituality and ethics. The Dalai Lama is even more radical than King in his notion of interdependence by including nonhuman species as a part of solidarity. He has declared that "the nature of nature" is interdependence. The existence of every being can be understood only in terms of its "dependent origination." Every transient thing, a product, arises in dependence upon the aggregation of causes, effects, and conditions. A thing or a phenomenon is dependent on the collection and the interaction of parts; these parts further break down into smaller particles. A thing only exists as the sum of its parts. Therefore, a thing only nominally exists. It does not exist in and of itself but rather through our consciousness.[2] Dependent origination offers a metaphysical framework within which one can understand cause and effect, identity and difference, truth and falsity.[3] The loss of identity is a characteristic of every existence as it points to the way things exist. Because of this fundamental interdependence, an individual's interest and the interests of others are inextricably connected.[4]

Such a high metaphysical awareness of human interdependence led the Dalai Lama to emphasize the necessity of global ethics: a universal sense of responsibility. As we are very much interdependent at every level, the Dalai Lama believes that the

---

2. The Dalai Lama, *Kindness, Clarity, and Insight,* ed. Jeffrey Hopkins and Elizabeth Napper (Ithaca, NY: Snow Lion, 1984), 55–56.
3. The Dalai Lama, *Ethics for the New Millennium* (New York: Riverhead Books, 1999), 45.
4. Ibid., 47.

challenge for today is to learn how to live with others.[5] He believes that humanity should deal with common problems as members of one global family. In an ever-shrinking world, selfish pursuit of self-interests ultimately brings harm to the self and others. Recognizing the extent and intensity of global interdependence, the Dalai Lama declares, "The only peace that is meaningful to speak of is world peace."[6]

The Dalai Lama believes that the shrinking of the world urgently requires the development of a sense of universal responsibility for common survival and mutual happiness. He claims that every human action has a universal dimension in a global society.[7] The question of how to relate to those outside the confines of one's own community is not a choice, but our destiny.

The Dalai Lama believes that respect for humanity and interdependence should be the foundation of global ethics. According to him, the only permanent human social categorization today is our shared humanity. Race, class, ethnicity, religious affiliation, and gender and all other categories are temporary. The Dalai Lama considers the development of this universalistic sense of human solidarity to be critical for the common survival and well-being of humanity in this ever-shrinking world.

Happiness

For the Dalai Lama, the idea of global ethics is intimately related to human happiness. The Dalai Lama defines happiness as the goal of every human life and spiritual endeavor: it is a natural human disposition to pursue happiness. Yet his idea of happiness is different from that of utilitarianism. He believes that the quest for happiness cannot be separated from the quality of human existence and spirituality. Although the achievement of happiness

---

5. Sidney Piburn, ed., *The Dalai Lama, A Policy of Kindness: An Anthology of Writings by and about the Dalai Lama* (Ithaca, NY: Snow Lion Publications, 1990), 15.

6. The Dalai Lama, *Ethics for the New Millennium*, 202.

7. Ibid., 161.

depends on a number of causes and conditions, it primarily depends on our ability to master, train, and transform our mind, namely our spiritual discipline.[8]

The Dalai Lama claims that true happiness comes not from self-centered love, but from love and compassion for others because one's happiness and the happiness of others are intertwined. One cannot be happy by hurting others. For the Dalai Lama, any quest for happiness that does not include care for others is futile. Gaining spiritual progress or maturity means transforming the self so that we become more eager and ready to help others.

Spiritual Discipline

According to the Dalai Lama, the principal feature of genuine happiness is an inner peace.[9] Inner peace is created and maintained by guarding against obstructive emotions (e.g., fear, anxiety, greed), while cultivating constructive ones (e.g., love, compassion, care). No external elements can create enduring happiness. Fixation on material things does not promote happiness. Achieving happiness requires the transformation of the self through "a radical reorientation away from our habitual preoccupation with self."[10]

Spiritual discipline aims to transform the basic human mindset or motivation, called *kun long* in Tibetan. It curbs destructive and harmful impulses and encourages compassion toward others. The ethical value of a particular action is determined not by its behavioral outward formality (expression), but by an inner quality, which is motivation. Since our actions are manifestations of our disposition, only when this disposition is wholesome can one's actions be called wholesome. This implies that external control of human behavior by law and order is not sufficient. External restraint only checks negative and harmful actions; it does not

8. The Dalai Lama, *Beyond Dogma: The Challenge of the Modern World* (London: Souvenir Press, 1996), 146.
9. The Dalai Lama, *Ethics for the New Millennium*, 55.
10. Ibid., 23.

excise the roots of these desires. Without cultivating positive desires of peace and love, we cannot avoid afflictive emotions and negative thoughts.

Meditation is a technique used to achieve this goal. Control of the mind through meditation is important because, according to Tibetan Buddhism, actions come out of the mind. The ultimate cause of human suffering and tragedy lies in the human mind. Unless we control our minds, we cannot tackle the root of human problems. Thoughts and emotions are not separate in Tibetan Buddhism.[11] Perception inevitably impacts affective dimensions.

On the basis of this spiritual understanding, the Dalai Lama is critical of the Western educational system that emphasizes knowledge, information, and technology at the expense of morality and spiritual development. Without positive development of individuals' minds and hearts, technological and bureaucratic efforts cannot be effective. Similarly, the Dalai Lama challenges the current form of capitalism, which glorifies material advance and growth. For the Dalai Lama, the major contemporary human problem in the West is the impoverishment of the mind and the good heart. Human desires are unlimited and unquenchable. Discontent engenders greed, disgruntlement, unhappiness, frustration, and anger. Materialistic attachment diverts attention from human self-development, self-restraint, and care for others, while instilling and fostering a sense of discontent, greed, and self-centeredness. It is antithetical to one's responsibility toward others. Only spiritual discipline can restrain these negative tendencies.

Compassion

The Dalai Lama's definition of compassion is not much different from King's idea of *agape* — a benevolent will toward others. Love is a compassionate moral consideration and action that contributes to the happiness of others. For the Dalai

---

11. The Tibetan word for disposition is *lo*, which includes the ideas of consciousness, feeling, and emotion (The Dalai Lama, *Ethics for the New Millennium*, 30–31).

Lama, compassion is the foundation of ethics, and compassion arises as one transforms one's disposition from self-attachment to self-emptiness. Compassion is a form of spiritual discipline. By showing compassion to others, one learns to be less selfish. By participating in the suffering of others, one can be more altruistic.[12]

To be compassionate does not require any formal religious training or membership. It is a part of a natural human disposition, an innate spiritual quality. The Dalai Lama says, "Love means wishing that all sentient beings should find happiness, and compassion means wishing that they should all be free of suffering."[13] The seed of compassion is within us. Through the practice of deep meditation, this quality can become the foundation of our ethics. Meditation is important because it helps us to overcome the negative emotions of fear, hatred, and anxiety. With less fear and more calm and self-confidence, one can be more open-minded and friendly toward others, thus more compassionate.

All positive spiritual qualities, regardless of religious and doctrinal differences, grow toward compassion and altruism. The Dalai Lama has argued that our concern for others, our compassion, must undergird every aspect and realm of our social action — religious, political, economic, and cultural. Lacking this feeling, our social actions become aimless and misleading, functioning only as the agents of destruction. In particular, the Dalai Lama has contended, the kind of affection and care we show toward the unfortunate is an index of our spiritual health, both individually and socially.[14]

Religion and Spirituality

The Dalai Lama's spirituality is ecumenical in nature. He rejects any exclusive form of loyalty, such as nationalism, tribalism, and religious fundamentalism, that upholds the welfare of one group

---

12. The Dalai Lama, *Kindness, Clarity, and Insight,* 30.
13. The Dalai Lama, *A Policy of Kindness,* 103.
14. The Dalai Lama, *Ethics for the New Millennium,* 169.

at the expense of others. He not only affirms the dignity and rights of every human being, including one's enemies, but also welcomes the participation of others in their liberation processes. He does not hesitate to cooperate with other groups and organizations working for a common cause; in confronting social evils, the Dalai Lama emphasizes cooperation among different social, cultural, and religious groups.

The Dalai Lama maintains that religions share some common underlying intuitions in dealing with human suffering and predicaments: they ultimately seek the good of humanity. Religion itself cannot be the goal, but only a means to achieve one's spiritual fulfillment: happiness. In the final analysis, he says all religions teach and promote the same values and messages of love, compassion, and forgiveness.[15] An individual should be allowed to choose his or her religion on the basis of his or her natural spiritual disposition and character. Diversity of religion is desirable and beneficial for humanity because no single religion is able to satisfy every human being.

The Dalai Lama sees a great deal of similarity among religions in the area of the contemplative life and practices.[16] He declares that "the basic purpose of every spiritual tradition is, after all, the transformation and mastery of the mind."[17] Therefore, religions must cooperate with one another to teach human beings how to achieve their disposition for peace and happiness.[18]

The Dalai Lama guards against the rigidity of institutional religion because it is, all too often, the source of intolerance to other religions. Like King, he is critical of fundamentalists, of their extremist attitudes and intolerance. From his perspective, intolerance is the expression of their lack of inner peace, which engenders all sorts of negative passions and attitudes of hatred, jealousy, and narrow attachment. This failure to achieve inner peace is a major cause of serious conflicts. According to the Dalai

---

15. Ibid., 20.
16. The Dalai Lama, *Beyond Dogma*, 156.
17. Ibid., 157.
18. Ibid., 151.

Lama, fundamentalists try to impose on others a transformation that they themselves have not yet achieved. Religious conflicts result not from the religions themselves but from those people who failed to transform themselves according to the teachings of their religion. They classically do not model what they preach.

Nonviolence

The Dalai Lama has demonstrated the same relentless commitment to the principle of nonviolence as did King. For the Dalai Lama, nonviolence is a minimum requirement of ethics: if one cannot bring good to others, then one should at least avoid harming others. Nonviolence does not only mean not harming others (nonmalfeasance), but also positively bringing good to others, namely, compassion. He conceives justice and peace as an organic unity. In order to achieve peace, we have to use peaceful means. Like King, the Dalai Lama rejects violence because violence begets violence[19] and is the cause of a new suffering. The Dalai Lama says that violence achieves only short-term objectives.[20] It is very hard to predict its consequences. One cannot build trust with violence; trust is the glue of relationship, and violence is inimical to trust. He opposes war because war legalizes maximum violence.

For the Dalai Lama, nonviolence is not merely a tactic for a less powerful people, it is a way of life, a spiritual discipline. Forbearance is the basis of nonviolence. In Tibetan Buddhism, *sö pa* is an important virtue that undergirds nonviolence. It is a Tibetan expression that means "able to withstand or bear." It connotes a resolute forbearance and fortitude in the face of difficulties.[21] *Sö pa* allows one to remain composed, peaceful, and unperturbed during adversity. *Sö pa* enables us not to give in to the negative thoughts and destructive impulses of hatred and resentment in the midst of our struggle against evil. The Dalai

---

19. The Dalai Lama, *Ethics for the New Millennium*, 201.
20. Ibid.
21. Ibid., 103.

Lama's idea of *sö pa* and King's notion of *agape* share similar moral values and concerns.

As King denounced calls from the black power movement, so too the Dalai Lama rejects violence despite the call and challenges from many young Tibetans. He has refused to support any violence, such as guerrilla warfare, against the Chinese, even in self-defense. The Dalai Lama confesses, "I am...Tibetan before I am Dalai Lama, and I am human before I am Tibetan. So while as the Dalai Lama I have a special responsibility to Tibetans, and as a monk I have a special responsibility toward furthering inter-religious harmony, as a human being I have a much larger responsibility toward the whole human family — which indeed we all have."[22] For the Dalai Lama, nonviolence is necessary for the long-term interest and future of Tibet because a free Tibet must live with China forever.

Ecological Ethics

The Dalai Lama's idea of interdependence, as shown in his ecological ethics, is more extensive and radical than King's. He has applied his nonviolent ethics not only to interpersonal relationships, but to ecological issues as well. Buddhist spiritual teachings of interdependence and ethics of nonviolence, which are mutually related, offer the resources for an ecological ethics. The Dalai Lama believes that environmental concern is a distinctive area in which Tibetan Buddhism can contribute greatly to humanity in a global society. He claims that an environmental concern has been innate to Buddhism from the beginning. Buddhism has always acknowledged the interdependence of all existing beings; therefore, compassion is not confined to the human species, but includes all living beings.

The Dalai Lama envisions that Tibetan people (and the Buddhists) will play a redemptive role in awakening this awareness

---

22. Ibid., 20.

among people in a technological and commercialized society, just as King envisioned the redemptive role for African Americans in the liberation of the downtrodden and the oppressed. In his Nobel Peace Prize address in 1989, the Dalai Lama suggested the transformation of the whole of Tibet into the Zone of Ahimsa (nonviolence), an exemplary place for environmentalism. His proposal of the Zone of Ahimsa called for the complete demilitarization of Tibet; the prohibition of the manufacture, testing, and stockpiling of nuclear weapons and other armaments; and the transformation of the Tibetan plateau into the world's largest park or biosphere, where strict laws of environmental protection would be enforced. In short, his vision conveys the notion of a peace sanctuary for Tibet, which deeply resonates with the unique history of Tibet as a peaceful Buddhist nation and nonviolent culture.[23]

Similarity

One sees a great deal of consonance between the Dalai Lama's Asian Buddhism and King's African American spiritual traditions. As the ideas of the sanctity of humanity, interdependence, and nonviolence were at the core of King's spirituality, the Dalai Lama also says that nonviolence and the interdependence of all sentient beings are two tenets of Buddhist teaching.[24] They share some commonality in their universal communal spirituality. The spiritual and moral similarities exist in terms of their emphasis on compassion, interdependence, and the power of truth, nonviolence, hopefulness, and so on.

Due to this common universal communal spirituality, and despite their different religious traditions, their notions of love and compassion are strikingly similar in terms of their emphasis on respect and empathy for others.

---

23. The Dalai Lama, *A Policy of Kindness*, 23.
24. The Dalai Lama, *Beyond Dogma*, 146.

For King and the Dalai Lama (and similarly for Mahatma Gandhi and Desmond Tutu), the onto-theology of interdependence undergirds their understanding of humanity and the universe. In spite of the enormous challenges and pressures of their struggles, they do not hesitate to extend their compassion and commitments to the causes of oppressed peoples beyond their immediate community. It is their unique quality to be able to see the commonality of humanity despite a plethora of differences. Obviously, their ecumenical spirituality is closely associated with their belief in the ultimate unity of humanity. Beyond their unwavering dedication and sacrifice for the causes of their own peoples, they place the well-being and the common good of humanity above the interests of their own groups. They approach the suffering of their peoples in the context of the suffering of all humanity, a spiritual transcendence of narrow religious confines.

King and the Dalai Lama maintain optimistic outlooks, despite the many difficulties and challenges surrounding them. They believe in some potential of good and progress within human nature, for the Dalai Lama Buddhahood and for King the *imago dei*. For example, the Dalai Lama says, "I believe that human determination and willpower are quite sufficient to challenge outside pressure and aggression. No matter how strong the evil force is, the flame of truth will not diminish."[25] Grounded in their spiritualities, they both believe in the ultimate triumph of justice over injustice in history.

King and the Dalai Lama emphasize the significance of spiritual practices, including contemplation, meditation, prayer, and worship, not only for personal well-being, but for the sustaining work of justice and reconciliation. Their ecumenical spiritualities affirm that any viable social change requires not only the prophetic critique of social evils but also a spiritual renewal of society (which includes the deepest sense of meaning and the value of society). They share the belief that spiritual practices

---

25. The Dalai Lama, *Kindness, Clarity, and Insight*, 64.

are important to inculcate this attitude of love and compassion against destructive and harmful impulses.

Pointing out the spiritual poverty of a materialistic world, they believe that any social order is not stable unless it is grounded in the deepest structure of human meaning and tested values and visions. Genuine peace and justice require not only democratic constitutional structures, but also the transformation of people's hearts. A mere judicial change, although necessary, is not sufficient. The well-being of humanity and our planet requires that the material blessings and advances be balanced with spiritual and moral growth and maturity.

These similarities are impressive, given the differences of their religious traditions as well as their political and social contexts. Like King, the Dalai Lama is respected and emulated by peoples across religious and ethnic boundaries. More important, such respect and emulation of the moral exemplars of different religions increase the possibility of mutual acceptance among the religions, thus weaving a shared moral fabric for a global society.

Difference

Despite their similarities, King and the Dalai Lama differ in the starting point and the emphasis of their politics. Although the Dalai Lama sees human existence as profoundly interdependent, he tends to emphasize the significance of individual spiritual discipline and transformation over social, structural changes. He believes that global peace begins with the inner peace of each individual:

> I think society can live in peace thanks to the inner peace human beings have developed through their intelligence. Thus, I believe that to have world peace we must first have inner peace. Those who are naturally serene, at peace with themselves, will be open toward others. I think this is where the very foundation of universal peace lies.[26]

---

26. The Dalai Lama, *Beyond Dogma*, 151.

The Dalai Lama believes that even if one may not be able to change external situations, one can change one's inner attitude toward the situation in order not to lose peace and tranquility. What one loses outwardly one may gain inwardly through self-cultivation of patience and tolerance. Thus the Dalai Lama contends that social transformation begins with the transformation of this inner disposition. For example, he says that the sophistication of our legal system alone cannot solve the problem of crime because crime has to do with a lack of ethical restraints that grow out of inner spiritual discipline.

In the Dalai Lama's ethics, there is no serious systemic analysis of power or injustice functioning through various social structures and institutions of society: how they interfere with, obstruct, facilitate, and empower human spiritual qualities and their development. It is not a surprise that the Dalai Lama is concerned with the institutions of education and the media since they serve as the primary social instruments affecting human dispositions today. Even when he discusses other social problems, his analysis remains very commonsensical, without any in-depth analysis of historical connections, problems, or suggestions of concrete resistance and transformation like King's "Beyond Vietnam" speech.

In comparison to the Dalai Lama, Martin Luther King, Jr., was much more confrontational and realistic in dealing with the social injustice of the world. King, under the influence of Reinhold Niebuhr, was deeply aware of the entrenched nature of collective egoism. King's primary focus was on how to transform a society, specifically unjust institutions and laws entrenched in collective egoism. One finds King's contribution lies in informing us how our dispositions and motivations are informed and shaped by our institutional structures, and that unless these structures (as the configuration of a collective egoism) are transformed, any individual transformation is limited. This collective egoism has to do with the spiritual state of a society and a nation.

Deeply rooted in their own seemingly disparate traditions of African American Protestantism and Tibetan Buddhism, King and the Dalai Lama offer valuable insights into human problems and ways to approach them. Just as African American Protestantism needs to learn from the mystical spirituality of Buddhism, so Tibetan Buddhism has much to learn from a Christian prophetical tradition. It is no accident that the Dalai Lama has told his followers to study Christian theology and doctrines thoroughly. This does not mean that Christianity has not developed a mystical spirituality; history shows otherwise. Nevertheless, as an articulate science of mind, Buddhism has much to teach Christians. Christian mystical spirituality can have a new relevance, articulation, and self-understanding in conversation with Tibetan Buddhism, which is best embodied in the Dalai Lama.

In terms of their primary emphases, the spiritualities of distinctive emphasis in King and the Dalai Lama are complementary. The two dimensions of the personal and the societal transformation must be conceived as balancing each other. In relation to social transformation, individual spiritual transformation is prevented from being asocial and ahistorical; in relation to individual spiritual transformation, a social transformation is prevented from being superficial or judicial only. As our discussion of King's idea of "a complete life" has shown, King's emphasis on social transformation should not be viewed as his disregard or rejection of individual well-being or personal spiritual experiences.

Toward Ecumenical Spirituality

In constructing an ecumenical spirituality, one may draw some insights and guidelines from King's and the Dalai Lama's spirituality. Among other common emphases between King and the Dalai Lama, ecumenicity, interdependence, human dignity, nonviolence, commitment to justice, and love offer us some parameters to figure out the contours of ecumenical spirituality.

Ecumenical spirituality is not an illusionary ideal. Great world religions all deal with the universal human problems of suffering, death, happiness, sickness, meaninglessness, sin, guilt, and other limit situations. They more or less require conversion (liberation or enlightenment) from self-centeredness as the precondition toward the achievement of a higher fulfillment. They offer some methods and solutions to help in our quest and journey toward the goal.

Ecumenical spirituality is critical for the enhancement of global peace and justice. To some extent, the rejection of religious fundamentalism depends on the ecumenical spiritual competence of each religion — that is, how each religion is able to reconstruct its tradition in a way that is morally relevant in response to the challenges posed by a global society. The reconstruction requires religious imagination, spiritual probing, theological acumen, and ethical discernment. At the same time, their ecumenism is inseparable from their public theological efforts and sensibilities. King and the Dalai Lama serve as eloquent public theologians of their respective religions. In coping with new challenges and issues confronting their religious communities, they have been able to reinterpret their traditions and reconstruct them in a way relevant to contemporary situations.[27] For example, King's vision of the beloved community was informed by the Christian idea of the dominion of God interpreted through African American spirituality. King saw in Jesus Christ a new universal humanity, just as the Dalai Lama understands the Buddha as the universal symbol of human enlightenment.

Ecumenical spirituality is not a syncretistic form of spirituality that replaces a particular-historical spirituality of a religious community. Rather, it is a form of spirituality grown within each religion in response to the common needs for justice and peace in a global society. Our study of King and the Dalai Lama shows that an ecumenical form of spirituality is feasible within each tradition, without suppressing a particular religious identity. In speaking to the public, they each retrieve the rich universalistic

---

27. For example, through the retrieval of religious visions and values, the liberation movement of Tibetan Buddhism has undergone changes by more explicitly embracing modernist ideas, such as democracy and human rights, including individual and women's rights.

thrusts and motifs within their particular spiritual tradition. One may say that they uphold a kind of internal universalism.

Ecumenical spirituality does not have a coercive binding power (like universal human rights), but exercises an alluring or exemplary force for people, for spirituality by nature cannot be imposed. Although not coercive, it may be presented as an exemplary form of spirituality that attends to the well-being of a common humanity and the earth. Ecumenical spirituality is embodied and expressed in the lives of global spiritual exemplars. They are global spiritual and moral exemplars because their lives embody the universal values of humanity in their spiritualities, which ordinary people may emulate regardless of their religious and ethnic backgrounds. The spirituality of these leading figures has a profound impact on the spirituality of their followers. Their lives have a pedagogic power over us because "one example is better than a thousand theories." These giants are familiar, respected, and visible symbolically to ordinary people. Their spiritualities are effective and instrumental in cultivating and promoting universal values, ecumenical dialogue, and cooperation among different nationalities, races, and religious groups, which are all necessary for the common human existence today. These spiritual figures embody and represent their respective traditions in many ways, opening new possibilities of relating to the tradition, to others outside the tradition, and toward achieving mutual understanding and collaboration. The roles of these spiritual figures are important as many successful nonviolent social movements are rallied and sustained around these figures. As such, these spiritual giants offer a critical antidote to the contemporary misuse and abuse of spirituality by religious terrorists and theocrats.

For global exemplars like King and the Dalai Lama, their spiritualities are crucial to the mobilization of religious groups for the common purpose of peace and justice, to the identification of areas of common spiritual quest, meaning, and even practices, and to collaboration to effect desirable social changes. Such exemplars can be instrumental in promoting dialogue and mutual

understanding among different religions. Such great spiritual figures help us to see the overlapping spiritual and moral sensibilities
that exist among religions. Furthermore, the existence of spiritual
moral exemplars makes it impossible to dismiss other religions as
evil or immoral. Finding a person one can respect and emulate
in other religious traditions facilitates mutual understanding and
cooperation, and leads to a new appreciation for other religions.
For example, reading Mahatma Gandhi and the Dalai Lama may
help a Christian rethink his or her narrow perspective toward
other religions. Global exemplars point out that although each religion's understanding of the ultimate origin, destiny, and method
of the salvation of human beings may differ, common endeavors
toward global peace and justice are possible.

Fortunately, an ecumenical form of spirituality is also found in
prominent spiritual figures of a variety of religious traditions —
people such as Mahatma Gandhi, Thomas Merton, Dorothy Day,
Mother Teresa, and Desmond Tutu, to name a few. There exists
a striking similarity among these figures and King, despite their
theological and doctrinal differences. In their spiritualities, they
reconcile the universal ethical demands (e.g., the universal respect
for human dignity and human solidarity) with the particularity of
their religious traditions. With deep roots in their own particular
spiritual traditions, they, like King, were active in the struggles
for justice and peace. They pursued those struggles of peace and
justice on the basis of their spirituality. They also advocated nonviolent resistance as a moral means of social change, emphasized
the moral responsibility of religious persons and communities,
and cared for the welfare of their opponents. They did not com-
promise their political radicalism against injustice, and were all
committed to nonviolence.

Ecumenical spirituality is enriched and grows through the exchanges and contributions of various religious communities. The
fruitfulness of mutual interaction and exchange is almost unlimited. For example, King's spirituality grew and deepened through
his learning of other religious traditions, such as Gandhi's and
white liberal theology and philosophy. Similarly, many of King's

spiritual insights, strategies, and practices were appropriated by other religious traditions for their struggles against injustice. Such exchanges among religious communities and spiritual persons may challenge one's religion to reexamine and retrieve one's own religious traditions and heritage. These interactions do not mean the surrender of one's own religious identity, but rather promote the expansion and enrichment of one's own tradition. In conversation with King and other spiritual leaders, religious communities in the world may consciously nurture and develop their own versions of an ecumenical spirituality as an alternative to religious fundamentalism and theocracy.

Conclusion

Contribution and Legacy

The sincerity and the authenticity of our beliefs are usually proof-tested in our actions and deeds, for these ultimately disclose what kind of persons we are. In the final analysis, spirituality is a matter of a *lived* faith, neither mere dogmatic confession nor conceptual ideals. For King, love, justice, and forgiveness were not just moral ideals or political slogans but how he lived his life. Nurtured in African American spiritual traditions, King naturally acquired several distinctive forms of communal African American values, such as beneficence, generosity, forbearance, forgiveness, nonviolence, improvisation, practical wisdom, and justice.[1] These values were engrained in his character as virtues, correlated with the communal and the political aspects of his spirituality. In his movement, King displayed an unyielding commitment to justice, the courage to stand against social evils, and the practical wisdom and prudence to discern a feasible means and method to achieve his objectives. His communal disposition was displayed in his extraordinary virtues of magnanimity, benevolence, and forbearance.

These spiritual and moral qualities, the communal and political virtues in particular, were unveiled through decisions he made, particularly at the critical moments of his life. For example, his faithfulness was demonstrated during the early stage of the Montgomery Bus Boycott. When he was urged by Daddy King to give up the boycott and return to Atlanta for his and Coretta's safety, he solemnly responded: "I have to go back to Montgomery. My

---

1. Peter Paris points out that the virtues King displayed were congruent with African qualities (Paris, *Spirituality of African Peoples,* chapter 6).

friends and associates are being arrested. It would be the height of cowardice for me to stay away. I would rather be in jail ten years than desert my people. I [began] the struggle and I can't turn back."[2] He knew that his father was deeply concerned about safety for him and his family. As a son with great respect for his father, making the decision was not easy for Martin. Although he was distressed that his decision would pain his father, he stayed the course.

Nurtured in African American spirituality, King evinced a magnanimous character. His beneficence was demonstrated by the almost unlimited scope of his goodwill toward people. He exercised forgiveness on many occasions. During the Montgomery Bus Boycott, King constantly urged his followers to be kind and polite to whites in standing up for the cause of justice and freedom. When his house was bombed, King gave a calming speech of forgiveness to angry crowds who gathered in front of his home at the news of the attack. His magnanimity was also demonstrated by his forgiveness of a woman in New York who almost killed him by piercing his chest with a letter opener.

King's commitment to justice and his love of humanity were demonstrated by his fights against poverty in the North. Despite his celebrated achievement against segregation in the South, the historic Selma march, and the subsequent passage of the voting rights bills, he did not stop there; he moved to the North. He rented a slum apartment on the south side of Chicago in January 1966, and moved in to live among its poor people. This decision shows that King's belief in the interdependence of humanity and his commitment to justice were not empty ideals.

King's moral commitment was perhaps revealed most unequivocally in his stance against the Vietnam War. On February 25, 1967, King gave his first full speech critical of the Vietnam War, knowing that his stance against the war was not popular and would alienate a large segment of his followers and political bases. It undermined his relationship with the Lyndon Baines

---

2. King, *Stride toward Freedom*, 144.

Johnson (LBJ) government — no small thing, since the SCLC's thirty-three-member board of directors, mostly comprising African American ministers, had a grateful attitude toward LBJ, a hero who gave sterling support to the civil rights movement. Yet once his mind was made up, King did not change his position on the war despite constant urging from his advisors and supporters who were concerned about the political cost of his opposition to the war — the loss of prestige and influence, financial difficulties for the SCLC, and the possibility of physical danger. Even King's confidant, Bayard Rustin, warned that King's anti-Vietnam initiative would split the civil rights movement, upset the LBJ government, and harm the cause of racial justice for African Americans. Whitney Young's fearful warning to King summarized the atmosphere of the time: "If we are not with him [Johnson] on Vietnam, then he is not going to be with us on civil rights."[3] Even the NAACP's sixty-member board passed a unanimous resolution opposing any effort to blend the civil rights movement with an anti–Vietnam War campaign.[4] King was being isolated from many of his friends, supporters, and previous sympathizers.

With this kind of opposition from within his own ranks, why did King persist with a stance that seemed tantamount to political suicide? King maintained that his antiwar position was consistent with his faith. His position was the expression of his solidarity with helpless and outcast people, such as the Vietnamese. This solidarity with common humanity was deeper and more fundamental than national, racial, or ideological unity.[5] He said, "We are called to speak for the weak, for the voiceless, for the victims of our nation, and for those it calls enemy, for no document from human hands can make these humans any less our brothers."[6] And he stood by his word. For King, although friendship with LBJ and African American civil rights leaders was important, this

---

3. James Forman, *The Making of Black Revolutionaries: A Personal Account* (New York: Macmillan, 1972), 369.
4. Oates, *Let the Trumpet Sound,* 438.
5. King, "A Time to Break Silence," 234.
6. King, *Trumpet of Conscience,* 25.

consideration could not take precedence over the fundamental values of his spirituality.

For the cause of humanity, King gave up his own personal comforts, reputation, and privileges — even his life. The Christ-like quality of his life was manifested in his decisions to stand for God's justice and love. At the end of his life, he frequently talked about bearing the cross, no matter the consequences:

> The cross we bear precedes the crown we wear. To be a Christian one must take up his cross, with all of its difficulties and agonizing and tension-packed content and carry it until that very cross leaves its marks upon us and redeems us to that more excellent way which comes only through suffering.[7]

The source of this faithfulness, courage, humility, and openness to truth was King's identity as God's minister. Whenever there was an opportunity to introduce himself, King introduced himself as a minister of God. Whenever questions were raised about the direction and course of his political movements, he returned to this fundamental identity: who he was, and what he was required to do as a minister of God. King believed that he was thereby called to serve all human beings regardless of their religion, race, nationality, and economic status. This spiritual identity shaped the courageous decisions King made regarding his involvement in the anti–Vietnam War campaign; he maintained that on the basis of his commitment to the ministry of Jesus Christ, his public stance and engagement were inevitable, because the campaign for peace and justice was a part of his Christian ministry.

King drew energy, strength, and a sense of purpose from God. His spirituality was personal, deeply rooted in his intimate relationship with his Lord. Yet his spirituality was different from the individualistic spirituality abounding today. King did not have

---

7. Martin Luther King, Jr., National Conference on Religion and Race, Chicago, January 17, 1963; cited in David J. Garrow, *Bearing the Cross: Martin Luther King, Jr., and the Southern Christian Leadership Conference* (New York: Vintage Books, 1988), [5].

any interest in personal spiritual experiences per se, either ecstatic or transcendental. From King's perspective, the reduction of spirituality into the interior of the self or self-absorption is distorting. It dangerously borders on solipsistic narcissism, being indifferent, or conforming, to the reality of injustice and exploitation. In his spiritual life, King was never solely concerned with his own personal perfection in itself. His relationship with God went beyond that. King could not think of human spiritual pursuits or religious commitments independent of one's service to humanity. The quality of inner transformation was tested and authenticated by the fruits of love and justice.

King's spirituality presents a third way between a theocratic/ fundamentalist form of spirituality and a therapeutic, individualistic form of spirituality. It was radical and militant, but different from that of theocrats whose spirituality is exclusive and self-righteous toward others. His spirituality was holistic and balanced. For King, an authentic spiritual fulfillment requires the transformation of both personal and societal dimensions, both the hunger for mystery and the hunger for righteousness.

King's spirituality shows a way for healing a nation where religious moral values are identical with pro-war and pro-rich, and political progressiveness is synonymous with secularism.[8] His communal and political spirituality offers a creative alternative ethics for being simultaneously Christian and public, religious and civic. His unapologetic Christian faith is a surprising challenge to the secular liberals who dismiss the relevance of personal faith and spirituality for the public life.

Like all of us, King was not a perfect person. He struggled with his shortcomings and personal flaws. King privately bore many traces of agonizing personal struggles. Written in the context of his personal struggles, his sermon "Unfulfilled Dreams" is very insightful in revealing the torment of his heart and his own moral resolution about personal sins. According to the sermon, a person

8. See Jim Wallis, *God's Politics: A New Vision for Faith and Politics in America* (San Francisco: HarperSanFrancisco), 2005.

should not be judged by one isolated mistake or incident of his or her life, but by the overall bent of his or her heart. For King, spirituality is the ongoing and consistent journey toward destiny. What is important is the consistent disposition, the direction of one's will, rather than every detailed behavior or action of a person. He noted, "What God requires is that your heart is right. Salvation isn't reaching the destination of absolute morality, but it's being in the process and on the right road."[9] King did not believe that one should first complete one's personal moral perfection, a goal impossible to achieve, before one can move to social realms by applying one's moral convictions. Dyson's comments on the issue are consistent with King's self-reflection:

> Character cannot be understood through isolated incidents or a fixation on the flaws of a human being during a selected period in life. Assessment of character must take into account the long view, the wide angle. Character is truly glimpsed as we learn of human beings negotiating large and small problems that test moral vision, ethical creativity, and sound judgment.... Character can only be glimpsed in a sustained story that provides plausible accounts and credible explanations of human behavior.[10]

Spirituality, in this respect, should be understood as a narrative script of one's life in its totality — a story that integrates and gives coherent meanings to various experiences and decisions. Spirituality is concerned with the overall directive or trajectory of one's heart, rather than an isolated, discrete behavior or action. Without justifying King's personal mistakes, one cannot deny that he was a deeply spiritual person, committed to following

---

9. Martin Luther King, Jr., "Unfulfilled Dreams," in *A Knock at Midnight: Inspirations from the Great Sermons of Rev. Martin Luther King, Jr.*, ed. Clayborne Carson and Peter Holloran (New York: Warner Books, 1998), 196.

10. Michael Eric Dyson, *I May Not Get There with You: The Real Martin Luther King, Jr.* (New York: Free Press, 2000), 166.

and doing God's will to the best of his ability. Despite personal shortcomings, King lived a dedicated life for others and God.

No one can deny that King gave his life for the vision of a new people and a new nation, and for the betterment of humanity. As Moses led the Israelites in the wilderness, and transformed ex-slaves into a new peoplehood through the giving of new values (the Decalogue) and a new vision, King tirelessly endeavored to forge a new people in this nation and the world. The motto, "To redeem the soul of America," was not a voguish political slogan for him. Moving beyond the struggles for African American civil political rights, King's actions reflect an authentic search for a new possibility of being a human and a community. He believed in the redeeming possibility of humanity. King was convinced that revolution begins within us, through the renewal and dedication of our hearts and minds for the highest cause of humanity. Through the example of his life, King awakened the divine qualities within his followers. In his brief life, King inspired many ordinary African Americans to respect and believe in themselves as God's children, and to stand up against dehumanizing power of social evils for their humanity.

King's spirituality was clear historical evidence of the transforming effects of Christian spirituality for a society. Through his ministry, King demonstrated not only that Christian spirituality could take a public form but also that public engagement itself, rooted deeply in spirituality, could be transformed and sublimated to a new level with lasting effects and meaningful results. He showed that a spiritually motivated movement can be even more effective than purely secular movements. A political movement with an integrating spiritual vision and practices can have a sustaining power and moral quality.

If King's life presents one of the noblest forms of a struggle to transform the soul of the United States and humanity as a whole, what do King's vision and ministry mean for us today, especially those who live in the United States, which is infested with violence, terror, and distrust? What did we learn from his life and service? Despite our annual national celebration of King's birthday, U.S. society is still far from achieving King's vision. Events such as the Los Angeles riots in 1992 and the war in Iraq launched in 2003 show how history repeats itself unless a lesson is learned from past failures, and unless the fundamental conditions and ethos of the nation are altered.

Of course, the world and its times have changed since King's death. The world has become even more interdependent and pluralistic through the global exchanges of people, ideas, goods, and symbols. After the collapse of the Soviet Union, the United States is currently the only superpower, enjoying unquestionable political, economic, and military dominance in the world. Yet our society is still wrestling with social problems similar to those with which King had struggled, such as racism, militarism, and classism. These problems continue and are even further exacerbated in different guises and forms.

Since King's death, white backlash exists in a clever, more subtle form. People may point to the political and legal achievements of the passage of the civil rights bills and the voting rights bills, but how much of those bills has now been compromised by various undermining conditions and revisions? The laws may have changed but not the ethos. White ethos still subtly embraces white superiority over nonwhites. The ethos of the nation has become more and more conservative. We witness the public expression of a mean, callous, and punitive spirit in our public policies, arrogant foreign policies, and the entrenched egoism of a ruling economic class. Obviously social problems are not confined to the social evils of racism, classism, and militarism. Newly identified problems, such as sexism and environmental justice, are interlocked with these issues.

Thirty-five years after King's death, the nation has regressed in the area of economic justice. For example, despite a few improvements of civil rights and the rise of the African American middle class, the social situation of poor African Americans is getting worse. King was right. Because precious financial resources and moral opportunity were squandered on the Vietnam War instead of targeting inner-city problems, urban poverty has been getting worse. Indeed, the habits of military adventurism and violence have dragged us into an unnecessary war in Iraq, while grave problems fester at home.

The disintegration of urban families and neighborhoods is horrifying. Erosive capitalism undermines civic virtues, social capital, and human solidarity. As a society, we worship money and power rather than justice and love. We place self-interest over the common good. As a result of our exploitation and overuse of natural resources, our ecological conditions are deteriorating, as the greenhouse effects show.

The ethos around the poor is extremely negative and punitive. The Welfare Reform Act of 1996 signed by Democratic President Bill Clinton indicated where white ethos was heading, and showed how entrenched their hearts were against economic rights for the poor. As a society, we do not help them, but instead accuse them of laziness, a lack of work ethic, and a poor choice of lifestyle. Both public and private spheres have given up on the urban areas. The idea of social reform is dismissed as the bankrupt liberal idea of a big government. This collective policy direction reveals the state of our collective spirit, which is mean, narrow, and punitive. King's concerns as regards urban African American communities have come true. There is evidence of anger, frustration, desolation, and nihilism, resulting from a long-standing and accumulated sense of rejection and marginalization. In turn, these negative qualities engender high rates of suicide, domestic and street violence, family abuse, and other social pathologies.

King realized that the urban problem could not be solved by one city government or agency, for the problem is the result of accumulated history-long negligence and exploitation. The solution requires, according to King, a massive and systemic intervention on the federal government level. Our nation has no will to solve urban problems. Tax cuts for the wealthy are made at the sacrifice of programs and funding for unemployed workers, job training programs, childcare assistance, and after-school programs.

The U.S. criminal justice system is infested by this rancor of revenge and vindictiveness, often in the name of law and order.

The law of "Three Strikes, You're Out," the increasing rate of litigations, and the fistfights between adults at children's sports competitions are all indications that we are infected by the culture of violence. In our cultural products, violence is almost glorified as a sign of strength and might. We see this in movies, videos, and computer games, and we hear it on radio and television talk shows.

The situation has recently grown worse, especially after the attacks of September 11, 2001. Violence takes on the nature of normalcy and necessity. Our nation glorifies military force ("shock and awe"). We spend billions of dollars on war and weapons at the expense of support for education, children, poor families, and health care. In a global society, the United States is perceived not as a peace broker but as a perpetuator of violence, both through the export of our culture and through our arrogant response to international political problems.

The rise of violence discloses the destitution of our spirituality. Sadly enough, we no longer believe in the power of love. Peace and love are regarded as signs of weakness or incompetence. Concern or care for others is socially discouraged as the traditional occupations of teaching, pastoring, nursing, and public service work are increasingly low-paid and unpopular. Only the assertion of Me, Myself, and I dominates.

What has happened to the spirit that sparked and led the movement that energized so many people to stand and commit themselves to the higher cause of humanity, to the fuller realization of democracy, and to the long-overdue healing of the pain and scars of racial divisions? What kind of wind or "spirit" is sweeping our public sphere today? Many moral indicators show that King's dream is dying in our nation today. In light of King's life and public ministry, one cannot deny that we face a deepening spiritual crisis in the United States.

Yet in our despair we know that we have to carry on where King left off. King's life calls us to stand against the spirits of Mammon and Mars. King's call for the fundamental reconstruction of American social values is still loud and clear. His life of commitment challenges our complacency, our self-indulgence, and our self-concern as they are revealed in individual career pursuits, competition, and achievement, with indifference to others. King's life of nonviolence and love challenges our nation in her arrogance, hypocrisy, and imperialistic hegemonic desire to control the world.

King is still alive through his dream. His dream is important for us, because as a metaphor of imagination and vision, a dream sets the horizon of one's moral epistemology. We are able to see and act only within the scope of our capacity for envisioning. King's dream cannot be killed, because his dream was larger than his life: it came from God. And his prophecy rings still in our ears because it is true. Raines is right:

> It is not difficult to silence a good man. But it is very difficult to silence a good man's dream, because it becomes the dream of others. You can kill good people, but you can't kill goodness.[11]

King's clarion call for the universal kinship of humanity cannot be more relevant and urgent than in our time and society. A global society, which is increasingly multiracial, multicultural, and multireligious, still needs to learn how to live together. As King astutely observed, "The real problem is that through our scientific genius we've made of the world a neighborhood, but through our moral and spiritual genius we've failed to make of it a brotherhood."[12]

King's idea of interdependence should be affirmed as a core value of our society. To accept and respect others as equal members of a common humanity, one family in God is a precondition for any viable global peace and justice. Religious communities need to work together to enhance the recognition of human solidarity and mutual understanding. As demonstrated by the Dalai

---

11. Raines, "Righteous Resistance and Martin Luther King, Jr.," 740–41.
12. King, "Rediscovering Lost Values," in *The Papers II*, 249.

Lama, Desmond Tutu, and Martin Luther King, Jr., this recognition of interdependence does not require a particular form of religious allegiance. It can be affirmed by many different religions on different theological grounds.

The blissful vision of humanity, the Promised Land in biblical terms, cannot be reached by one people, one race, one religion, or one nation, no matter how powerful it may be. The achievement of this vision will be possible only when, like the ancient Israelites, a new humanity, a new peoplehood is born through the divine disciplines of love and justice. If there is to be peace, we have to learn to live together. And in order to live together, we have to accept the sanctity and the solidarity of humanity. Unless we do so, the vision of the Promised Land will remain distant and unreachable. King's profound communal spirituality is telling us today that the Promised Land is possible only when the whole of humanity works together in deep awareness of its interdependence. The Promised Land will open itself to humanity as a whole and not to individuals or an individual nation, race, or class. *Only "We, as a people, will get to the Promised Land."*

This is the challenge that King poses for all of humanity living in this ever-shrinking world. Toward this end, King is our inspiration, our vision, and our way.

Bibliography

Works by Martin Luther King, Jr.

King, Martin Luther, Jr. "Creative Protest." The King Center Archives, February 16, 1960.

———. "Gay Lecture." Baptist Theological Seminary. The King Center Archives, April 19, 1961.

———. "Interview on World Peace." *Redbook*. The King Center Archives, November 5, 1964.

———. *The Martin Luther King, Jr. Companion: Quotations from the Speeches, Essays, and Lectures of Martin Luther King, Jr.* New York: St. Martin's Press, 1993.

———. *The Measure of a Man.* New York: Christian Education Press, 1959.

———. *The Papers of Martin Luther King, Jr.* Ed. Clayborne Carson. Vol. 1: *Called to Serve, January 1929–June 1951.* Berkeley: University of California Press, 1992.

———. *The Papers of Martin Luther King, Jr.* Ed. Clayborne Carson. Vol. 2: *Rediscovering Precious Values, July 1951–November 1955.* Berkeley: University of California Press, 1995.

———. *The Papers of Martin Luther King, Jr.* Ed. Clayborne Carson. Vol. 3: *Birth of a New Age; December 1955–December 1956.* Berkeley: University of California Press, 1997.

———. "Speech at the Staff Retreat of SCLC." Penn Center, Frogmore, South Carolina. The King Center Archives, May 1967.

———. "Statement at *Pacem in Terris II* Convocation." Geneva. The King Center Archives, May 28–31, 1967.

———. *Strength to Love.* New York: Harper & Row, 1963.

———. *Stride toward Freedom: The Montgomery Story.* New York: Harper & Row, 1958.

———. *A Testament of Hope: The Essential Writings of Martin Luther King, Jr.* Ed. James M. Washington. New York: HarperCollins, 1986.

———. *The Trumpet of Conscience.* New York: Harper & Row, 1967.

———. "Unfulfilled Dreams." In *A Knock at Midnight: Inspiration from the Great Sermons of Rev. Martin Luther King, Jr.,* ed.

Clayborne Carson and Peter Holloran. New York: Warner Books, 1998.

———. Untitled paper on Vietnam. The King Center Archives, April 30, 1967.

———. *Where Do We Go from Here: Chaos or Community?* Boston: Beacon Press, 1967.

———. *Why We Can't Wait.* New York: Harper & Row, 1963.

Other Works

Allen, Diogenes. *Spiritual Theology: The Theology of Yesterday for Spiritual Help Today.* Boston: Cowley Publications, 1997.

Ansbro, John J. *Martin Luther King, Jr.: The Making of a Mind.* Maryknoll, NY: Orbis Books, 1982.

Assensoh, A. B. *Rev. & Dr. Martin Luther King, Jr., and America's Quest for Racial Integration: With Historical Testimonies from King's Former Classmates, Close Friends, and Colleagues.* Ilfracombe: Stockwell, 1987.

Baer, Hans A., and Merrill Singer. *African American Religion: Varieties of Protest and Accommodation.* 2nd ed. Knoxville: University of Tennessee Press, 2002.

Baldwin, Lewis V. "Martin Luther King, Jr., Black Church, and Black Messianic Vision." *Journal of the Interdenominational Theological Center* 12 (Fall 1984/Spring 1985).

———. *There Is a Balm in Gilead: The Cultural Roots of Martin Luther King, Jr.* Minneapolis: Fortress Press, 1991.

———. *To Make the Wounded Whole: The Cultural Legacy of Martin Luther King, Jr.* Minneapolis: Fortress Press, 1992.

———. *Toward the Beloved Community: Martin Luther King, Jr., and South Africa.* Cleveland: Pilgrim Press, 1995.

Battle, Michael. *Reconciliation: The Ubuntu Theology of Desmond Tutu.* Cleveland: Pilgrim Press, 1997.

Bennett, Lerone. *What Manner of Man: A Biography of Martin Luther King, Jr.* Introduction by Benjamin E. Mays. Chicago: Johnson Publishing Co., 1986.

Bridges, Flora Wilson. *Resurrection Song: African-American Spirituality.* Maryknoll, NY: Orbis Books, 2001.

Bush, George W. Address to a Joint Session of Congress and the American People, September 20, 2001. *www.whitehouse.gov/news/releases/2001/09/20010920-8.html.*

Calloway-Thomas, Carolyn, and John Louis Lucaites, eds. *Martin Luther King, Jr., and the Sermonic Power of Public Discourse*. Tuscaloosa: University of Alabama Press, 1993.

Carson, Clayborne, ed. *The Autobiography of Martin Luther King, Jr.* New York: Warner Books, 1998.

Carter, Lawrence Edward, Sr., ed. *Walking Integrity: Benjamin Elijah Mays, Mentor to Martin Luther King, Jr.* Macon, GA: Mercer University Press, 1998.

Chan, Simon. *Spiritual Theology: A Systematic Study of the Christian Life*. Downers Grove, IL: InterVarsity Press, 1998.

Chinula, Donald M. *Building King's Beloved Community: Foundations for Pastoral Care and Counseling with the Oppressed*.

Chireau, Yvonne P. *Black Magic: Religion and the African American Conjuring Tradition*. Berkeley: University of California Press, 2003.

Coban, Helena. *The Moral Architecture of World Peace: Nobel Laureates Discuss Our Global Future*. Charlottesville: University Press of Virginia, 2000.

Colaiaco, James A. *Martin Luther King, Jr.: Apostle of Militant Nonviolence*. New York: St. Martin Press, 1993.

Collins, Kenneth, ed. *Exploring Christian Spirituality: An Ecumenical Reader*. Grand Rapids: Baker Books, 2000.

Colston, Freddie C. "Dr. Benjamin E. Mays: His Impact as Spiritual and Intellectual Mentor of Martin Luther King, Jr." *Black Scholar* 23, no. 2 (Winter–Spring 1993): 6–15.

Cone, James H. "Black Theology–Black Church." *Theology Today* 41, no. 1 (1984): 409–20.

———. *Martin and Malcolm and America*. Maryknoll, NY: Orbis Books, 1991.

———. "Martin Luther King, Jr.: The Source of His Courage to Face Death." *Concilium* 183 (March 1983): 418–27.

———. *The Spirituals and the Blues: An Interpretation*. Maryknoll, NY: Orbis Books, 1991.

———. "The Theology of Martin Luther King, Jr." *Union Seminary Quarterly Review* 40, no. 1 (1986).

Dalai Lama XIV. *The Art of Happiness: A Handbook for Living*. New York: Riverhead Books, 1998.

———. *Beyond Dogma: The Challenge of the Modern World*. London: Souvenir Press, 1996.

———. *Ethics for the New Millennium*. New York: Riverhead Books, 1999.

———. *Freedom in Exile: The Autobiography of the Dalai Lama*. New York: HarperCollins, 1990.

———. *The Good Heart: A Buddhist Perspective on the Teaching of Jesus*. Boston: Wisdom Publications, 1996.

———. *Kindness, Clarity, and Insight*. Ed. Jeffrey Hopkins and Elizabeth Napper. Ithaca, NY: Snow Lion Publications, 1984.

———. *Live in a Better Way: Reflections on Truth, Love, and Happiness*. New York: Penguin Compass, 1999.

———. *My Land and My People*. New York: Warner Books, 1997.

———. *The Way to Freedom*. San Francisco: HarperSanFrancisco, 1994.

Davis, George W. "God and History." *Crozer Quarterly* 20, no. 1 (January 1943).

Deats, Richard. *Martin Luther King, Jr., Spirit-Led Prophet: A Biography*. New York: New City Press, 2000.

Downey, Michael. *Understanding Christian Spirituality*. Mahwah, NJ: Paulist Press, 1997.

———. *Worship: At the Margins: Spirituality and Liturgy*. Washington, DC: Pastoral Press, 1994.

———, ed. *The New Dictionary of Catholic Spirituality*. Collegeville, MN: Liturgical Press, 1993.

Downing, Frederick L. *To See the Promised Land: The Faith Pilgrimage of Martin Luther King, Jr.* Macon, GA: Mercer University Press, 1986.

Dreyer, Elizabeth A., and Mark Burrows, eds. *Minding the Spirit: The Study of Christian Spirituality*. Baltimore: Johns Hopkins University Press, 2005.

Du Bois, W. E. B. *The Souls of Black Folk*. New York: Dover Publication, 1994.

Du Boulay, Shirley. *Voice of the Voiceless*. Grand Rapids: Eerdmans, 1988.

Dyson, Michael Eric. *I May Not Get There with You: The Real Martin Luther King, Jr.* New York: Free Press, 2000.

Fairclough, Adam. *To Redeem the Soul of America: The Southern Christian Leadership Conference and Martin Luther King, Jr.* Athens: University of Georgia Press, 1987.

Fisher, William H. *Free at Last: A Bibliography of Martin Luther King, Jr.* Metuchen, NJ: Scarecrow Press, 1997.

Flip, Schulke. *He Had a Dream: Martin Luther King, Jr., and the Civil Rights Movement*. New York: W. W. Norton, 1995.

Fluker, Walter E. *They Looked for a City: A Comparative Analysis of the Ideal of Community in the Thought of Howard Thurman and Martin Luther King, Jr.* Lanham, MD: University Press of America, 1989.

Forman, James. *The Making of Black Revolutionaries: A Personal Account*. New York: Macmillan, 1972.

Franklin, Robert M. *Liberating Visions: Human Fulfillment and Social Justice in African American Thought*. Minneapolis: Fortress Press, 1990.

———. "Martin Luther King, Jr., as Pastor." *Iliff Review* 42 (1985): 4–20.

Frazier, E. Franklin. *Negro Church in America*. New York: Schocken Books, 1966.

Garrow, David J. *Bearing the Cross: Martin Luther King, Jr., and the Southern Christian Leadership Conference*. New York: Vintage Books, 1988.

———. *Martin Luther King, Jr.: Civil Rights Leader, Theologian, Orator*. 3 vols. New York: Carlson Publishing, 1989.

Gutman, Herbert. *The Black Family in Slavery and Freedom, 1750–1925*. New York: Vintage, 1976.

Hansen, Drew D. *The Dream: Martin Luther King, Jr., and the Speech That Inspired a Nation*. New York: HarperCollins, 2003.

Hanson, Bradley C., ed. *Modern Christian Spirituality: Methodological and Historical Essays*. American Academy of Religion Studies in Religion, no. 62. Atlanta: Scholars Press, 1990.

Harding, Vincent. "Dangerous Spirituality." *Sojourners* 28 (January–February 1999): 29–31.

———. *Hope and History: Why We Must Share the Story of the Movement*. Maryknoll, NY: Orbis Books, 1990.

———. *Martin Luther King, the Inconvenient Hero*. Maryknoll, NY: Orbis Books, 1996.

Häring, Bernard. *A Theology of Protest*. New York: Farrar, Straus and Giroux, 1970.

Herskovits, Melville J. *The Myth of the Negro Past*. Boston: Beacon Press, 1958.

Hopkins, Jeffrey, ed. *The Art of Peace: Nobel Peace Laureates Discuss Human Rights, Conflict and Reconciliation*. Ithaca, NY: Snow Lion Publications, 2000.

Howard, M. William, Jr. "Martin Luther King, Jr.: Challenge to the Church." *Princeton Seminary Bulletin* 8, no. 2, New Series (1987).

Huggins, Nathan I. "Martin Luther King, Jr.: Charisma and Leadership." *Journal of American History* 74, no. 2 (September 1987).

Ivory, Luther D. *Toward a Theology of Radical Involvement: The Theological Legacy of Martin Luther King, Jr.* Nashville: Abingdon Press, 1997.

Khabela, M. Gideon, and Z. C. Mzonlei, eds. *Perspectives on Ubuntu*. Alice, South Africa: Lovedale Press, 1998.

King, Coretta Scott. "Foreword," in Richard Deats, *Martin Luther King, Jr., Spirit-Led Prophet: A Biography.* New York: New City Press, 2000.

———. *My Life with Martin Luther King, Jr.* New York: Henry Holt and Company, 1993.

King, Martin Luther, Sr. *Daddy King: An Autobiography.* With Clayton Riley. New York: William Morrow, 1980.

Lassiter, Valentino. *Martin Luther King in the African American Preaching Tradition.* Cleveland: Pilgrim Press, 2001.

Lawrence, Bruce. *Defenders of God: The Fundamentalist Revolt against the Modern Age.* San Francisco: Harper & Row, 1989.

Lebacqz, Karen, and Joseph D. Driskill. *Ethics and Spiritual Care.* Nashville: Abingdon Press, 2000.

Levine, Lawrence. "Slave Songs and Slave Consciousness: An Exploration in Neglected Sources." In *American Negro Slavery,* ed. Allen Weinstein and Frank Otto Gatell. New York: Oxford University Press, 1973.

Lincoln, Eric, ed. *Martin Luther King, Jr.: A Profile.* New York: Hill and Wang, 1984.

Lischer, Richard. *The Preacher King: Martin Luther King, Jr., and the Word That Moved America.* New York: Oxford University Press, 1995.

Macquarrie, John. *Paths in Spirituality.* Harrisburg, PA: Morehouse Publishing, 1992.

———. "Spirit and Spirituality." In *Exploring Christian Spirituality: An Ecumenical Reader,* ed. Kenneth Collins. Grand Rapids: Baker Books, 2000.

Mafico, Temba J. "The African Context for Theology." *Journal of the Interdenominational Theological Center* 16, nos. 1–2 (Fall 1988–Spring 1989).

Mays, Benjamin. *Born to Rebel.* New York: Charles Scribner's Sons, 1971.

Mbiti, John. *African Religions and Philosophy.* New York: Praeger, 1969.

McClendon, James, Jr. "M. L. King: Politician or American Church Father?" *Journal of Ecumenical Studies* 8, no. 1 (Winter 1971).

McGinn, Bernard. "The Letter and the Spirit: Spirituality as an Academic Discipline," *Christian Spirituality Bulletin* 1, no. 2 (Fall 1993): 1, 3–10.

———. *The Presence of God: A History of Western Christian Mysticism,* vol. 1: *The Foundations of Mysticism: Origins to the Fifth*

Century. New York: Crossroad, 1992; vol. 2: *The Growth of Mysticism: From Gregory the Great through the Twelfth Century.* New York: Crossroad, 1994.

McGrath, Alister E. *Christian Spirituality.* Oxford; Malden, MA: Blackwell, 1999.

McIntosh, Mark A. *Mystical Theology: The Integrity of Spirituality and Theology.* Malden, MA; Oxford: Blackwell, 1998.

McKnight, Gerald D. *The Last Crusade: Martin Luther King, Jr., the FBI, and the Poor People's Campaign.* Boulder, CO: Westview Press, 1998.

Mikelson, Thomas. "Mays, King, and the Negro's God." In *Walking Integrity: Benjamin Elijah Mays, Mentor to Martin Luther King, Jr.,* ed. Lawrence Edward Carter, Sr. Macon, GA: Mercer University Press, 1998.

Mitchell, Henry H. *Black Belief.* New York: Harper & Row, 1975.

Moses, Greg. *Revolution of Conscience: Martin Luther King, Jr., and the Philosophy of Nonviolence: Critical Perspective.* New York: Guilford Press, 1997.

Oates, Stephen B. *Let the Trumpet Sound: A Life of Martin Luther King, Jr.* New York: HarperCollins, 1994.

Ogleby, Enoch. "Martin Luther King, Jr., Liberation Ethics in a Christian Context." *Journal of the Interdenominational Theological Center* 4 (Spring 1977): 33–41.

Owen, Thomas C. "Some Problems in Contemporary Christian Spirituality." *Anglican Theological Review* 82, no. 2 (Spring 2000): 267–81.

Paris, Peter J. *Black Religious Leaders: Conflict in Unity.* Louisville: Westminster/John Knox Press, 1991.

———. *The Social Teaching of the Black Churches.* Philadelphia: Fortress Press, 1985.

———. *The Spirituality of African Peoples: The Search for a Common Moral Discourse.* Minneapolis: Fortress Press, 1995.

Piburn, Sidney, ed. *The Dalai Lama, A Policy of Kindness: An Anthology of Writings by and about the Dalai Lama.* Ithaca, NY: Snow Lion Publications, 1990.

Pollard, Alton B., III. *Mysticism and Social Change: The Social Witness of Howard Thurman.* New York: Peter Lang, 1992.

Prozesky, Martin, ed. *Christianity amidst Apartheid: Selected Perspectives on the Church in South Africa.* New York: St. Martin's Press, 1990.

Raboteau, Albert. *Slave Religion: The "Invisible Institution" in the Antebellum South.* New York: Oxford University Press, 1978.

Rauschenbusch, Walter. *Christianity and the Social Crisis*. New York: Harper & Row, 1964.

Reagon, Bernice J. "Songs of the Civil Rights Movement, 1955–1965: A Study in Culture History." Ph.D. dissertation, Howard University, Washington, DC, 1975.

Schneiders, Sandra M. "Feminist Spirituality." In *The New Dictionary of Catholic Spirituality*, ed. Michael Downey. Collegeville, MN: Liturgical Press, 1993.

———. "A Hermeneutical Approach to the Study of Christian Spirituality." *Christian Spirituality Bulletin* 2, no. 1 (Spring 1994): 9–14.

———. "Spirituality as an Academic Discipline: Reflections from Experience." *Christian Spirituality Bulletin* 1, no. 2 (Fall 1993): 10–15.

———. "Spirituality in the Academy." *Theological Studies* 50, no. 4 (1989).

Sebidi, Lebamang J. "Toward a Definition of Ubuntu as African Humanism." In *Perspectives on Ubuntu*, ed. M. Gideon Khabela and Z. C. Mzonlei. Alice, South Africa: Lovedale Press, 1998.

Senghor, Leopold. "Negritude and African Socialism." In *St. Anthony's Paper*, 15, ed. K. Kirkwood. London: Chatto and Windus, 1963.

Shupe, Anson, and Jeffrey K. Hadden. "Is There Such a Thing as Global Fundamentalism?" In *Secularization and Fundamentalism Reconsidered*, ed. Jeffrey K. Hadden and Anson Shupe. New York: Paragon House, 1989.

Shutte, Augustine. *Ubuntu: An Ethic for a New South Africa*. Pietermaritzburg, South Africa: Cluster Publications, 2001.

Smit, J. H. "Ubuntu Africa: A Christian Interpretation." In *Ubuntu in a Christian Perspective*, ed. J. H. Smit, M. Deacon, and A. Shutte. Potchefstroom, South Africa: Potchefstroom University Press, 1999.

Smit, J. H., M. Deacon, and A. Shutte, eds. *Ubuntu in a Christian Perspective*. Potchefstroom, South Africa: Potchefstroom University Press, 1999.

Smith, Ervin. *The Ethics of Martin Luther King, Jr.* New York: Edwin Mellen Press, 1981.

Smith, Kenneth L., and Ira G. Zepp, Jr. *Search for the Beloved Community: The Thinking of Martin Luther King, Jr.* Valley Forge, PA: Judson Press, 1998.

Smith, Theophus H. "The Spirituality of Afro-American Traditions." In *Christian Spirituality: Post-reformation and Modern*, ed. Louis Dupre and Don E. Saliers. New York: Crossroad, 1989.

Sopa, Geshe L., and Jeffrey Hopkins. *Practice and Theory of Tibetan Buddhism*. New York: Grove Press, 1976.

Soros, George. *The Bubble of American Supremacy: Correcting the Misuse of American Power.* New York: Public Affairs, 2004.

Thurman, Howard. *Deep River and the Negro Spiritual Speaks of Life and Death.* Richmond, IN: Friends United Press, 1975.

———. *Disciplines of the Spirit.* Richmond, IN: Friends United Press, 1977.

———. *Jesus and the Disinherited.* Boston: Beacon Press, 1976.

Tutu, Desmond. *Crying in the Wilderness: The Struggle for Justice in South Africa.* Ed. John Webster. Grand Rapids: Eerdmans, 1982.

———. "God's Dream." In *Waging Peace II: Vision and Hope for the 21st Century,* ed. David Krieger and Frank Kelly. Chicago: Noble Press, 1992.

———. *Hope and Suffering: Sermons and Speeches.* Ed. John Webster. Grand Rapids: Eerdmans, 1984.

———. *No Future without Forgiveness.* New York; London: Doubleday, 1999.

———. *The Nobel Peace Prize Lecture.* New York: Anson Phelps Stokes Institute for African, Afro-American, and American Indian Affairs, 1986.

———. *The Rainbow People of God: The Making of a Peaceful Revolution.* Ed. John Allen. New York: Doubleday, 1994.

———. *The Words of Desmond Tutu.* Ed. Naomi Tutu. New York: Newmarket Press, 1989.

Vaughn, Wally G., and Richard W. Wills, eds. *Reflections of Our Pastor: Dr. Martin Luther King, Jr., at Dexter Avenue Baptist Church, 1954–1960.* Dover, MA: Majority Press, 1999.

Wallis, Jim. *God's Politics: A New Vision for Faith and Politics in America.* San Francisco: HarperSanFrancisco, 2005.

Walzer, Michael. *Exodus and Revolution.* New York: HarperCollins, 1985.

Washington, James M. "Jesse Jackson and the Symbolic Politics of Black Christendom." *Annals of the American Academy of Political and Social Science* 480 (July 1985): 89–105.

Watley, William D. *Roots of Resistance: The Nonviolent Ethics of Martin Luther King, Jr.* Valley Forge, PA: Judson Press, 1985.

West, Cornel. *Prophetic Fragments.* Grand Rapids: Eerdmans, 1988.

Wilmore, Gayraud S. "The Black Messiah: Revising the Color Symbolism of Western Christology." *Journal of the Interdenominational Theological Seminary* 2, no. 1 (Fall 1974): 8–18.

———. *Black Religion and Black Radicalism: An Interpretation of the Religious History of Afro-American People.* 2nd ed. Maryknoll, NY: Orbis Books, 1983.

Acknowledgments

Excerpts from the following are reprinted by arrangement with the Estate of Martin Luther King, Jr., c/o Writers House as agent for the proprietor, New York, NY. All rights reserved:

"Creative Protest," a speech delivered by Dr. King in Durham, NC, during the lunch counter "sit-down" by Negro students (The King Center Archives, February 16, 1960); "Interview on World Peace," *Redbook Magazine* (The King Center Archives, November 5, 1964); *A Knock at Midnight: Inspirations from the Great Sermons of Rev. Martin Luther King, Jr.,* ed. Clayborne Carson and Peter Holloran (New York: Warner Books, 1998); *The Measure of a Man* (New York: Christian Education Press, 1959); untitled paper on Vietnam (The King Center Archives, April 30, 1967); *The Papers of Martin Luther King, Jr.,* ed. Clayborne Carson. 3 vols. (Berkeley: University of California Press, 1992, 1995, 1997); "Speech at the Staff Retreat of SCLC at Penn Center," Frogmore, SC (The King Center Archives, May 1967); "Statement at *Pacem in Terris II* Convocation" (The King Center Archives, May 28–31, 1967); *Strength to Love* (New York: Harper & Row, 1963); *Stride toward Freedom: The Montgomery Story* (New York: Harper & Row, 1958); *A Testament of Hope: The Essential Writings of Martin Luther King, Jr.,* ed. James M. Washington (New York: HarperCollins Publishers, 1986); *The Trumpet of Conscience* (New York: Harper & Row, 1967); *Where Do We Go from Here: Chaos or Community?* (Boston: Beacon Press, 1967).

Index